IMAGES OF TRUTH
Religion and the Art of Seeing

A *Joint Publication of*
The American Academy of Religion
and the Society of Biblical Literature

Volume 3
IMAGES OF TRUTH
Religion and the Art of Seeing
by
John W. Dixon, Jr.

IMAGES OF TRUTH
Religion and the Art of Seeing

JOHN W. DIXON, JR.

Scholars Press
Atlanta, Georgia

IMAGES OF TRUTH
Religion and the Art of Seeing

by
John W. Dixon, Jr.

© 1996
The American Academy of Religion
The Society of Biblical Literature

Library of Congress Cataloging in Publication Data
Dixon, John W.
    Images of truth: religion and the art of seeing / John W.
Dixon, Jr.
        p.   cm. — (Ventures in religion ; v. 3)
    ISBN 1-55540-277-1 (cloth : alk. paper) — ISBN 0-7885-0183-6
(pbk. : alk. paper)
    1. Image (Theology) I. Title. II. Series.
BV150.D55   1996
291.3'7-dc20   95-39872
                                                CIP

Printed in the United States of America
on acid-free paper

To: Susan and Judy and Miriam and Joe and Frank and Daniel and Elizabeth

TABLE OF CONTENTS

PREFACE

Umberto Eco has said that a sign is anything that can be used to lie. Since images are signs, then images can be used to lie. The assertion also supposes that signs and images can be used to tell the truth.

What kind of truth can an image tell?

How do we know when an image is being used to tell the truth and when to lie?

A sign is something used to indicate something else, to point to it and, in the process, make certain kinds of assertions about it. It is, therefore, an instrument of communication and a way of stating truth or falsehood. Since images are one class of signs, they too function in the same way. But images are not only signs. They are one of the means for organizing our lives.

One of the superstitions of intellectuals holds that human life is ordered and controlled by ideas, our kind of things. Well and good — so long as we recognize that ideas are not exhausted by verbal statements but include other forms as well. Music, for a central important example, is a fundamental means for ordering our emotional lives. We could learn much about ourselves and our own people by comparing the sickly sweet, crooning sentimentality of the popular music of my boyhood with the wild, abandoned, grossly sensual, popular music of today. These, too, are ideas, ways of ordering emotions, desires, attitudes, relations, into rhythmic patterns that are one component of human life.

Similarly, stories, narratives, are fundamental means for organizing the thoughts, fears, desires, ambitions, all the feelings and purposes and actions and relations that make up human life. To know a people's or a person's narrative is to know something fundamental about that form of human life. A people or a person without a narrative, without a place in a narrative, has lost an essential component of a human life, one of the means for separating humans from animals, who have no narrative.

Music and story are two of the fundamental means of human thought, two basic sets of ideas, ordering human experience and purpose. There are others. Ritual includes both the formal liturgies of religion and the less formal, still rigorous, rituals of athletics. Festivals, the time out of time, are another mode. (A rock concert might be considered an orgiastic festival, not necessarily saying all there is to say about those indulging in it.)

Human life is understood only by grasping all of these ordering principles, including the "ideas" of the intellectuals, in their particular relations and interactions. Academics, intellectuals, have responsibility for one of these essential components but intellectuals are human before they are intellectuals and their work is shaped by their raw human emotions (fear, ambition, love, desire, lust for power, etc.) and their narrative and their sense of the shape of narrative, the rhythms of their music, their participation in ritual, all the things that shape their understanding of evidence.

Human life is lived as bodies in the world, relating to the world by the whole act of bodily participation in the world, which is the totality of perception. Ordering the whole of perceptual participation is a primary human responsibility. Music is not an abstraction but a way of ordering sound to give shape to time and emotions. Dance and athletics are shapes of bodily movement and drama in space.

Vision is one of the fundamental perceptual modalities. The image is the most important means for ordering vision into meaning.

The image is normally a picture, a representation, of something or someone and goes far toward determining our thoughts and feelings about that thing or person. Our sense of what a man or a woman is or ought to be is shaped by many of the images that so clamorously surround us. The images in advertising, often squalid, shape many attitudes and hopes and visions. The images of living or once living persons shape our sense of what we ought to be. How can we trace the affect on American character of the grave, sad, majestic, wonderful face of Abraham Lincoln and all we know of the words and acts embodied in that face? The image and the dramatic roles of the movie actor Marion Morrison (a.k.a. John Wayne) shaped the sense of manhood governing the attitudes of millions of American men. Such illustrations are legion.

Since this book is necessarily short, it cannot be comprehensive. Choices have to be made. It is intended for beginners and cannot be technical without essential preparation. Images are not simple things. Which aspects of images will make them more accessible to the beginner? It is one of the offices of a preface to indicate what choices have been made and why.

To start with a distinction that will have to be examined further in the body of the book, images are two things. First, they are representations of something else. That is, they look like, resemble, represent, re-present, something other than themselves. Second, they are made objects, things, with a character of their own. Within these basic characteristics, they have a variety of functions and qualities.

Traditionally, images were studied almost exclusively as art, with the distinction of value the word implies. Images that were not made as art were not ignored but they were definitely in an inferior position. The distinction between "high art" and popular art is no longer supportable. At the same time, it must be said that most — not all — the works I present are drawn from the traditional body of art and that choice will have to be defended.

That traditional history of art was founded on the history of styles. Despite its present eclipse, the history of styles is still an essential aspect of the history of art, but it is irrelevant to this book.

Style was traditionally defined as form and form treated as part of stylistic development. If the history of style is irrelevant to this study, that would seem to eliminate the study of form. Form, however, is far more central to the making of images than its function as an adjunct of style and will feature prominently in this account. The distinction will be developed later.

Some critics, rather than historians, treated form as an "aesthetic" value, without reference to anything outside itself. While the pleasures of form are not irrelevant to this study (the quality of form that gives delight is traditionally a means for the glorification of God or the gods), the claim of "art for art's sake" is manifestly inadequate and is generally ignored.

"Iconography", the study of the represented subjects, has been a vital part of traditional art history. Inescapably, it will be central to this book.

More recently a major development in the study of images has been "semiotics", the image as a sign of something basic in the social and political ordering of a culture. This is inescapably true; images are made for human purposes, some conscious and intended, some unconscious, and those purposes will shape what the image represents and how it is represented. The essential principle, over-simplified, is that the image (and all cultural products and social/political arrangements) are designed to secure the power of one group over another, a socio-economic class, one gender (male) over the other, an ethnic group over others. These claims are related to the understanding of all cultural products as emerging from psychosexual history and desire.

Since these things are undoubtedly integral parts of the making, and therefore the studying, of images, they will be present in this study but not focally. The reasons for putting them in a subordinate position are complex and this is no place to be arguing the appropriateness of the various contemporary "post-modern" disciplines. A brief statement will have to suffice; an essential point needs to be made.

Everything human is made up of a complex of causes and purposes; no one of them can be selected as the only one or even the only important one. We all belong to a particular social and economic class, a gender, a nation, an ethnic group. We are all subject to the pressures of various desires and emotions. We are all, critics, image makers, spectators, involved in all of these all the time. Since all these forces, these energies, are present in all of us, we cannot isolate one (except for observation and study). The necessary critical act is to see how a particular image emerges from the struggle for meaning that is the source of the personal and common work.

Images can rightly be used as evidence for something else, which semiotics normally does. Such use makes them into documents in another study. In this book, however, we need to see images in their own right, as statements of the truth, or what some people have felt to be the truth. What, then, do we do?

An image is an object. It is first of all a thing, made by an artisan. This elementary (and elemental) fact is of the greatest possible consequence. The making itself is a process of forming a physical material. Both the making and the resemblance are complex intellectual acts which involve not only the process of making but also a number of assumptions (including gender, class, etc.). The forms as well as the subject (the represented thing) can be seen as signs of many things.

From birth (should we say from conception?) human life is worked out within, by means of, the body's interaction with its physical, material world. "Man", said Montaigne, "though he sit ever so high above the earth, yet he sits on his own tail." Making is a physical act, an act of the body. In order to represent something the artisan has to see it, feel it, which is the complex act of perception. In order to make something, the artisan has to see the material, the tools, the evolving process of making. At the same time, the spectator (in this study, often the worshipper) has to see the image, which is a physical act related to but not the same as the act of making and seeing of the artisan. This is a technical problem that is more than simply technical; it involves the deepest movements of our nature. It lies, perhaps, on the other side of this preliminary study.

Inescapably, the beginning of the understanding of images as with their making is the physical object, which is to say that the image has to be treated as a "work of art". But this book is supposed to be about images, not about art. It is also and inevitably about art. We are not concerned with literary images, with the politician's or the advertiser's image. The images that concern us are made visible in the forming of matter so they are all art, whether or not that was the intention of their maker. Despite decades of attempts, there is no definition of art that distinguishes definitively between art and other made objects. Some images were made as "art", that is, as objects to be looked at in their own right. Other images were made purely as functional objects, without regard to their status as art. All are art and subject to the same kinds of interpretations.

It is equally true that a great many people, probably a majority, use images without any regard at all for their character or their quality as art. (I consider this problem directly in Chapter 6, "The Artless Image".) To them it is a sign of something, often something exceedingly precious to them. This situation cannot be ignored.

From the many possibilities inherent in these distinctions, I have chosen to concentrate on the image as subject and the image as form. These are not two separate things: the image exists for us only as a material formed to represent the subject.

I make this choice for two reasons. In the first place, it studies the most elemental quality of the image. Whatever else can be done with the interpretation of images (and there are many other things that can properly be done), this is where it begins. Everything else depends on this.

In the second place, it is the aspect of the study most important for those (meaning most students) who will not be professionally students of religion. However much we need to know about the image as sign, the study of signs depends on learning, on scholarship, which, so far as students are concerned, is something done by somebody else. The principles and procedures developed here should enable students to work with images in their own right. "Their own right" is an ambiguous phrase. It refers to the right (if inanimate objects have rights) to be seen for itself, for what it is, not solely in its relation to something else. The phrase also refers to the right of the student (beginners and professionals) to see images in relation to ourselves, as embodiments of some form of truth that has relevance to me. All artifacts made in the past are also immediately present to us now.

The instructions to the writers of this series encourage them to offer an argument, a reasoned position that can provoke discussion and counter-argument. One argument of this book is simple: the study of images is indispensable to the study of religion.

By means of the image we know something about religions we could not otherwise know. In academia, knowledge is still too linked to verbal propositions for that assertion to be received comfortably. Nevertheless, however small a part imagery plays in the teaching of religion, imagery is increasingly acceptable as a part of the scholarly literature on religion, particularly as it is summarized in textbooks. Such books once appeared without illustration; they now use illustration as ornamentation and enlivenment of the text, showing the things religious people do.

The image is something more than ornament and illustration. It is something more than a sign. That "something more" is crucial, fundamental, and unless we can identify it my argument fails.

Images are not only part of the evidence for what people in religion do, they are evidence for what the people mean.

Every image is a work of art. This is not a value judgment; it may be bad art, inadequate art, false art, but it is art because it is a physical material formed by a human being for the distinctively human purposes of statement, expression, instruction, devotion, etc. Or, for the embodiment, the incarnation, of meanings that cannot be set out in any other way. The principle of that forming is the "something more" that cannot be translated into any other language, despite the inevitable necessity of pointing to it by words. Therefore, the stages of my argument:

1. As human beings, we are inescapably involved in the physical world in all our workings, just as all organisms are.

2. Perception in all its modes is primary because it is the means for our dialogue with the world of our placement. Perception has primacy, not merely as means (which could be conceived as providing data for an independent mind), but because its various modes provide the possibility for the different modes of our thought.

3. The image as sign is a necessary part of our knowing. The image as work of art is the organization of the experience and the modes of

perception into something new that goes beyond all we share with other organisms. It organizes the perceptual interaction with the world into structures of meaning which are not in addition to or an ornament to the basic human experience but definitive of it. The image is an essential instrument in the origin and development of human consciousness.

4. Since religion (in all its senses) is the most basic of all human acts that determine human meaning and purpose, the image, as a prime element in the structure of human consciousness, is indispensable to the study of religion.

The foundational argument in #1 and #2 is large, beyond the limits of a short book. It goes to the heart of what we believe about the nature of the human and the way humans know. The argument I will summarize is not original with me; it has been made and is still being made by others. Consequently, much of the earlier part of the argument will have to be made by reference, allusion and brief summary in order to get to my main responsibility, the setting out of a procedure for grasping, or being grasped by, the image.

Since this is an introduction to the study of the use of images in religion, I have confined attention to those images that have traditionally been used in religions. This does not take into account the imperative force of imagery today, marked by the invention of the repeatable image (the image that can be reproduced by the printing process), the discovery of photography as the culmination of the repeatable image and a seismic shift in representation. High speed, mass production printing meant the wide distribution of images. Film brought movement into the image and extended the time and conditions of its experience. Television is a culmination of these developments. Finally, the development of digital imagery makes possible the manipulation of imagery far beyond anything previously possible.

This new "image world" affects how we see images and thereby creates a major problem for the religions; the spiritual world, the imaginations of people is more formed by that image world than by anything religious institutions do. We cannot ignore the shift in our own sensibilities since they are the means whereby we apprehend our world. Certain aspects of the present argument are not affected: traditional images remain what they were and technology impinges on the study in making easily available a vast store of images of those images.

ACKNOWLEDGEMENTS

I would like to offer my special thanks to Marjorie Kinsey for a useful critical reading of an earlier version of this book; to David Morgan for an equally useful reading of the same early version, for an additional reading of Chapter Eleven and for advice on other issues; and to that prince of editors, Willliam Scott Green, who does not intrude but makes an author do his best work.

Section One

The Image as the Suspension of Time

In which certain fundamentals of the human experience are dramatized by the experiences of a solitary tourist.

1

THE IMAGE AS THE SUSPENSION OF TIME

The originating problem of the image, of art, is the relation between movement and stasis, between process and structure, between time and the timeless, between presence and absence. The function of the image is the suspension of time.

I once visited the Greek island of Mykonos in the heat of the summer. The brilliance and the power of the sun was nearly unbearable, pulsating with physical force from the whitewashed walls, bearing down with painful weight against the body. The shade of walls was a refuge from the violence of the sun against vulnerable flesh. Odors were an intensity of experience, odors of sun-baked herbs from the barren hills above the town, of cooking from houses and restaurants. Vision was an immersion in the whiteness, in the intense blue of the sky, in the narrowness of the streets, the narrow streets as a winding penetration among the heavy cubes of whiteness, the white planes of walls penetrated by the darkness of doors and windows, the cubic forms of the buildings. Dust was the taste of dryness in the mouth. There were the sounds of children playing, the talk of women, the cobbler's hammer, the creaking of boats in the harbor.

Mykonos enclosed me on all sides. Wherever I was I was conscious that there was something behind and to the sides, as a looming presence. The earth was solid under the stones beneath my feet, bearing my weight. The sky was blue lightness above. The buildings filled my field of vision, under sharp focus in the center, a blur of wall and whiteness at the edges. As I moved there was a succession of solids and voids in an uninterrupted flow. Beyond what I was seeing there was the sense of other things, spaces, the extension of the sea, the mystery of the horizon. What I had just seen shaped what I was now seeing; I emerged from the enclosure of a narrow street into the releasing openness of a plaza, then back into the winding pathway of a street.

3

Time passes as it must but I felt suspended in space. Subliminally I knew time passed; it must be getting close to lunch time; the sun is lower in the sky, it is nearly time to go back to the ship. Yet now I felt suspended out of time, moving through space.[1]

The experience of Mykonos was three dimensional, involving all the senses immersed in both space and time, a totality of sensation.

I look at my slides projected on the screen in our living room. The room is a pleasant 68^0. Odors are the mild ones of a middle class house. Mykonos has become a rectangle of colored light on a screen. The sky and the buildings are cool white against cool blue. Narrow streets and the massed cubes of houses become a pleasing arrangement of flat patches of color. My eye reconstructs the depth from flatness. It no longer contains me. I am here, the image is there and is something other than the vanished Mykonos. What I had experienced in time, through motion, my body heavy on the ground, is now a single, detached, abstracted image, suspended before me, to be looked at in the single experience of vision. The image is absolute stillness, absolute quiet.

One reason for all those devices that we put between us and the image, the critic's learned chatter, the collector's display, the historian's industry, the explainer's system, is to protect us against the terror of that stillness, that silence.

The image serves both memory and contemplation. From the image I reconstruct the experience in my mind, relive in memory what is now irretrievably past and gone. Time is suspended.

Equally, the image is a thing in itself, a reminder of something other than itself but itself an object, colored light on a beaded screen before me. Is it art? In the old sense of "art", no. It is a tourist snapshot, made only as a reminder. But of course it is art, an object made for the human function of memory, an object that serves the human purpose of contemplation. While visiting Mykonos, I was a part of a total experience, an active process involving all my senses. The image is an abstraction from that process, taking from it the single experience of colored shapes, sensory experience reduced to the single act of vision. I am reminded of the earlier experience but now, in detachment, I can contemplate it, think about it. Change and

---

[1] This is a sensation common to all intense physical and emotional experiences. It is one of seveal reasons for the popularity of sports and other games as well as rituals. The time of the event is marked at the beginning and the end and, for the duration, ordinary time is suspended. The only experienced time is an element of the game.

process are stopped in thought, in a distinctive act of seeing that interprets my experience of Mykonos.

Years later, I returned to Mykonos in October, which is other than the heat of the summer. The sun was not violent pain but pellucid light, playing softly on the white surfaces of the massed cubes. My senses were not so powerfully involved, overwhelmed. I could now contemplate the beautiful forms of Mykonos. Memory was now the memories of my images of Mykonos, closed away in my slide cabinet. I saw streets and houses. I also saw streets and houses as images of themselves, images of my past experience of Mykonos.

My experience of time is now more complex. I am set apart from my ordinary time into the space of Mykonos but I remember, and remembering is the presence of past time. My experience of Mykonos is not so immediate, so pure, as it was the first time, for now I stand a little apart from it to contemplate what is happening to me.

I described my experience of Mykonos almost entirely in terms of complex perceptual experience. That is too simple. I was there from a distant and different country and people, a visitor, a voyeur, an intrusion, not knowing the meaning of the speech I heard in the street, not knowing the names of the people, nor who lived within those walls. I did not only see; I was seen. As what? A stranger, economically useful but otherwise irrelevant, a brief appearance, plodding wearily through the hot streets, then gone. In my image of the world, I am at the center, the world and time spread out around me. To the people of Mykonos I was a minor, unimportant incident in a world that is centered on each of them.

That little church, so often photographed, so picturesque in tourist advertisements and post card souvenirs, is to them an intersection of lives, a place of devotion, the enactment of the dramas of christenings, of marriages, of death.

What of all this can any image show? What is the use of the image? In the face of its obvious inadequacy, how could any image be spoken of as "realistic", "representational"? Are images of no greater use than words in capturing the real, the true?

I spoke of three distinct experiences of Mykonos: the experience from within, for those who enact their lives as a part of Mykonos; my own intense, brief immersions in the experience of Mykonos; my images of Mykonos that serve memory and contemplation. These do not exhaust the experience of the images.

What of those who have not been to Mykonos but see my images? They have no memory of Mykonos to draw on so Mykonos is only a series of images on my screen. For them, it is an imagined experience built up from the information in the images. It cannot serve as reconstruction but as presentation. They can participate in the beauty of Mykonos, insofar as the image selects it, in the beauty of the images to the restricted limits of my own skill as a photographer. They may know more about Mykonos than they did before. They can experience almost nothing of what it was like to be on, in, Mykonos. They see Mykonos as an imagined reality, seen through a window. For them as for me, the distant is made present but present only in part.

Could I, in any way, make my experience of Mykonos present to them? No. Were I a painter, I might show something of the light of the sun but never the feel of the sun on my flesh, never the sounds and odors, never the sense of the streets and houses behind and beside me. Had I the skill, such paintings might show something of my feelings about Mykonos, "express" those feelings, but only by distorting appearance. My images of Mykonos are colored shapes.

We have not yet done with Mykonos and its use.

I went to Mykonos only to see; my images of Mykonos serve the single purpose of the memory of vision. But very little of life outside the world of the tourist is given to the single experience of vision; we act, work, love, worship. The image is involved in that world as well, still as record and memory and contemplation but also as way of coping with meaning and purpose, with something more nearly like the wholeness of experience. For instance:

The idea of an image as a window originated in Renaissance Italy and has been present in the understanding of Westerners ever since. It is an unusual idea in the use of imagery. More common is the image made famous by E.H. Gombrich, the hobby horse. For the child, resemblance plays very little part in the making of the hobby horse (it is adults rather than children who want realistic dolls). A stick that can be held in the hand and straddled is sufficient as a substitute for a real horse. The only thing necessary is that degree of functional relation and that it be manageable. The child cannot manage a real horse but can the pretend horse.

The stick as hobby horse is a true image. It is a representation but not (as the word usually implies) a representation of appearance. It is a representation of function and relation. It might be called, as Gombrich does, a substitute but only if the word "substitute" is not understood as something inferior. The hobby horse is not an inferior horse; for the child, it **is** the horse. Were it an accurate representation of appearance, if it 'looked like" the horse, it would lose the capacity for that function.

Many years ago, we were going through a museum and arrived at Brancusi's "Bird in Space", a famous piece of modern, "abstract" art. It is a tall, elegantly and gracefully curved, ovoid form of polished brass, nothing more. One of our daughters ran over, read the label, and started to laugh. I said to her, "Wait a moment. Think what it would look like if he had shown the appearance of the bird. It would sit there, showing feathers and beak and claws, just a lump of brass. This is the bird in space. He's showing you the flight of the bird!" With the singular capacity of a child, her face reacted with delight. Ill. 1

But Brancusi has not distinguished between an eagle and a dove, which is useful to know.

In other contexts, a passport or driver's license, the reproduction of appearance is the necessary function. It is a mistake to oppose "appearance" to "reality"; appearances, too, are part of the real.

There are realities of personality that survive alteration of appearance. Equally, the personality can alter with no change of appearance. Representation is not responsible only to appearance or to function.

The power of representation of appearance is suggested by the strange place of illusionistic art in the imagination. Wax works have an entrancing touch of the macabre about them, an almost numinous fascination. The contemporary sculptor, Duane Hanson, using the resources of modern technology, has carried the principle of the wax works beyond entertainment into the major arts. The amazing, the uncanny, the slightly frightening, appeal of all such figures is that of the painted corpse displayed in the coffin. That which was alive or might be alive is dead and yet retains the appearance of a living form. The illusion is astonishing and never complete; there is an inescapable dialogue between life and death.

The only nearly complete illusion I know of is some of the more expensive plastic flowers. The illusion is so accurate that sometimes only touch can tell the difference. So the plastic flower is not a part of the experience of the uncanny, the dialogue between life and death. It is simply a lie. It has all the appearance of the true flower, except everything that reminds us of its true nature, the changing, the transitory.

The only way to deny death is to deny life. Flowers are beautiful because they die.

The photograph is a different matter. It reproduces certain appearances with great precision but, by its difference of scale, is more a memory of the thing than an illusion. Hence women often have a corner of their house devoted to photographs of their family.[2]

Photographs are a type of the image as the abstraction of reality from time, with its use and its loss. Illusion is the extreme case and few images go so far, even in the sometimes entranced concern for appearances. There is so much more to true experience than appearances, indeed so much more in appearance than illusion. Something, not always appearance, is abstracted from the process of time and held before the mind for contemplation, used by the mind for contemplation.

The image makes the distant present and the un-manageable manageable. It can represents the appearance or the function or some interaction of the two or some other aspect of reality that is not appearance or function. It is not, is never, never can be, merely a record of an immediate experience, the prolongation of a moment. Pressed too far, this becomes sentimental. It is never correct to say "art is" or "art does", since the idea of "art" is a construction in our own minds for some one or another of our purposes that are often not at all agreeable to the original work. Art works, which are what we have of "art", are as varied as human beings are, great or squalid, true or false, honest or dishonest, competent or incompetent. Most art works, like most of us, are some combination of human virtues and vices. True or false, they all represent some attempt to transcend time. Our task is to determine what purpose they may have in thus denying one of the essentials of experience.

....all time is always now.
T.S. Eliot

The art work, the embodied, em-mattered image, lifts immediacies out of the flow of time, thereby suspending time into memory and contemplation.

The present is the moment between past and future. It is not a moment without dimensions; it is prolonged or contracted in the immediacy of events. For the animal, the present is all there is. Its memory is learned responses and associations, not the holding of the past in consciousness for contemplation and use. Having no true memory, it cannot

---

[2] Among those I know it is always the women who establish such a household shrine. I do not know if that is always true.

have hope. Having no hope, it cannot plan; its purpose is solely to be what it is. It will die but does not know that it will die. It can have fear but its fear is the immediacy of a threat, not the general dread of our inescapable knowledge that we are going to die. Animals have intelligence, animals can love, and both can be carried out over time. Neither is available to them for contemplation, for thought.

We live between memory and hope. Memory gives meaning. Hope gives purpose. To destroy either is to destroy the human.

The process of time cannot be stopped. The image can abstract some moment of that process to hold in suspension for contemplation. What does that do to history?

What is "history"? The events of the past? The relics of the event? The reconstruction we make of the events?

The past is gone, irrevocably. All that remains are its artifacts, some of which are documents from or about the past. With these artifacts, we use our rhetorical devices to construct an image of the past. All images are responsible to the integrity of the material they work with. Since the artifacts were made by people like ourselves, they are entitled to the courtesy of careful attention; we cannot deal arbitrarily with the things they made for their purposes. Whatever the intrusion of our own processes, it is their world we try to see.

At the same time, the artifacts are part of our world. The time suspended is held in trust by us, for us. To turn them into evidence only is to deny their force and insights. They are present now, with us, not set apart as though they no longer matter except as we use them for our own purposes. The ancient Egyptian, the modern Navaho, are not something other than ourselves to be observed from a physical or intellectual distance. They are people like ourselves, living in their own situation, coping. What they do, what they make, can be, if we have the honor and the courage, parts of ourselves to enlighten and enliven our own coping.

What use do we make of the suspension of time?

Section Two

The Image and the Construction of the World

In which, by the consideration of myth, fable, and biology, and by means of imagined reconstruction, certain fundamentals of the human circumstance are proposed as the origin of imagery.

2

The Construction of the World

A Myth and a Fable

We cannot understand images unless we understand where we are as human beings, what we are trying to do in our world and how we do it. My experience of Mykonos differs only in intensity from our common experience; we do not, cannot, sit apart from the world, able to explain its reality by this or that formula or belief. We are incessantly, always, involved in the world, involved with our whole organism. Explanation — philosophy or theology or physics — is a function of our organism, necessary to our fullest human life, but it depends from the totality of the involvement.

The image is an essential part of the particular human involvement.

Images are made by human beings for human purposes. We cannot understand human artifacts unless we have some understanding of people, who make them. That understanding is only in part a matter of certain knowledge. It rests, rather, on interpretation, on belief, on commitment, the kind of understanding that is best set forth or made manifest in myth and story, not explanation. Let us see what we can do with an ancient myth and a modern mythical story.

The Myth

"In the beginning was the word...". No. "In the beginning was the Logos...".

What is the Logos? Not words, speech, but the Word, the creative breath of God, the spirit of God hovering over Chaos, bringing all things into being.

13

In that phrase, John the Evangelist established part of the controlling myth of Christianity and, therefore, of Western culture. "Logos" was divine reason, the word as the principle of reason and order in things. John deliberately used a parallelism, "In the beginning God created...", "In the beginning was the Logos....". For John, the Logos was Jesus as the Christ, a great principle of the Christian myth but not our point at the moment, which is: What was in the beginning? The Logos as the creating spirit of God brought all things, including the human, into existence. It was the Light of God, before there was the sun as the earthly light, the Word of God before there were words. What does this have to do with words? What is the beginning of the human? What is the place of language, of human speech, in the making of the human?

What is the seriousness of speech? Is the beginning of speech the beginning of the human?

For help let us turn to another part of the founding myth. In the second creation story in the book of Genesis, the writer says, "And out of the ground the Lord God formed every beast of the field and every fowl of the air, and brought them unto Adam to see what he would call them: and whatever Adam called every living creature, that was the name thereof." (Genesis 2: 19)

The confused state of the text and the charming picture of the animals and the birds parading past Adam to be named obscures the importance of this part of the myth. For most of us a name is arbitrary, meaning little. For a few, the terrible mystery of naming has become the central problem for the mind. For the ancients, for early people generally, a name is not arbitrary but emerges from the nature of the thing, the person. The name calls the thing into being, into thought. The name of the Lord was a terrible thing for ancient Hebrews, who would not speak it publicly.

The name was a spoken word, issuing from the mouth of Adam, but it was not a casual thing. It was part of the nature of things, bringing them into consciousness. Words are a part of the nature of the self; to speak is to throw something of the self into the public domain, to make the self vulnerable. For many of the ancients and "primitive" people, speech is to be used only with care and deliberation. To chatter is to offend against the human.

So speech is the first act of the human? Not quite, for there is an act that precedes the naming: "...and brought them unto Adam to **see** what he would call them;..." To name them Adam had first to <u>see</u> them; to see them was to grasp the nature from which their name issues.

In the beginning was the image....

THE FABLE

Let us look now at the popular fable.

Stanley Kubrick's film "2001", begins with a vast panorama of a primeval landscape. Animals are gathered around a waterhole, searching for food, idly playing. An anthropoid is playing with a thigh bone, pounding other bones to make them jump. Well and good; animals play. Suddenly there flashes through his mind pictures of striking other animals and killing them. (Here film has the advantage of the other arts since it can show the mind's first work as pictures, images; **show,** not argue.)

Animals perceive, see, have images on the retina which become full images in their brains and thereby are the means of their interaction with the world. No animal, as animal, could imagine this. "Imagine" here is not the thinking of that which is not, but a thinking in images of what both is and can be.

This creature did not "invent" the "club"; invention and club are names we, in our symbol systems, have given to acts and things. This creature as yet had no names, no language, no words. He <u>saw</u> and what he saw was the potential act within a thing, part of the full nature of the thing. This is abstraction, the basic human art. It is also metaphor, which is not simply an ornament in language but a far more fundamental human act: seeing the structural likeness between two different things and acts, making an object that is a representation of the other thing or, as in this case, the act.

In the beginning was the image. The anthropoid had become human.

The next scene shows this humanoid with others like himself, each carrying a bone-club, driving other anthropoids away from the waterhole. We presuppose the teaching that took place off screen and we see social organization, the band with its leader moving with new purpose. An inexorable process had begun. The image, the thing, the act, imposed logical necessities. The process required speech; both things and acts had to be named.

To act with intention with the other and on, or against, the other is to be aware of the other as other. To be aware of the other is to be aware of the self. The metaphoric image is the beginning of the consciousness of the self.

Beyond the film, this human would have taken the next step. Having seen the potential within the bone, achieved an image of the potential act, he would have seen the inadequacy of the bone, which did not fully represent the act; the image, the mental picture of the act, now had to be embodied in a better object, a more accurate representation of the act, an object made according to the image. This was craft, a fundamental enlargement of the repertoire of human thought.

It is presumption to think we can reproduce the mental processes of anyone. It is beyond presumption to think we can do it with those who were at the beginning of a process we do not understand. We must try, for much depends on the conclusion.

The image of the act — not the object, club, but the act, clubbing — was an act of the mind, the earliest act of imagination, the awareness of future possibility in the immediate. To see clubbing within the bone, to see the image of form, the abstraction of the true form from its approximation in the bone, is again a mental act. The club is a representation of the mental image.

In the fable, the simple act of the metaphoric imagination immediately involved desire, desire for control of people, of economic resources (the waterhole). It involved power as domination, as hierarchy of leadership, of teaching. With the initial image was born all the dimensions of the human.

What about the word "club"? We can barely even guess when language came into being, or why or how. It is conceivable to say that, originally, the word was a pointer to the thing, a sign, a signifier related to a signified, a necessary tool. The tool is so useful it is difficult to remember that the word does not refer to the thing but to acts of imagination. The speaker uses it as a part of the act of will, to direct attention. For the hearer the word directs perceptual attention in the form of an image. The word represents the image in the mind, not the thing.

Later, words began to emerge from different kinds of abstractions. Words in their relations began to weave their own structures which seem to describe the real but are still representations of images in the mind, even when the interaction of the words generates the images. No verbal construct, or concept, describes the real. It represents the mind's grasp or construction of the real.

All this is fable and not history. The process was almost certainly something like this but, in the fable, it could have been a tool, a basket or pot (unfortunately, in story telling, war is more interesting than weaving). In history, it certainly was all of them, laboriously achieved over millennia. In myth and fable we deal in summary. This is the image as the first true act of thought.

It is well to remember that this first human is not a mere figment of an imaginative reconstruction. He is flesh of our flesh and bone of our bone and mind of our mind. It is a long road from his club or her pot to our technology, but it is a continuous road.

THE IMAGE AND THE CONSTRUCTION OF THE WORLD

So far the making of things as images of acts, of tools for purpose. We need to take a closer look at the creatures making the tools, for they are ourselves. The creatures made the tools and became human; the tools in turned shaped the humans who made them. What is the human?

It is always risky to begin the understanding of truth from the work of the scientists, since science is rapidly changing. Certain things, however, may be true for all.

We can no longer think of ourselves as substantial, independent beings, somehow involved in the matter of the world because we inhabit bodies, yet able to stand apart from the world and observe it with a detachable mind. We are inescapably part of the world. All creatures, anthropoid, humanoid, ourselves, are part of the organic, biological, order, which is, in turn, dependent on the working of physics and chemistry.

We think we live in a world of things, other than ourselves. But the world is not like that. The very solidity of things is a construction. Things, including our own bodies, are, we are told, mostly empty space, elementary particles held in tension.

As laymen in physics, most of us have a hard time grasping this dissolution of solid matter into its particles. Even when we try to follow, we imagine smaller and smaller things, molecules, atoms, protons, neutrons, electrons, sub-nuclear particles. But particles are not things. They are particular focal points of energy in rhythmic concentration.

The core of things is not substance but rhythm.

1. The world, physical "reality", is made up of particles as particular concentrations of energy in rhythmic tension. Rhythmic relation is the reality of substance.

2. These particles cohere into larger units by structured relations, particles structured into atoms, molecules, on up through inorganic forms, elementary organic forms, reptiles, animals, humans, on through the universes to the cosmos. Relation is as real as substance.

3. Each such unit is a part of a larger unit which in turn is part of still larger and more comprehensive, more complex units. Each level in the hierarchy of being has a character which is more than the sum of its parts. (This is known as its "emergent properties.") The whole is not accounted for by its parts but the parts by their place in the whole.

Now we should try a difficult act of imagination, the "world" as it truly is and not as we ordinarily imagine it to be. It is easier to do for the world that existed before the intrusion of the human into it. Do not think of trees, and grass and water and dinosaurs. Those are names human beings have applied to certain imagined units. Instead, imagine a vast, pulsating web of interlocked particles, interacting structures of relation, thinner here, thicker there, more independently mobile here, less there. It possesses no qualities such as color, which is a name for experiences of — more names — "light" on the human "retina". This is the hierarchical order of the real from the tiniest particle or wavicle to the outer reaches of the cosmos.

The basic conditions of physical reality are relation and structure, energy and rhythm, hierarchy.

Organic life occupies a middle position in the hierarchical order. The animal occupies a central position in organic life. The human, in every respect but one, is an integral part of the animal. The one, decisive, difference is a matter of constant debate. It can be most directly stated as self-consciousness. Dogs think. They do not think about what it means to be a dog. They are unselfconsciously a part of nature. Because we ask the question, we are forever separated from that union with nature.

By nature we are a part of nature. By nature we are apart from nature.

We have arrived at the basic characteristic of the human, its paradox and its tragedy and its responsibility. Animals have a world distinctive to each; the world of the fly is not the world of the wolf. But their world is given to them, by their place and nature. Humans live in the same world but they have an additional burden, caused by the fatal duality of human existence: they must make a world.

Such a statement is unintelligible to many people, for whom the world is inescapably there, given, other than ourselves. Some have assumed the reality of a given world, a reality that can be known, described, explained, by the reasoning intelligence. Some existentialists use a dramatic analogy: we are thrown into existence, into the world, which has its reality but a reality we can never know; we can only cope as best we can with the conditions of this unknowable, mysterious, threatening, reality. This won't do.

To be self-conscious, to be aware of the self, is, necessarily, to be aware of the other. To be aware of the self as over against the other is to raise all manner of questions. What am I? What is the other? Some of the others are like myself, most are very different. Why? How am I related to the other? How ought I be related to the other? The problem is both descriptive and normative.

The other is in space, there. I am in space, here. Relation, no longer a part of nature, is enacted within space. Self-consciousness brings with it the awareness of space as having significance. The relation between the self and the other is a line. "We" is a collection of these lines surrounded by limits. Relations are enacted among these selves; generating the forms of relations. Being human is inseparable from purpose.

Some of these forms are established by nature. As we do, animals live in pairs, in groups, in hierarchies. As animals do, we hunger and thirst, we desire, we fear, we sleep. Once the forms are human and not simply animal, they have to be made, intentionally.

So far science with an overlay of imagination. The further we go with this imagination the more we have to rely on fable but still a fable illuminating reality.

We left our humanoids armed with their bone-club, acting as a group, controlling the waterhole, killing for food. The first man who made a club, the first woman who made a pot, irretrivably altered the world, and thereby made a new world. The first act of making, fulfilling the image of the act, began the process of building up the repertoire of images and ideas necessary for coping with the world they were making: abstraction and metaphor, shaping of form to purpose; hierarchy of leader and led, teacher and pupil; the consciousness of the self and the other, we and they; the ontological and moral problems of the self and the other: how **am** I related to the other?, how **ought** I to be related to the other?

Each principle, each image generates others; once begun, the process develops inexorably. The principle of abstraction, once established, functions for many other things; if clubbing can be seen in a bone, containing can be seen in a shell or a hollow in a rock. The Greeks are often credited with inventing the idea of invention but earliest people would have done it constantly.

The self is here; the other there. There is a line between the two. We are here, they are there. There is a line around us, a line between us and them.

The line around us becomes a fence, a wall, a new shape. Walls and fences require openings, doorways, joining movement and shape. Shelter is not merely sought but made, round or square according to materials and their required techniques, new shapes and forms. Again, doorways, perhaps windows. The line from us to them becomes a path, movement, transition, enmity or friendship.

One shape of clubbing becomes a stone, chosen for its weight, shaped in symmetry to balance with its handle. The pot is shape as volume

The body stands and moves with weight on the earth. Arms are cylindrical, heads spherical. Hills are pyramidal, triangular, the desert a plane surface, vines a catenary curve.

Even fable cannot contend with the multiplicity of things and shapes and acts that are parts of the apparently simple "primitive" society, nor with the intensity of thought that went into all these acts of discovery and of making.

"Thought" is a critical term in this argument. We cannot know how much "thinking" they did in the form we identify as thinking, manipulation of verbal patterns in propositions. But their thinking in images, in the forms generated in material as realization of the images, was thinking of a very high order. It was also a matter of making their world.

If the imagined description is reasonably sound, the process of making the world becomes clearer. It is first of all a matter of craft, which is an intimate, organic involvement with the matter of the earth in order to make the things necessary to the imagined world. Craft, however, is more than the simple making of useful objects. It establishes (and transforms) relations. Just as the initial image, the metaphorical image linking possibility and form, set a process in motion, so the making within relations begins the process which generates culture. Culture is made up of things, embodying the images of acts and relations and purposes. At some point, probably a very early point, the process began to involve ritual and narrative, themselves embodying the image of order and process that defines the world of that culture.

If there is any doubt where this argument is going, it is to demonstrate that the image is essential to human thought, not incidental or peripheral. Images are not things we think about. Images are things we think with. There is more.

It seems, or once seemed, reasonable to think that human evolution produced people much like ourselves who then generated their culture. Culture, therefore, was considered something other than nature and human thought was detached from nature. It is now evident that the generation of culture considerably preceded the completion of human evolution and significantly affected the course of evolution.[1] As organisms, we are inseparable from the instruments of our culture, just as culture is very much a part of the organic order; the opposition between nature and culture is a false one. The tools, the ordering of things, that are the manifestations, representations of our images are parts of who and what we are. The mind is the work of our whole organism within our culture.

It follows that the repertoire of images and their manifestations in things and the ordering of things is an inventory of the instruments of thought and, therefore, an account of the basic structures of the mind.

MAKING AND THE PRINCIPLE OF TRUTH.

The first bone used for striking (or the first leaf used for carrying water) had an uneasy fit between its form and its function; it was an approximation of the truth. The metaphorical image that gave rise to this primitive form made possible the perfecting of the form. The act of striking (or of carrying) has its own nature which is fulfilled best by certain forms; the imagination of those forms fulfilled the act.

---

[1] There is no reason to think human evolution is complete. It is simply that the scale of human evolution is so large, hundreds of thousands of years, that we in the short time of human history cannot detect it.

It would be well at this point if the reader were to look closely at "primitive" tools, preferably as they survive in museums, but it can be done in books. Note the careful balance worked into the stone, the provision for attaching the handle, the fit between handle and stone. Their tools and weapons are **true**. Their truth is conditioned by circumstances; the craftsmen had available certain material, certain techniques. There is sloppy, careless workmanship in primitive artifacts, just as there is in all things human but, at their best, their works are, inescapably, true.

This can be tested further by a visit to the local hardware store. Look at the tools displayed on the wall. They are remarkably beautiful, which may or may not be to the present point. They are also true, as an exact fit between what they are and what they are intended to do.

It would be well to keep in mind this account of the truth. It does not solve all our problems; the possibility of truth in words is not so easy to determine as the truth in the primitive club or the modern hammer. Yet we would do well to bring the same disposition of spirit to the problem of truth in words. But our present concern is truth in images. The craftsmen could make the thing that corresponded to the needs of the function, the thing as metaphor of the function. The image has the same responsibility but also it has far graver possibilities of falsehood.

So far we have been dealing with the practical matters of human development. The metaphoric image is insight into the function of things and the generation of objects to fit those functions. Its is the foundation of all the later argument but it remains true that these are not the images that concern us primarily in this study. The images that concern us are a different embodiment of the mental image: pictures, representations, that are made with human intention. Within the larger body of these images, we are concerned with those that are specifically religious. That function requires a separate chapter.

3

RELIGION, SYMBOL AND THE IMAGE

*I*t is difficult to discuss religious images and the role of images *in the study of religion without having some understanding of the definition of religion. It would be equally difficult to get on with the study of images if first there had to be a definition of religion.*

It is not simply that there is no scholarly agreement on such a definition, which is true, or that the variety of religions is so great that there are few features common to all, which is also true. The real problem: to define religion is to deny the very thing the adherents of a religion consider the most important thing about it. To them, their religion is an account of how things are; to define it is to subsume it under something other than itself, to set it apart as though it were something within the whole of how things are. This is the dilemma, the enervating paradox, of the scholarly study of religion; to account for religion, perhaps even to describe it, is to presume an order of things that includes religion, an order that then becomes its own religion.[1]

One way of partially evading the dilemma might be to revert to the fable and try to place the symbol in the mental work outlined by the fable. This should complete the grounding of the image in whatever it is we are calling religion.

THE IDOL AS SYMBOL

First, we can attend to the prophet Isaiah in one of the most remarkable accounts of the making of images:

---

[1] An good overview of the problem is Winston King's entry, "Religion" in the *Encyclopedia of Religion*.

23

All who make idols are nothing, and the things they delight in do not profit; their witnesses do not see nor know, that they may be put to shame. Who fashions a god or casts an image that is profitable for nothing....?

The carpenter stretches a line, he marks it out with a pencil; he fashions it with planes and marks it with a compass; he shapes it into the figure of a man, with the beauty of a man, to dwell in a house. He cuts down cedars; or he chooses a holm tree or an oak and lets it grow strong among the trees of the forest; he plants a cedar and the rain nourishes it. Then it becomes fuel for a man; he takes a part of it and warms himself; he kindles a fire and bakes bread; also he falls down before it. Half of it he burns in the fire; over the half he eats flesh, he roasts meat and is satisfied; also he warms himself and says, "Aha, I am warm, I have seen the fire!" And the rest of it he makes into a god, his idol; and he falls down to it and worships it; he prays to it and says, "Deliver me, for thou art my god!" (Isaiah 44: 9-10; 12-17)

Isaiah was a very great prophet but a very bad anthropologist; the principle he missed is essential both to the understanding of religion (his and the one he condemned) and to the understanding of images. For Isaiah, it was ridiculous to think that a block of wood could be used to cook food and warm people and, at the same time, be carved into a god. He was moved to contemptuous sarcasm; it was wholly outside any possibility of comprehension since God, the author of creation, is wholly outside that creation.

For the image maker, however, it was precisely *because* the wood contained the possibility of fire, a primal form of energy, that it could also be a god. The fire, the god, the energy, were different manifestations of the same thing; to make the image was to make the divine energy present, to make it possible to *participate* in that energy (participation will be a major theme of the following pages).

Isaiah's principle is a powerful part of the history of religious imagery in ways to be considered later. It is a form of <u>iconoclasm</u> (which means literally the breaking of images but is used for the extreme forms of the condemnation of images). It is also a minority view; however powerful iconoclasm has been at intervals in history, most peoples most of the time have felt the need for images, or, if not literally for images, some localization and specification of the energy. This localization and specification create the *sacred*, the thing or place or act that contains the vital energy. The iconoclastic religions are the great monotheisms, Judaism, some forms of

Christianity, and Islam. Yet they, too, consider certain things and places as set apart, containing the power of the divine. (Unfortunately, they have designated the same place. I do not know if Isaiah would consider Jerusalem an idol.)

Isaiah was a precise observer and reporter; it is well to pay close attention to this passage. He makes clear that, for his image-making enemies, the god is present in the image and the image is the object of worship. He accepts without question the fact of representation, which is not an obvious thing; the image "looks like" a man. It also posseses "the beauty of a man", which is also not obvious. It is worth noting for later use that Isaiah is strikingly sensitive to the ordinariness of the world, the tree in the forest, nourished by rain, the carpenter going about his craft.

Unwittingly, Isaiah has shown us the symbolic imagination at work, the ability to see the fire, the wood and the sacred energy as one. Yet, for the maker of the image, the wood alone is not enough; it must be shaped into the image, the representation of a man with the beauty of a man. The most important aspect of the story is the transformation of the wood into the image of the human body, the transformation of the human body into symbol. The vital energy of the body, the "life force" of the body, is the presence of the sacred energy.

In the previous chapter, we looked at the imagination in its most concrete workings. How does the process of making the sacred image compare with that work? Perhaps they should not be identified with each other; the sacred image is different from the club. The difference, however, is not so great as might be supposed, and the character of the earlier image may clarify the character of the sacred image.

The metaphoric imagination, as we looked at it earlier, is a practical thing, seeing the interlocking of form, function, and purpose, the act implicit in the bone, the fittingness of the bone, then the club, to the act. The symbolic imagination is not basically different; it is the metaphoric imagination in a different mode, seeing the primal energies of life in the thing (the wood; the representation). The emergent image is also a function, a tool in its own right. We might make a distinction in the kind of tool involved here; the one serves the practical function of conquest and power, the other the impractical function of reconciliation with the powers of the world. There is no reason to think they would have thought of it in such terms, which belongs to our more analytical mental processes. Such a reconciliation is hardly "impractical".

The symbolic imagination works in different modes but the one that will most concern us is indicated by Isaiah's description: the maker of the image falls down before it and worships it and calls it his god. The image is more than a function; it becomes a god.

Something else Isaiah could not have grasped: the image could be seen as a god <u>because it was an image</u>. This requires underlining because it is one of the most powerful motifs in the history of imagery: the very fact of resemblance, that an inert material should take on "the figure of a man", is uncanny, a great mystery, a magical act inspiring awe and desire. The resemblance does not have to be great for the image to have this quality of re-presenting the original.

Even though reproductive technology has created a world drowned in imagery, so that images of all kinds are a constant presence, this motif is as powerful now as it ever was. The elite may consider images harmless but demagogic politicians know better. Those who draw crude sexual images on toilet walls know better. Those who carry photographs of the beloved or who have a corner of their house devoted to a gallery of family photographs know better. Rulers still put their images in public places, not as a sign but as their own presence.

Such images are not only the presence of the represented, they themselves have a kind of life and personality. Several years ago I visited a church in Rome to see a fine fifteenth century sculpture of the Madonna and Child. Attached to the wall next to this image was the story of a miracle, told in cartoon style. A young man, much devoted to this image, was severely injured in an automobile wreck. The <u>image</u> (not the Madonna) left its niche, went into the street and healed the young man. Revolutions, as recently in eastern Europe, are always marked by the destruction of the image of the former ruler.

It is time now to revert to the fable and see how it might have been possible for the imagination to reach this point. While the body is one of the most powerful of the images, it is only one symbolic image; the symbolic imagination sees the relation and interaction, the resemblance of appearance, form or structure among things and so makes up a vocabulary of images. So long as we know we are dealing with a parable, a fable as parable and not history (the "origin of religion"), we might thereby get some sense of the fullness of thinking and the way thinking becomes transformed into religion.

Even in outline, the road from the making of a tool to the religious imagination is not a simple one. Making becomes thinking. More than tools needs to be discovered or made; we must first see how it would have been possible to grasp the principle of meaning, of truth, finally those things we, not they, call religion.

MAKING AND THE SYMBOLIC IMAGINATION

Let us return to the processes of the metaphoric imagination because they determine the course of the human mind, which is the source of all imagery. We began with our first humans developing their humanity by means of the metaphoric process that sees the relation between things and acts. The imagination, the image in the mind, was the essential principle in this process, for it enabled them to see function within the form, then to make a form that better fitted the function. The next step would have been a more complex act of the imagination: contemplating a task and imagining the form that would accomplish that task. We might postulate further even more complex acts of the mind: imagining a new function, then imagining the form that accomplishes that function. Or seeing or imagining a form and then imagining the function that form can serve.

It was possible to dramatize what could have been the first act of human thought, the making of the club. It is not so easy at this point because we cannot tell from surviving artifacts which process generated them. Some things can be said as summary.

The first acts of thought were not only directed toward the immediate task; they constituted the generation of the mind.

Our own understanding of the work of the mind, thinking, centers on words and the ordering of words into propositions that supposedly represent the real. We do not know and cannot know how language originated nor what role it played in the process we are fumbling with by way of this fable; we can suppose that it was generated within and because of this process of the imagination and became an integral part of it. Eventually, language would have take on something of an independent role as did all the acts of the imagination, but none could ever free itself wholly from its relation to the others or its dependence on the basic act of thought: imagination as seeing the relation of things to each other, of forms to function.

Certain conclusions follow:

1. At its origins, perhaps always, thinking is inseparable from matter and from the craft that shapes matter. This thinking in and by means of the physical material is done by the body that does the shaping. The

physical material and all those things that can be called "matter" are inseparable from the articulations, the desires and the skills of the body.(The qualification is necessary because there are "immaterial" things, such as human relations, that are parts of the making of the work of art. More of that later.)

2. The made thing has a purpose, since function is inseparable from purpose. Since purpose is in the future, the whole act of making generates a sense of the future and the possibility of planning toward the future. Out of this, at some unidentifiable point, there emerged one of the most characteristic human features: hope.

3. Continuation of the act of making along its stages of use and development depends absolutely on memory, which is the creation of the past. A decisive difference between the human and the animal is the imagination of the past and of the future.

4. The meaning of a form is its function (or: the function of a form is its meaning). The meaning of the function is what it does. (In order not to sound unduly materialistic, I should add that function, which we might postulate as practical in its initial formulation, becomes far more complex a short time thereafter.)

5. Meaning and purpose, form and function, generate one of the essential attributes of the human: truth. Truth is not a verbal statement of the real, as we so often understand it. Truth is the making of a form that fits the function. Truth is in the fitness of form to material, of the materialized form to its chosen function, of the function to the immediate occasion. Falsehood is a failure of any one of these.[2]

We are not accustomed to using truth and falsehood as applied to tools but we should become accustomed to it. In the originating act of thought in the fable, the bone was a partial truth. Used to dig a hole, the thigh bone would have been false, whereas a shoulder blade begins to serve as an early form of the spade. A hammer is a fine instrument of the truth. Used to nail fine walnut furniture, it would be used to lie. Truth is not an abstraction; it is inherent in the situation, in the materials and their proper forming according to their function. There is a truth in words but it

---

[2] Those who are familiar with contemporary controversies will recognize the range of these assertions. So long as it was believed that truth was something statable in words, the discovery that words can be highly deceptive was catastrophic. Those of us who did not believe in the adequacy of verbal statements in the first place endured the new revelation with a certain equanimity of spirit.

does not consist of abstract statement of an abstract Truth. It is the fittingness of statement to the immediacies of the occasion.

Truth is an intelligible notion when we are dealing with clubbing and digging, the proper and efficient performance of an identifiable function. It becomes a good deal more difficult when it is a matter of evaluating the function. When is it permissible to use the club? Against whom? At this point words become one of the essential instruments. We have no way of knowing when such questions became problematical to people. It is likely that patterns of habit were established early and not questioned for a very long time. Kubrick's fable assumes cooperation within the group, enmity and warfare against the other group. We might wish there had been a determining cooperation among groups but, regrettably, Kubrick is probably right. (It is not necessary to think that all early cultures were alike. Perhaps some developed their thinking around cooperation. The possibility of cooperation is part of the present human constitution, formed by evolution.)

(We will have to deal later with the problem of truth in art. When, under what conditions, is an image, a work of art, true?)

This much being said, we need to go further into the nature of forming.

FORMING AS CIRCUMSTANCE AND PURPOSE

Forming is not an abstract process, however much it depends on the immaterial image in the mind. Forming is always the forming of matter under particular circumstances. Forming thus generates not only specific tools but the whole process of forming to purpose. This forming is literal in terms of all the tools and instruments developed but it included also the forming of villages, dwellings, the structured relations that are a part of the culture. There is more.

Humanity began in the ability to shape things and relations into a human world. This alone is not enough; the made things have a function, which is their meaning, and a purpose. Inevitably, the principles of meaning and purpose became part of their imaginative processes. Inescapably, the sense of meaning and purpose would have to be applied to human life. There is no reason to think that this was an event. We might guess, as part of the fable, that it was simply part of the process of becoming human. As their own existence became a problem to them, they did not "think about it" in our common sense of thinking as verbal propositions;

they thought about it with the mental instruments they had developed: the things of the experienced world; metaphor; abstraction; made forms.

Again, we must imagine what it was like among these early people, remembering that they were like ourselves, only lacking all the explanatory devices developed with our technology. They were immersed, as we all are, in the processes of the organic world. At the same time, they were set apart from these processes by their consciousness of them. They, we, are simultaneously within and outside nature. The human situation creates the possibilities of human purpose.

The three possibilities: to return to the lost identity with nature; to escape from the involvement with nature; to find some reconciliation between the two. All religions, however complex, are defined by their disposition toward this problem and these solutions.

All images are made of formed matter; all matter is part of nature; the artisans, therefore, are inescapably involved with nature and its workings, wholly unable to live the ascetic "life of the mind" or the mystical escape from the hard uses of this earth.

The image makers are a special class of artisans. They work in matter but also and often represent this or that aspect of the human involvement with nature.

It is impossible for humans either to be reabsorbed into the unities of nature or to escape from involvement with nature. By nature we are a part of nature. By nature we are apart from nature. There can only be temporary accommodation which inevitably collapses of its own necessary failure to reconcile the contradictory poles of human existence. This is the inescapable tragedy of human experience. Every accommodation to the mystery of the world changes that world so the accommodation is no longer adequate to cope with it. No human construction can transcend the inevitable failure, no explanation escape from the process of change. The work must always be re-done, constantly.

These are not so much three purposes as three classes of purpose. Most structures of purpose in human history (that is, most religions) have sought one or another means of absorption into nature or some means of harmony with nature. The attempts to escape from it are few and belong largely to the great monotheisms (but the oriental polytheisms, immersed in the natural processes, have their own movements of ascetic withdrawal from the earth). The attempt to find a creative reconciliation of the two great purposes is extraordinarily difficult and correspondingly rare.

Whatever the purpose, the means for establishing it are the same. We might call it the "vocabulary" of religion and therefore of religious imagery. A full inventory of this "vocabulary" would be an enormous project, for it would be nothing less than an account of the total human experience of the world. The specification of it for each particular peoples is too large for even an outline sketch. The suggestion, however, should be enough; it is partly a matter of our being aware of the world we live in.

It does require an extension of our imagination because we are sheltered from the world by our technology. Early people experienced nature constantly and in full force; one of several purposes in the consideration of Mykonos was to evoke some sense of those rare occasions when we are outside that shelter and experience nature with full intensity. Most of us never experience true hunger or feel the inescapable darkness of night or the constant presence of animals or the difference between path and forest. We know nothing of the hunt, the making of weapons, the tracking of the animals, the complexities of the kill. We do not depend on gathering food, knowing where to gather it, which kinds are good, which poisonous. We do not know how to make the needed baskets or storage pots or the multiple, necessary uses of fire. All these, all the many others, constitute the necessary human experiences. They are also the vocabulary for the construction of their imaginative world.

THE SYMBOLIC PROCESS

We are now entering the field of the symbolic process, essential to religion.

As Isaiah knew, the human body is the first class of the infinite resources available to the imagination. The body has weight as it stands and moves on the earth. Its motions are infinitely varied in possibility but shaped by the necessities of its occasions; abstractions of these motions become the vocabulary for the dance which, as ritual, is a major statement of religion. The body and its parts have their characteristic shapes which are first those of the organism, then, in abstraction, geometric. For example, arms, legs, fingers, are cylinders, the head a sphere, etc. (African sculpture is the most extensive statement of the possibilities of abstracting geometric forms from the shapes of the body. Not until the Greeks and subsequently the Italian Renaissance has there been much interest in the internal ordering and articulations of the body.) The hand grasps, strikes, cups, caresses, gestures, pulls, pushes, scrapes and on and on; (one of the delights of studying Picasso is his fascination with the multiple shapes and acts of hands).

The human body and its infinite possibilities are common to us all; nature presents itself to us in the particularities of a region. Even so its acts and forms are nearly infinite. We experience nature first of all in terms of its energies, fertility and generation, fruitfulness and decay, death; also, their opposites, the deadly — literally deadly — sterility of drought and desert. Then there are all its motions, heat and cold, tranquillity and storm. Nature is stone, wood, earth, water, air, fire, vines, plants, trees, the undulating planes of desert, grasslands and seas, the enclosing valleys between mighty hills. Nature has its geometries. Hills are pyramids or cones, tree trunks are cylinders.

Human work creates whole new classes of shapes and actions, walls, passages, tents, houses, pots, paths.

The things of the world, including those unseen things that are the inner meaning of our geometrics, are inescapably part of this process of making the world. They become symbols, which are more than simply things. For the things to become symbols the metaphoric process must first discern the essential shape, the form directly related to the function, which is the meaning of the thing and the vocabulary of meaning for the symbolic imagination. Things have to be seen in themselves before they can be used symbolically in the construction of the world.

Walls are planes, masses and surfaces. They are obstacle, shelter, enclosure, limit and boundary. Doors are rectangles, passage, vulnerability, relation. Many things are multiple in function and therefore in symbol: rivers are water, depth, motion, limit, road, barrier, danger. Water is tranquillity, danger, life necessity, destroyer, deep mystery, motion, stillness. Water is a different thing with different symbolic potency to desert people and coastal people.

So far we have dealt with things as form and function, together with all that can be abstracted from them. Understanding the symbolic imagination on this model has a danger we should be careful to avoid. It would probably be false to their mental operations to think of the generation of the club (or the pot or whatever) in wholly instrumental terms, as though the makers could be apart from experience, making decisions about it. That is rather too much like our own analytical mental operations. It would certainly be false to the process of making the sacred image, which is a mode of life as much as a mode of thought.

The sacred images become symbols only by their joining with the characteristically human acts and feelings. It is one thing to apprehend nature as energy. It is quite another to see nature in terms of life. There are, first, all those things about life that are inescapably parts of the human and apparently parts of the rest of nature. The chief of these is will, the ability to act to purpose. I said "apparently" to distinguish most of us from our earlier ancestors. It seems that, at least for some of them, all nature is alive and has will. The stone willfully trips me. It was a decisive moment in the history of the human imagination when things became merely lifeless things. (But we still kick the chair that intrudes into our path.)

As soon as we talk in these terms, we run the danger of stumbling into ancient scholarly debates having to do with the origin of religion, debates that have mostly died of their own inability at resolution. It is not my purpose to become involved in such debates, only to point to things and attitudes that make up the human mind. Life is energy. Energy is power. Energy is an awesome thing in itself and impinges on our consciousness as power, the power of the sun, of the storm, of the river, of the burgeoning fertility of nature. Without energy, life gives way to death. Both death and life are mysteries.

The term "mystery" is double: things I don't know are mysteries to me but many of them are not mysteries to other people. Mystery is also that beyond understanding and explanation. We now know more about the conditions of life and death than our earliest ancestors did but life and death are as much mysteries to us as to them.

The other animals do not so much remember as learn. They have no future so they cannot plan. They simply are. We, alone among all the structures of the hierarchical order, live in the past and the future. The present is the moment between memory and hope. We look back and around for meaning. We look forward for purpose.

This is the inescapable paradox of the human. We can never escape from our involvement with nature. Despite the eternal yearning, we can never again be absorbed into nature. We are forever divided, therefore forever defeated.

All creatures are going to die. We are the only creatures who know we are going to die.

Still avoiding, if possible, all suggestion of "the origin of religion" and thinking of it only as fable, we might perhaps have the ingredients of religion: the power of imagination to see the identity of things; the sense of the energy and mystery of the earth and all its things, natural and made; the fateful split at the heart of human purpose; the awareness of past and future, of memory and hope; the awareness of the inevitability of death.

Religion is the human response to all these things and begins with all the things designated at one time or another as the origin of religion: fear of power and energy and the desire for propitiation; awe and the desire to worship; awareness of the power and energy and the desire to participate in it or to use it for human purposes (magic).

All questions concerning the specification of these matters can be left to the account of specific religions, not to speculation about origins.

All these things, responses, emotions, become part of their own form of making. This making goes beyond the area of this study since it includes myth and ritual, the narrative and the act that accounts for the mystery and enables the worship or to participate in the energy. But in the whole, myth and ritual are inseparable from places and things. The place is the sacred place, set apart as peculiarly containing the energy, the thing is the sacred thing representing the primal energies.

The place, defined and enclosed, is the beginning of architecture. The thing, carved or painted, is the beginning of art. Both are images of order and process, the way the world is made, the way the world inescapably, ineluctably, **is,** for those who are part of that world.

To grasp, to be grasped by, to comprehend, to understand their imagery is to participate in the world of another people.

Interlude

Summary and Definitions

Wherein various matters are offered for review and preparation; to be used for reference or preparatory reading.

An Annotated Glossary

Image

1. An image is a made object—drawn, painted, printed, carved—that represents something other than itself. The reference here is not to the concept of a person or thing (e.g., the politician's image).

2. The image is a selection from the total perceptual experience. The visual image, however much affected by the rest of the perceptual experience, is a selection of things seen from a point of view.

3. Our perceptual experience of the world is an experience of the whole organism, all the senses and modes of awareness functioning simultaneously. (Emotional involvement and personal relation significantly affect perception. Fatigue, state of mind, curiosity, degrees of physical awareness, modify the immediacy of perceptual experience.)

4. The image serves the purposes of memory and of interpretation.

Elements of the Image

1. Representation
   a. Subject: the things, persons and actions shown by the image.
   b. Sign: the subjects as pointers to something other than themselves.
2. Form (see Appendix for a fuller treatment of form)
   a. As interpretation of the subject.
   b. As representation, by means of its structure, of some structure or principle from the experienced world.
   c. As expression; a direct statement of feelings, etc.
   d. As form-world.

37

A form-world is the integrated set of formal properties of a person or a culture.

Representation and form are separable only for investigation; by nature they are inseparable.

REPRESENTATION

The term "representation" has two important references:

1. The first is political and applies by analogy to images: the senator represents the people of his state, in that he acts for them, stands for them. In politics other than the democratic, the king represents the people, not as chosen spokesman but as their equivalent. When Louis XIV said, "L'etat, c'est moi" ("I am the state"), he was speaking a serious politics, although one most of us would reject.

2. The second: the image as resemblance, as imitation of the subject. Imitation is never simple; the most exact reproduction of appearances (which is possible only with very simple subjects), still extracts the image from its context, both place and time, and consequently alters it decisively. Representation as imitation is always and by necessity, selective. The principle of selection is a purpose of interpretation. Representation as imitation is determined by cultural conviction and so is a means of understanding the semantics of the image.

"Representation" re-presents appearances but also characteristics of experienced reality that are other than or within appearances.

Appearances are on the surface but they are not superficial. While the distinction between appearance and reality is sometimes useful, it is problematic, since appearances are a part of reality. It is useful when it is understood that appearances often are the manifestation of realities that are not palpable or immediately accessible to vision. Furthermore, the appearance of a human artifact can often, even usually, manifest a reality, such as the flight of the bird, that is not present in the immediate appearance.

The double meaning of representation defines two major types of images, particularly images as used in religion:

1. Representation as standing for, in the place of, that which is represented, is the principle of the *idol*, which contains the divinity, the sacrality, represented. This is "re-presentation", making the sacred present.

2. Representation as resemblance makes possible the principle of the *icon,* which does not contain the sacred but give access to it.

The worshipper prays to the idol, but through, by means of, the icon. This distinction is fundamental in principle, but rarely appears so clearly in actual religious experience.

A further, psychological, consequence of representation as resemblance is the progressive detachment of the spectator from the image and the consequent encouragement of the sense that the world is something other than ourselves to be looked at from the outside.

FORM

Since representation normally involves actual physical resemblance, the making of a form that in some sense is like the form of the subject, this is the locus of analysis.

The form does several things:

1. Form is the means of the imitation, which is always selective.

2. Form is interpretative, in that it selects the aspects and the qualities of the subject that fit the maker's understanding of the subject

3. Form is expressive, the statement of the maker's feelings.

4. Form, considered as representation and in itself, has its own semiotics and semantics.

All these definitions require further development in the analyses to follow.

THE STUDY OF IMAGES

Emerging from these preliminary distinctions is a basic account of the image: There are three principal disciplines for the study of images.

1. The image is, first of all a subject, the representation of something other than itself. The study of subjects is iconography. Every culture, every religion, has its characteristic and distinctive iconography, the body of subjects that make up its imagery

2. Since the image is a made object, a thing, it has form. The form is simultaneously the embodiment of the subject and the means for its interpretation.

3. An image is a sign as well as a subject. The study of signs is semiotics.

4. Subjects, forms and signs have meaning. The study of meaning is
semantics.

These disciplines interact and interlock in so many ways that they
cannot rightly be followed as separate modes of investigation. They are
modes of our awareness of the complexity of images.

For example, the crucifixion is a common subject in Christian imagery,
appearing in many forms throughout Christian history. It is part of
Christian *iconography*. As a subject, it can be represented in a number of
different ways. The head of Jesus can be represented as hanging in quiet
resignation. Or contorted in suffering and pain. Or raised in triumph over
pain. These (and the many other possibilities) are interpretations of
meaning, the *semantics* of this image. The crucifixion and the cross are signs,
signs of Christianity, of a Christian church, etc. These are elements in the
visual *code*, the study of which is *semiotics*.

To many, the cross is a sign of persecution, oppression, enmity, hatred.

The cross, as a sign, is also a symbol since its meaning is wider than
its particular sign function. It marks the center where the arms of the cross
intersect. It is direction, radiating out to the four cardinal directions.
Vertically, it is the world tree, an element in many mythologies. Thus the
cross is subject to both semiotics and semantics, reference and meaning.

Both as subject and as sign, the crucifixion, as all subjects, is
independent of the nature of its particular embodiment; it can be of wood
or bronze, it can be large or small, simple or elaborately ornamental. Its
semantics, its meaning, is dependent on and determined by its form, so
formal analysis is basic to the understanding of images.

The psychic or political needs of critics of different periods of time
will determine where the emphasis lies among these three major categories.
A generation ago, students of imagery concentrated on the artistic image
(meaning images they judged to be high quality), with a corresponding
emphasis on form as independently valuable. At present, during a time
when people increasingly identify themselves with a group, the emphasis
has shifted to the semiotic codes as determined by the political interests of
the group. This emphasis is justified, for all images of consequence are
coded in many ways by the personality and interests of the maker and the
patron, by social and political interests and images, by the variety of
purpose present among those who make and use the image. The danger
lies in emphasizing only one of these codes at the expense of the others
and the common neglect of form as the means for the interpretation of the
subject.

Since an introductory study cannot deal in depth with all of these, choices have to be made. At various points in the study, I will illustrate one or another of these coded involvements but I will place primary emphasis on the image as subject and the form as an interpretation of the subject as well as an embodiment of meaning in its own right.

THE ELEMENTS OF ANALYSIS

Every image is a made object, a thing. As a made object, every image is a work of art. This is not a statement of value; it may be bad art as well as good art. Every object, every thing, is made up of component elements: matter, form, content.

I. Matter

The physical material the image is made of, together with all its qualities and characteristics.

II. Form

The shapes and relations imposed on the material by the hand and mind of the maker of the images (the artist).

III.Content

All the things communicated through and by means of the form.

Missing from the list is the element considered by most people as the image itself: the representation of some thing or person from the experienced world. This is something of a pedagogical stunt to emphasize an important issue: the represented subject — the subject "matter" — is part of the material. It is shaped, presented, re-presented by the form.

Content is identical with what most people think of as meaning; it is the chosen term because meaning seems to be separable from the formed material whereas content is not.[1] Content includes the semantics and the semiotics of both the represented subject and the form

Form is both the representation and the interpretation of the subject. Understanding images requires knowing the energies embodied in the subject and selected for the image. The purpose of the analysis of form is the interpretation of the content.

---

[1] Even professional literature often uses "content" as synonymous with subject. This is a pity. We already have a good term for the subject. It would be better to save content for something not present in the term "subject".

Form is so complex that an outline of it will be deferred to an Appendix, together with the outline of a scheme for analytical interpretation.

RELIGION AND MAKING

In the fable, the first act of making was the beginning of the human. Once begun, the process was inexorable: having become human, these people, unable to be anything other than nature, had to make a human world.

A common term for the description of this human world is "world-view" (the more portentous sounding German word is "Weltanschauung"). The term supposes that there is a world out there, over there, which we can see in various ways. This is a mistake.

By nature, we are apart from nature. In that capacity, we look at nature, "reality", from outside and have opinions about it and views of it.

By nature, we are a part of nature. There is certainly a physical reality out there, with its characteristic relations and interactions. We are not apart from that reality but inextricably involved in its processes. In that capacity, we do not have views of it or have opinions about it. We are a part of it.

Because we are a part of those physical processes and because we are something more, we have to make all those things and acts that constitute our world. "World" is the reality of the given things and the processes of our involvements in them

The word "makes" is not an analogy; the world is composed of the things made by the minds and hands of human beings, including all the abstract structures and energies, the symbolic forces, within those things. The things made as ways of coping with the necessities of the immediate world are themselves symbols and the models for the making of symbols.

The general categories of both the making and the understanding of the physical and symbolic worlds include such things as space, time, cause and generation, matter and the natural order. Equally they include the responses that are a part of being human: desire, fear, love, hate, the whole repertoire of human feelings and emotions that are an integral part of the real and of our ways of knowing the real.

They include also reverence, awe, desire, terror, mystery.

To understand the religion of a people it is necessary to do (at least) two things:

1. Analyze and interpret the structure and processes of their world in terms of the full range of categories that we apply to the making of worlds. This requires the analysis of all the things and institutions of their world. Images are among those things and both the things and the institutions are themselves images of order and process.
2. Grasp the character and the quality of their responses and the images that embody those responses and define their sense of the sacred.

The dimensions of religion.

1. Every religion contains, or is, a "world-view" that is more than a view of a separate world but that world in its completeness as defined by the imaginative ordering of the people. The first step in understanding a religion is to grasp its world with all the sympathy, participation and understanding possible.
2. Every religion, if it is to be more than a mere philosophy of life, is a response through all possible human agencies to the power and mystery of life. This is the numinous (Otto) and the sacred (Eliade).
3. Every religion, as part of its world and its pattern of living in the world, has a moral structure that involves a conviction of how the self is related to the other and how it ought to be related to the other.[2]

Some elements of religion (for the study of images).

1. Idol: an image that contains the divinity or sacrality.
2. Icon: an image that gives access to the divinity or the sacred, without containing it.

We cannot know when images were first made, only those that are the earliest to survive for us. We do know that later images became complex in their character and in their motivation. The first images were made as an essential part of the making of the world. More surely than most of the evidence that survives, it reveals that world to us.

The first stage of understanding a religion is the account of the structure and energies of its world, then within that world the defining sense of the sacred.

---

[2] Some cultures keep their moral code detached from the formal ordering of their religion. It is, nevertheless, a part of their religion in its totality.

Section Three

The Evidence and the Argument

In which certain groups of images are analyzed as demonstrations of the role of images in the religious life and of the function of images as primary theological thought. These include the earliest images of organic energy and geometric order, images of the earth, of space as symbol and human context, of the body in several modes.

4 | THE FOUNDATIONS

> ...and they themselves [the Paleolithic peoples] were racially
> exhausted, having bequeathed to all humanity a foundation
> of ideas upon which the mind could raise its structures.
> ....Gertrude Rachael Levy

We know nothing of the origin of religion. We can look at its earliest manifestations in the caves of south-western France and the plains of southern England.

So far we have tried to imagine the mental world of our earliest ancestors and the things that were the instruments of their thinking and of their coping with their world. That coping included the things made (and done) under the conditions of the energies and the structures that surrounded them. These made things included images, things that looked like other things. We cannot know when images were first made, only those that survive to us. We do not know why early people made images. We know a good deal about what we think are the earliest images. These introduce the elements of the making of images.

The title of the chapter itself contains an argument: earliest people were not other than ourselves. They were people like ourselves with the considerable and consequential difference that they lacked the technology that shelters us from the immediacies of the physical earth. In a manner sketched out earlier in an imaginative reconstruction, they made the things of their world. They also made images as among the means of coping with their world.

PALEOLITHIC IMAGES

Stone age people are not parts of a foreign and distant past. They are not merely our ancestors. They are dimensions of our selves. As the earliest peoples had to develop the elementary processes of human life and thought, so the Paleolithic and Neolithic peoples established the basic symbolic modes that are still part of our heritage and our psychic operations. The ideas (imagistic, not verbal) of these periods are fundamental in human development and the key to the purposes of this chapter is the epigraph.

For the earliest period, the Paleolithic era, the evidence is almost exclusively European, raising a question about Levy's expansive "to all humanity". The limitation is a necessity; there is too little evidence of images from the Paleolithic period in other regions. We do not know if the evidence has disappeared or has not yet been discovered or whether images played so limited a role in the early development of the non-European cultures. Evidence from the Neolithic period seems comparable everywhere so perhaps that would be true for the earlier people.

The evidence for Paleolithic imagery consists primarily of paintings found in the caves of south-central France and northern Spain. It is difficult to determine when they were painted; they seem to have been common over many centuries, say from around 25,000 to 12, 000 BCE.

The subject matter of Paleolithic cave painting consists almost entirely of images of animals on walls deep inside caves. (There are also a few representations of the human figure, some outlines of hands, a few non-representational signs.) The paintings do not occur in habitable caves. They are often found very deep, past dangerous obstacles, requiring a perilous journey to reach them. While many are on the walls and vaults of large rooms, many are found in almost inaccessible places, under low ledges, high up in chimney-like formations.

Only fragments of evidence suggest how they were used. Some have injuries on the surface around the region of the heart, suggesting that weapons were ritually thrown at them. There are a few figures in other caves molded from clay; some have the heads smashed. Footprints in the clay of some of the floors suggest a ritual procession. Occasionally these prints were made by groups of boys, suggesting an initiation ceremony.

It is difficult to reconstruct the life of these our ancestors. They lived in small groups, took shelter in shallow caves, used stone tools, fed themselves from what they could get by hunting animals and gathering food, buried their dead with ceremony. We can only imagine their mental life: they were few in number and small while the world was huge, teeming with life, fecund, nourishing, dangerous. Death was close and frequent, decay as much a part of life as growth. The night was huge and terrible, the seasons remorseless in their changing, the earth powerful in its inescapable imperatives. Their desires were immediate and elemental: food, drink, shelter, sex.

They were a hunting-gathering people, nomadic, moving with the seasons, the migration of the herds, the shift in availability of gathered food. Their corporate life had no center, no fixed location. Hunting was a deadly danger but also the occasion for combined activity. Their world was the world of nature unmodified by much human activity, a world in movement and change. The emptiness of space could be filled by the enormous energies of the herds, constantly shifting and moving, overlapping, interweaving, the common energies of unhidden copulation, the terrible energies of the predators. The sun and growth. Night and death.

There is more we need to know, want to know and, in the absence of their words and only a faint shadow of their ritual, can never know. What we have is surely one of the greatest inventions of human history, experience transmuted into a system of images that copes with the complexity of life and sustains a genuinely human existence.

The cave is the first great architectural form, not architecture as built but as deliberately chosen symbolic space. Constructed architecture has both an inside and an outside. The cave is all interior, its defining edges the surface of a vast, amorphous, unshaped mass. It has passage ways but no defining direction, no axial organization; walls, floors, ceilings flow into each other.

The cave is the entry into the earth. The earth is source and origin of life and in death receives life back into itself. The cave is the womb of the earth, the passages the entry into the womb.

The treatment of the animals varies greatly. Some are simple outlines, others are painted surfaces (they were done at different periods of time with long gaps in between). They demonstrate a high degree of abstraction: hair can be represented with a series of lines, bodies are elongated to emphasize their grace, legs are sometimes tiny, to place emphasis on the bulk of the body. They are often in movement or give the suggestion of movement. This liveliness, so essential a characteristic of animals, is *gesture*.

The modern eye is conditioned by images in frames, organized around the coordinates of the vertical and horizontal. The energies and vitalities of our organic life are the same as those of all organisms but they are lived out in the context of an ordered geometry, roads and streets ordering the flat surface of the earth, the verticals and horizontals, the remorseless right angles of our buildings framing our lives[1] To eyes trained

---

[1] There are exceptions to this generalization, parks, some forms of festival buildings, but they are normally felt as amiable exceptions. The modern period has gone further

by such ordering and centering, there appears to be no intelligible relation among these images. They are crowded, often overlapping, arranged at random over the irregular surface of the cave. There is no dominant direction, no axial organization of this fecund life. To a sense of order conditioned by 5,000 years of axial ordering, this appears to be a deficiency, that they had no coherent sense of order. In actuality it is a sense of order quite different from our own, an indifference to controlling directions, to frames, an acceptance of the uncentered infinite.

The center is one of the great inventions of history, one of the fundamental hierophanies. So powerful is it in our own imaginations that it is difficult to imagine an image world that is not centered.

Description has already become analysis, for we are here approaching fundamentals. The things I have been describing are the **structure** of the cave paintings: the sense of the unbounded, the uncentered, the sole emphasis on the vital energies of the great animals, the entry into the earth. What can all this "mean", which is to say, what kind of content can we point to verbally?

Since the specific experience of the work in place is often so vital to the purposes of the work, it is necessary to rely on the description of a personal experience.

Ill. 2   Lascaux, in south-central France, is the most famous and perhaps the finest of the caves. I saw Lascaux by means of its floodlights. At one point, the guide turned off the floodlights and used a flashlight for a few moments. The effect gave a little sense of how the paintings might have looked originally, illuminated by little lamps. A part of an image was strongly lit, the rest progressively dimmer. This light gave a sense of how they were supposed to be seen. The walls pulsated with animal energy. There was a sense of being surrounded by, immersed in, the unrestrained energy and vitality of the animals.

The effect was awesome. The floodlights made the paintings into exhibits, as in a museum; it was possible to be detached from the images, an object lesson in the way we experience the world sheltered by technology.[2] In the dimmer light, the space suddenly became mysterious,

---

than any other since the earliest times to soften, even dissolve, the rigidities of this geometry.

[2] This is not a value judgment, in the contemporary fashion of extolling the merits of the primitive. Their experience of the world is not superior to ours, only different. Or, to put it differently, to judge their experience as superior to ours, or wiser or truer, is merely to accept their religion without demonstrating why it should be judged superior.

the walls merely the edge of the vast mass of the containing hill; the observer becomes one with the vital energy of the animals and the earth. This was truly the experience of the numinous. The pulsating animal energy of the walls is an archetypal experience.

The people who made these images were people like ourselves, probably not much different in appearance, certainly no different in degree of intelligence. Their minds would have been furnished with a quite different set of mental tools, of imaginative structures. We must be careful in attributing our experiences to them. But this may be the occasion for us to experience their experience and, therefore, share their intention.

Among the most common of the sign forms on the wall are those of the vulva, the external triangle of the female sexual organs. Several caves have molded representations of breasts. There are a few, but only a few, images of the phallus; the phallus would have been as great a power for them as for any later people but it was not so much a symbolic power, not so often used in imagery; it rarely appears on the walls (unless some rather strange feathered shafts are signs of the phallus). However much male sexuality was among the physical powers of the earth, it may not have been associated with reproduction and the symbolism of the caves is basically fertility, generation, fecundity.

The animals are the decisive elements of this fecundity, the embodiment of extraordinary energy. They are the greatest animal images ever made. Their appearance is summarized with uncanny accuracy, permeated by the force of vital life, which is "gesture".

The imprint or silhouettes of hands may simply be a sign of human presence. They may also be a celebration of the bodily feature that makes humans superior to animals, that gives humans a control over the earth that no other creature has. The hand is the means for liberating the human from imprisonment in the habits of matter and animality.

The evidence of injury to the paintings, usually over the heart areas, led early anthropologists to suppose the images were part of "hunting magic", ceremonies to ensure the success of the hunt. Such an interpretation is determined by a sensibility which assumes that events are determined by cause. It is more probable that the ceremony was motivated as the imagery was, to give ritual embodiment to the wholeness of the action. The animals are the vitalities of the earth; the hunt is the death of the great animal. As the animal is awesome, awe-full, so the death of the animal is terrible. Such vitalities are not to be trifled with in simple, causal, practicality. The animals are to be dealt with honorably; among more modern "primitive" peoples, the slaughtered animal is often ceremoniously brought back to the place of the people, set up on a seat of honor, made the object of propitiatory ritual designed to placate its spirit, to give honor to one who deserves honor and respect. Some cave paintings almost certainly represent the same ritual.

Some interpretation sees a similar "sympathetic magic" directed toward ensuring the fertility of the herds. We cannot know if this was in their minds but it is not necessary either to exclude such a causal factor or to make it the only motivation. Fertility is one of the primal powers of the earth and the images preserve this fecundity for the sake of the ritual. It is a mode of participation.

They surely did not make images as we do, a form to "look like" something else. A representation for them was nothing like a work of art is for us, something other than ourselves that gives us "aesthetic" satisfaction. As best we can reconstruct their thinking (more than guesswork, less than certainty), the image was the animal in a different mode, brought to vigorous life in the cave, on the wall of the cave. This is based on a coherent principle, or image, of order: the earth and all things and creatures in it are made of a common substance. Therefore, all things are alive, permeated with the same force and energy of life. Only distinction of form identifies the different elements of life. It was essential to give the images as much of the form of the animals as possible to give them the necessary actuality. They are the thing itself, purified, freed from the adventitious, fixed into permanence, lifted out of, beyond, time, yet pulsating with the energies of life.

The key word becomes participation, participation of a kind that becomes indispensable for the understanding of so much religious imagery. It was certainly not the participation of a subjective, psychologistic kind, the psychic act we call the "spiritual". It would have been direct and immediate. The people entered the womb of the earth as a return to the source of life. The extraordinary act of making an image, a representation, within this earth womb, would have been a matter of fulfilling, making present, and directly participating in this vital energy. (It is a mode of what would later be called *sacrament*.)

We may have here an explanation for the location of the images. Many are found in large halls and passageways, accessible, although with difficulty. Others are found in remote places and almost hidden. In some cases, the painter would have to lie down and slide under a ledge to paint the animal on the underside. It was not necessary for the images to be seen, only to be there.

The famous "well scene" at Lascaux (it is in a deep, roughly circular, natural pit) provides a clue to their use of images. On the wall of the "well" there are two animals, a rhinoceros and a bison, the latter apparently transfixed by a spear, its intestines spilling out of the wound. In between there is a man, drawn with a crudity and lack of skill all the more striking given the very high quality of the animals.[3] Ill. 3

The man, wearing what appears to be a bird mask, is standing, arms thrown back and out, his head back and his penis erect. This is clearly a shaman figure and one of the few bits of evidence we have of the ritual connected with the actual hunt, here perpetuated in the cave. The shaman is a person, man or woman, who is the intermediary between the human world and the world of the spirits, often sharing qualities otherwise distinct. Thus the bird mask, since shamans are often identified with birds, able to fly into the world of the spirits. This figure, presumably in ecstatic trance, is manifesting the male energy of the erection; equally, shamans often assume the clothing and roles of the other sex, affirming the basic unity of the vitalities of life. The ritual, the hunt, are parts of a single act and one with the energy of reproduction

The other distinctive Paleolithic image is the carved figures of women, obese or pregnant (or both), faceless, both arms and legs diminished in favor of the prominent body. The focus is so exclusively on the fertile body that it would seem to account for the figures. Ill. 4

Most of the surviving figures are small enough to be carried in a pocket or hung around the neck. Often the legs taper to a point as though they were stuck in the ground. Circumstances suggest that they were used by women. The figures may be causal, to help ensure or encourage the fertility that was essential to the survival of the tribe. It is not necessary to assume causality as we understand it but, again, participation; as the image is fecund so will the woman, participating in the evident power of the image, be fertile.

---

[3] A curious error has handicapped interpretation of the figure. An early photographer photographed the scene as though the bison were standing on level ground, which made the man appear to be lying on the ground. With a misplaced trust in the accuracy of photography, most interpreters have tried to make up a dramatic illustration of a "prehistoric tragedy". Quite apart from the fact that the painters at Lascaux paid only casual attention to direction, in fact the man is standing erect and it is the bison which is at an angle. For some reason, the early photographer tilted his camera.

These figures are commonly referred to as "Venus". "Venus" is a misnomer, and falsifies what is going on; Venus was a goddess in a specific religion. There is no reason to think this figure represents anything that we would call a goddess; we should not superimpose our own inclinations on ancient evidence. Almost certainly these people had no sense of particular divinities (the existence of divinities would establish a dominance of symbolic direction, which was lacking).

Symbolically, religiously, what we have is a world dominated by organic energies. The cave itself is more a place than a center and the order represented in the cave is without a center, without dominant direction. There is no indication of divine personalities. We might presume, judging from the power of the images, that their ceremonies were intended to establish a continuity between human life and the energies of the earth.

We have here a profound essay on the sacrality of the earth and of organic life, on the continuity of all things, on participation in the character and the qualities of the natural order, on a reintegration into the vital energies of the earth.

NEOLITHIC IMAGERY

Paleolithic hunters generated images that were part of the foundation of all later life and thought: the cave; the animal; the fruitfulness of the bodies of women, the earth. The Neolithic revolution absorbed, sustained, built on that foundation. Complexities of development will have to be reduced to a few types.

Roughly, we are dealing with the change from a hunting-gathering society to a food producing society, with all the momentous consequences of such major differences in the means of economic production and political organization. Instead of roaming freely over a wide and ill-defined area, people now settled in villages with all the consequences such a movement entailed by way of a new social order. Sowing and harvesting requires a different order of control and cooperation, a shifting of responsibilities between men and women, the invention of new forms of containers and of houses, with a resulting change and increase in the imaginative vocabulary. As the great herds moved north, there was a change to domesticated animals with all that entails for the imagination. Instead of the shifting places of a nomadic people, villages were now points in the landscape connected by the lines of established paths.

Neolithic imagery takes a remarkable turn: geometric figures and geometric abstraction. This is a basic addition to the vocabulary of images.

Our evidence may be distorted by loss; most of what we know we learn from the ornamentation of pottery. Within these limits, the evidence for a profound shift in thinking is great. Ill. 5

1. The making of the pot itself is a revolutionary intellectual act; it involves not merely modification of a natural material as in the making of stone instruments but its transformation (by fire). Once established, transformation would have been a major technical procedure and a basic addition to the symbolic vocabulary.

2. A pot is the forming of emptiness, of volumes, of a clear distinction between inside and outside. For Paleolithic people, the image of space was determined by the vastness of the landscape and the irregular space of the cave; space now becomes geometrically regular. Whatever its functional usefulness, the pot retains its spiritual symbolism. In many cultures, the making of pots and baskets is the prerogative of women, presumably developing from their function as gatherers. (Hunting and gathering require quite different perceptual and motor skills. The survival value of these different skills would have affected the evolution of men and women, which may survive to our own day.)

It is conceivable (we cannot know for sure) that women were peripheral to the hunt; the symbolic significance of women might then have been confined to what we can see in the images, fertility and reproduction. Now it is possible, even probable, that as custodians of a major economic and symbolic principle of corporate life, their own symbolic authority would have changed and considerably increased.

3. After its crude beginnings, the best way to make pots is on the wheel: the primacy of the circle by means of rotary motion, the eternal return of movement on itself. Ornamentation is itself a prime motif, the addition of an element that has no functional value other than beautification with both expressive and symbolic value. The ornament often takes the form of continuous bands, clearly defined rectilinear fields, various continuous patterns (meander, spirals, zigzag, etc.), and abstract fauna.

"Abstract" does not mean "non-representational". It means to select from the myriad elements of "reality" those aspects of it that are considered important. In that sense, Paleolithic images are highly abstract; the representing elements are chosen for their vividness of reproduction of certain appearances and their intensity of organic energies. Organic forms in Neolithic imagery are abstracted toward their underlying geometric structure.

The making of pots was accompanied by weaving, both as fabrics and the plaiting of reeds, vines, grasses into mats. This is another aspect of geometry in the opposition of warp and woof and their resolution into a flexible plane surface.

This shift in techniques is related to the underlying shift in the structure of the economy. Agriculture establishes not only a different social order, a different diet, but a different relation to time. Hunting and gathering requires a submission to movement and change, the seasonal migration of the herds, the constant change in the food supply, the great repetitions. Planting requires a deliberate awareness of the future, the ability to plan forward, the ability to calculate (how much grain must be preserved as seed for the next season?), the division of fields, the exact observation of weather (deceived by an early spring, planters who do not understand the passage of time might destroy all their seed). Thus we have not only the establishment of space as shape but the discovery of time as succession, articulated by number.

Paleolithic people knew bilateral symmetry, a prime part of geometric abstraction. An exactly balanced stone ax functions best; spear points, etc., are symmetrical. They did not use it in their imagery. In the Neolithic, symmetry becomes a fundamental principle of abstract order.

This vocabulary of geometric pattern is not exhausted in the rectilinear patterns of pots, of plaiting and of weaving. It includes also a variety of curvilinear patterns, particularly in association with such great burial mounds as New Grange in Ireland. These patterns are often spirals, sometimes complex spirals making symmetrical forms. They are placed so prominently at the entrances and along the passage ways that they probably were signs with a generally accepted meaning which is lost to us.[4] We are again dealing with an archetypal form that is continuous throughout the history of image making.

The human race in its stone age development discovered or made the fundamental vocabulary of formal images that has served the present.

---

[4] The difficulty of interpretation is demonstrated by the variety of meanings attributed to such signs. For Levy they are signs of "conditional entry". For Gimbutas, they have more meanings but are usually considered signs of the regenerative powers of the "goddess". Both interpretations are stated with equal confidence. I am more persuaded by Levy.

We see here two fundamental spiritual dispositions. These appear in dramatically simple form among early people but they are as basic to us as they were to them. All attempts to define the order of things lie between the poles of organic vitality and geometric abstraction. Symbolic forms and images manifest one or the other of these orders (more commonly some adjustment of the relation between the two) or merge from and, therefore, represent some resolution of this polarity.

Given the extraordinary proliferation of both forms and images since the stone age, this may seem unduly excessive. Excessive, yes, for the additions to the vocabulary of images are of fundamental importance. Unduly excessive, no, for all later developments take place within the defining limits of these two primal motifs of the human situation. This is dramatically illustrated in the enterprise of the twentieth century which, under the burden of dead forms and exhausted images, has sought to return to elementals and has, therefore, explicitly isolated these two dimensions of human experience, in the pioneering work of Kandinsky and Mondrian.

MEGALITHIC IMAGERY

"Megalithic", the period of the great stones, is an important part of the Neolithic period. The best known and the most fully developed megalithic culture is that of western Europe, extending in a great arc along or close to the Atlantic seaboard from Spain to Scandinavia.

The megaliths occur in different forms:
1. Single vertical stones, often reaching to great heights; the menhir.
2. Long avenues of menhirs, two or more rows often extending for a mile or more.
3. Circles. The most famous of these stone circles, Stonehenge, is   Ill. 6
   one of a kind, not typical of the rest.
4. Graves. These take two forms:
   a. The dolmen, two or more vertical stones capped by other stones, then covered with earth.
   b. The passage grave. A long, narrow passage made from large stones, capped by stones, ending in a large dolmen-like space, dome-like, the whole covered with earth.

The graves are clearly the cave in the sacred mountain.

These great stones are a central part of Neolithic religion; do they belong in the study of imagery? If so, what are they images of?

Unfortunately there is no answer to these questions, since we do not know what they were intended to be, or, except for the graves, how they were used. Many prominent interpretations are guesswork on the basis of modern presuppositions.

The megaliths are the greatest recognition of the symbolic power of stones, not as images but as part of the religious vocabulary that later becomes part of images. The menhir may seem (deceptively) the easiest.

The menhir (Welsh for "long stone") is an upright stone planted in the earth. Hundreds are present along the Atlantic coast of western Europe and in other parts of the world. When they are isolated, there is no sure way of knowing why they were erected or how they were used. When, as is often the case, they are combined into circles, avenues, etc., we can begin to make reasonable guesses. They are often parts of or associated with formations that are clearly vaginal and uterine; it is reasonable to suppose they are phallic. What have we said when we have said that? It appears that there are only a few possibilities of interpretation.

To the extent that the people had begun to orient themselves toward the sky, the menhir is a connecting point between earth and sky and so is part of an image of the cosmos, and a center. Since the sky is a constant presence and, in the sun and rain, a necessity of life, this orientation must have been present in some way from the beginning, the sky, by means of the rain, impregnating the fecund earth. If, as I am supposing, the idea of divinities and, therefore, "sky gods" was poorly developed, then the menhir becomes a focus of energies.

To the extent that their orientation was toward the earth, the menhir was something like the phallus of the earth. The crudity of such modern terminology as "phallic symbol" is altogether misleading; there is no reason to think that, under some psychoanalytic compulsion, they erected phalluses. Rather, the energies of procreation which are essential to all life are here brought to a focus. The symbolic process is chiastic; the menhir is not so much a "phallic symbol" as it is a concentration of the potency of the earth; the phallus itself is the manifestation of the same potency that is in the menhir. The one is a symbol of the other and both are means of participation in the primal energies of the earth.

Late examples, usually in other areas, are carved as phalluses. Later modifications of the menhir begin to make its symbolism accessible. Some smaller stones are modified (by the addition of abstract facial features, some indications of breasts), into a female figure (the Great Goddess? The Mother Goddess? Or__?). Others had the male genitals fixed to the front.

This led directly to the Greek herm (a pillar with the male genitals on the front and often the head of Hermes on the top. Herms stood at the entrance to houses, at street corners and other intersections. Ancient Greece was considerably less modern than we often think.)

In Greece, we have a vivid illustration of the most important development of the menhir, into the column on the one hand and, by way of the column, the most important of sculptured images, the standing human body.

The stone circles are equally obvious —and more complicated. They are, at least, circles with all the symbolic power of circles, roundness, the condensed statement of the horizon, the localization of the circle of the sky, the eternal return of movement on itself, the center.

If they were simply enclosures for sacred ceremonies, they are not images even though, as the first definition of architecture, they become part of the language of images. If they were representations of the circularity of the sky, then they are images.[5]

Some of the grave mounds are more obviously images. The grave-temples of Malta are in the form of a recumbent female figure. Many of the less elaborate grave mounds are entered by a restricted hole along passages decorated by representations or signs of the vulva.

THE GODDESS AND THE BIRTH OF DIVINITIES

Both Paleolithic and Neolithic people made images of women who are either obese or pregnant. It is a mistake to call them either "fertility figures" or "goddesses". The failure of imagination that causes this terminology may be a failure in the understanding of images.

Scholars are word mongers by trade and extend their own concern to a conviction that all truth is statable in words. Therefore, an image is not an independent way of knowing or of being related to the world. It must be an image <u>of</u> something else. Clearly these are representations of

---

[5] They were not "prehistoric observatories". An observatory is a scientific instrument for the systematic study of astronomical phenomena. The circles involved close observation of such phenomena, perhaps even using them for prediction, but there is no reason to think this was for anything other than ritual purposes. While many of the circles show some types of orientation, the phenomenon is fully demonstrable only at Stonehenge, which is undoubtedly the greatest of the prehistoric circles but also absolutely unique in several respects. It has little to do with Avebury, one of the largest and formally most eloquent of the circles.

the female body; they are often composite figures, woman and bird, woman and snake, etc. As such they are assumed to represent something other than themselves and, therefore, they are "goddesses". They are not images of something; they are something.

What is a goddess, or any divinity? A complex question; at a minimum the word assumes a being, probably somewhat like a human but greater in some respects and probably invisible, possessing the power of affecting human life. There is no reason to think any of these figures were goddesses in this sense.

Equally, there is no reason to think they weren't, except the psychology of images. Calling the figures "goddesses" superimposes our intellectual concepts on a people whose thought processes were undoubtedly different. We can never fully explain the "mythical" importance of things like the human body if early representations of the body are always representations of a divinity.

As the menhir would appear to be the concentration of masculine potency, so the female figures would be concentrations of the female powers, which are clearly more complex than the male. All human life is the same at all times but for prehistoric peoples it was stripped to its primal essentials. The earth is fruitful and the source of fruitfulness; death itself is a return to the earth.

We can never know the ritual that was the context of the images nor can we know the stories that grew up around them, the myths, the drama of the history of the people, the action and response that gave names to the images, changed them from embodied energies into personalities, translated the image into a divinity.

These images did not necessarily represent the goddess; the images made the later goddess possible. The image is an instrument of thought; only the image made possible the process of thought whereby it was possible to conceive a being not identifiable with the beings of the earth, not other than the beings of the earth, but giving body to the felt but unseen energies of the earth and of flesh.

The image did not represent a divinity conceived apart from the image. The image created the divinity, as Isaiah saw, without understanding what he was seeing.

We have seen our ancestors determining basic, foundational themes, developing them with an uncommon eloquence and profundity. What they accomplished was not superseded but absorbed, transformed, combined with other fundamental themes. It remains now to isolate some of the great symbolic forms: the representation of the earth, the ordering of space as cosmic image, the human body and the sacred narrative.

5

IMAGES OF EARTH

IMAGE AND CONTEXT

E very image is part of a context. Images are made by people. Every person is an individual with desires, fears, prejudices, beliefs, all the things that make up a human personality. Every person is part of a particular society, a particular culture, participating in, in part formed by, all the attitudes and convictions, the general purposes and prejudices of that culture. Every image is a part of those personal and cultural worlds, part of their prejudices and purposes.

All these interweaving, interlocking forces make up the context of the image and no image can be fully understood without grasping that context. Equally, no work of any consequence is explained by its context; the maker of the image is a human being, not simply determined by the context but able to use it to a human purpose. Freedom is never unlimited or unconditioned; we are never so determined by our context that we have no freedom to act within it.

"Context" is not a difficult word to define; the difficulty lies in determining its relation to the work. Context includes all those things that go into the making of the image. The image has an immediate function which will affect what it is. It is bound into a social and economic system in several ways: its function is worked out within the institutional ordering of society; the production of the images depends on an organized system of training, of workshops, of financial support for obtaining materials and distributing the product, etc. The artist-craftsman is a human being, belonging to a particular social class, a particular gender, participating in the convictions and the prejudices that go along with these locations. All societies make use of particular systems of signs, codes of communication, and the image system must work within those codes.

63

However much we would like to ignore these factors in the making of the work and concentrate on that aspect of it that concerns us (the religious), we cannot; any image, every work of art, is inextricably bound up with all of these restrictions, possibilities, affects, purposes. Here, it is not possible to take up all the elements that make up the image; I have chosen instead to concentrate on the image as a product of the insight of its maker into the issues that we can describe as religious.

For prehistoric images we know almost nothing about the context, beyond a few educated guesses. The only possibility for understanding those images is by analysis and interpretation of their form, the structural principles of their making. This circumstance is useful pedagogically; it emphasizes the decisive act of making and the analysis of the form of the making. Also it considerably simplifies the task of analysis; we can't busy ourselves taking into account those things we cannot know. Sadly, this is simplification by falsification; what we don't know is the function of the works for those who made them and that, for them, was the most important thing about the images. We can, respectfully, try to grasp what they are "in themselves", which inevitably means what they are to us.

To carry the study into different areas where we know a great deal about the context, I have chosen three very different examples, all having to do with the placement of humans within a landscape, each providing an image of the earth and the human place in it. The first provides a transition between the prehistoric and our own day.

Ill. 7   NAVAHO SANDPAINTING[1]

Navaho sandpainting[2] provides a transition because certain defining elements of Navaho culture are Neolithic[3].The mistake comes in confusing the Navaho with prehistoric people, using the one to interpret the other and shoving contemporary people out of the way as though they, too, are

---

[1] The motive for this selection and the similar use later of African sculpture, is not the condescension so often involved in "multiculturalism". The quality of the works is so high, the intellectual achievement so considerable and the imagery so distinctive in its achievement as to make them central to this discussion.
[2] It can be called more accurately "dry painting" because commonly materials other than sand are used: pollen, powdered minerals, etc.
[3] Obviously, this is not entirely true. After so long contact with white culture, the Navahos have adopted a great many aspects of that culture. Religions, however, are always conservative and the Navaho particularly so; it remains basically Neolithic.

distant in time. Navaho work is more serious than that. They too are very much a part of our world.

Paleolithic peoples concentrated almost exclusively on the organic energies of life. Neolithic people concentrated, less exclusively, on the formal ordering of geometric abstraction. It has been some time since either Africans or Navaho could be called fully Neolithic; their present cultural problem has been the disturbing one of grafting modern technology into a Neolithic culture. Insofar as they retain their traditional art forms, they represent something that is neither Paleolithic or Neolithic. In each case we have, formally, neither the pure animal energies of Lascaux nor the pure geometric abstraction of the Neolithic but energies under the control of geometry. Each represents a high level of abstraction and intellectual control of the image.

Navaho mythology is full of drama, change, movement, transformation. Navaho sand painting is precise, exact, rigidly directional, reducing everything to geometrical schema. Its parts are all elegant signs of natural and supernatural things and beings, divinities, lightening, corn, snakes. The painting is made on the earth, of earthly materials; its use is healing. Each painting is part of a cycle in a ritual prescribed for the particular problem. Each is a part of a process to restore the patient to harmony and beauty. The mythical narrative is told in a delicate eloquence of portrayal. The energy is that of the living earth, its light and color, its things, brought into the harmony of the design.

The whole complex, the mythology, the psychological analysis in the diagnosis and the healing ritual, the chanted story, the painting, its making, use and destruction, combine into what may be called one of the most profound philosophical acts on this continent.

It is not only professors in universities who think.

Navaho culture is part of twentieth century America but its circumstances are quite different. The religious culture is basically Neolithic but we can know[4] virtually everything necessary of the context, the function, the purposes of their imagery. This knowledge cannot be transferred back to prehistoric works; Navaho imagery and the rituals it is a part of are extraordinarily complex and a part of a long and complex

---

[4] "Know" should be in quotation marks. We can know in the sense of "have information about" but we can know it properly only by apprehending it fully and somatically, with feeling as well as "mind".

development. Prehistoric imagery, in contrast, is very simple. That does not mean that their mythology and ritual were simple but that we can never know what they were. This also means that in this case as in all imagery remaining, the best we can do is a vastly oversimplified summary, a series of pointers and suggestions on how to pursue further study.

Navaho sandpaintings are functional objects. They are also very beautiful, which is part of their function. They are essential parts of the ritual and are destroyed by their use in the ritual or after its completion.[5] They are not made by independent craftsmen but by singers, those performing the ritual. In contrast to our normal use of the word "ritual", it does not mean here the formal worship of God or gods. The Navaho do not have divinities in the sense familiar to us; the "Holy People" are personified powers that both generate the forms of the earth and are the inner form of all earthly things. The ritual "sings" are the formal center of Navaho religion; they are basically healing rituals and the sand paintings are parts of the healing. They are not separate works of art, even though the singers have no objection to their reproduction and use as works of art.

Illness, accidents, are disruptions in the essential harmony of things. They may have been caused by an enemy, by misconduct of some kind, by violation of ritual responsibility. Healing is restoration of harmony, reincorporating the person into beauty.

Navaho country is almost frighteningly austere for the outsider, extraordinarily beautiful, high and open, spread out beneath the sky and the sun. It is one of the great sacred landscapes. To a people without a technology to shield them and to outsiders willing to respond, the world is immediately present, each item in it present with distinction and clarity. There is earth, sky, sun, moon, water, eagle, snake, corn, lightening, wind, colors, number; the myths and the paintings are an inventory of the Navaho world. The earth abides, in its order, its harmony, its beauty.

The Navaho mythology, not to be considered apart from their representation in the paintings, is an extensive and detailed analysis of human and earthly order. It is one of the most profound accounts of the human condition ever brought forth on this continent north of the area of the pre-Columbian Mexicans. Considering the ghastliness of the Mexican

---

[5] We have records of hundreds of the paintings, all copies of originals. A few of the copies have been made by Navaho chanters, most by white people, notably Franc J. Newcomb.

analysis, the Navaho account is more humane and certainly more balanced, harmonizing the powerful with the gentle.

The analysis (and synthesis) is accomplished in narrative and not in abstract statement; this should not deny it the term "philosophical" except by an arbitrary definition of philosophy. "A Navaho might well ask a professor of philosophy how the dawn looks, and finding the professor unable to picture the dawn either verbally or plastically might scornfully contend that the white man's idea of the dawn had not been worked out to its ultimate conclusion." (Reichard 1977: 75)[6]

The paintings are repeated exactly from inherited designs. There are some hundreds of these designs, distributed among the various chants, each of which is known by name and serves as the appropriate healing ritual. (There may have been as many as twenty-eight of the chants but many have fallen out of use; the world intrudes on the Navaho as it does on the rest of us.) Every item in the painting represents something, just as everything is accounted for in the narrative of the myth. Thus the whole of the natural world is present in the wholeness of Navaho painting.

Each "item", each thing, is represented by an extraordinary degree of abstraction. Unlike African sculpture, which abstracts natural forms into distinct organic shapes, Navaho abstraction is systematically geometric with minimal attention to organic form. Nature is vividly present in the representations, in the materials and their natural colors, in the allusions, but the burgeoning vitality of nature is strictly controlled by geometry. There are several different compositional patterns. All are symmetrically balanced. The favored pattern is a circle (always open on one side), strongly centered, with marked elements radiating from the center in the four dominant directions.

All is brought into harmony by the controlling power of geometry.

From my breast may the pollen of dawn instruct me
From my back may the pollen of yellow evening light instruct me
From the soles of my feet may the pollen of earth's little whirlwind
        instruct me

---

[6] This may be an occasion for a note stressing the issue here. Since we are constantly engaged in translating the image into words (and that is what this book is doing), there is a natural tendency to think the words are the equivalent of the image, or can replace the image. Words in their various functions are essential to our full humanity but the translation of the image into words is simply one of those functions; it does not replace the image, whose function is the determination of the specific and the concrete.

From the top of my head with sky, sunray, bluebird pollen being
 instructed, may I walk.
Earth's little whirlwind pollen will instruct the tip of my tongue
 Now restored to youth according to beauty may I be
 Being instructed I walk.
                    Extract from the Shooting Chant,
              quoted in Newcomb-Reichard 1975: 25

Time is present in the ritual, present as the course of life in steady
movements of the natural order, night and day, the turning of the seasons.
But time has no place in the painting. There is only the spreading out of
the space on the earth, marked by the vivid signs of the first people and
the earth's creatures.

Facing the task of apprehending these images, the first thing we
should learn is humility, the giving up of any sense of personal superiority
because of our complex technology. Lack of reading and writing is clearly
no bar to the attainment of the highest level of poetic eloquence, as even
the little extract quoted above indicates. It is certainly no bar to the
attainment of great precision of thought, an exactness of conclusion, that
makes Navaho philosophy important. It is important also because it takes
seriously, as so many philosophies do not, the complexities of human
feelings, of the narrative interaction of the human and the powers of the
earth.

It is a philosophy developed under the conditions of a particular
earth, as one of the means for coping with the complex conditions of that
earth. We who live on a different part of that earth under very different
conditions would find adoption of Navaho principles an abdication of our
own responsibilities. There are aspects of it most of us would want to reject;
an overpowering obsession with harmony denies innovation, which is a
disturbance of harmony. Even a wish that we might control the
depredations of our restless search for innovation might makes us reluctant
to adopt such a principle as a guide. Rather, we are obligated to do as well
under our conditions as they have done under theirs.

A working assumption of this study has been that two of the poles
of religious seeking are the attempt to escape from nature and the attempt
to return to nature. The Navaho project is an attempt to achieve a harmony
between the human and nature. Their route to that harmony is not the
only one.

The landscape painting of the Southern Sung dynasty in China and
the painting of the Italian Renaissance are among the finest examples of

self-conscious intelligence anywhere in religious painting. The comparison of the two may illuminate the issues of religion in painting. Let us first look at the Chinese painting by Ma Lin which we can compare with Giovanni Bellini's *Ecstasy of St. Francis*.

MA LIN, *SCHOLAR RECLINING, WATCHING RISING CLOUDS* Ill. 8

The general subject is the same, a figure in a landscape. There is a considerable difference in function between the saint and the scholar, but even that difference counts in the comparison. The form, and therefore the content, are wholly different.

One way to approach the Chinese painting is to note the things that have been eliminated, then the things emphasized.

Color has been eliminated altogether (strictly speaking, since black and white are colors, hue has been eliminated). Color is one of the most sensuous, sometimes sensual, aspects of experience. It is a prime means of emotional expression and its elimination where it might otherwise be expected creates a distance from the sensual and the emotionally expressive. Texture is very nearly eliminated, thus avoiding the tactility of experience and a sense of the immediate, tangible involvement with things. Modeling in the western sense of using light and shade to establish three-dimensional identity is absent. The shape of things is clearly evoked but not their weight and solidity. Things are seen more in terms of their interior surfaces than their contours and the edges of the painting itself remain undefined. The edges are there because a painting is a finite object but there is no sense that edges are a frame confining the landscape. The edges of the painting represent a more or less arbitrary stopping point in a continuum that extends on all sides, merely a selection from the infinite vastness of the natural order.

There is no emphasis on any axis that might tend to fix the gaze into the geometric shape of the painting. The painters were too sensitive to ignore the shape of the painting surface, which is clearly vertical or horizontal, but the painting is not defined by the axes of the shape. Rather, in a horizontal painting, a road or a river meanders along the surface with the casualness of experience. In a vertical painting, a stream or a path meanders down the mountain. Light comes from no place in particular and is evenly spread over the surface of things, not accenting one more than another. There is no single focal point by which the painting is controlled; rather the eye wanders over the surface.

In the general elimination of so many elements of experience, all the greater emphasis is placed on the chosen few. The most important of these is line and we have here an apt illustration of the content given to a part of the formal language. Whereas line in the Navaho sand painting is a powerful separator, here it unites. Exactly the same kind of line is used for the representation of nature and of the human form; by nature we are a part of nature.

The characteristic shape of things is established by delicate tones and by subtle modulation of sinuous lines. The term "characteristic shape" is important. The artist does not select his lines and tones in order to describe separately existing things but to evoke the characteristic inner life of each thing within the whole. It is not possible to stress this point too strongly. What is meant by "the inner life of things"?

We begin with a term that applies better to western art than to Chinese: "*gesture*". Gesture is not merely the expressive movement of the hands and arms but the characteristic attitude and action of everything. The use of the term can be extended to things since every thing has its characteristic gesture, its way of standing on the earth or a table or the floor, of swelling or shrinking. A pine tree is rooted in the earth and sways in the wind very differently from an oak tree. Painters may describe the shape and texture of trees but, unless they capture the gesture, the paintings are inert, informative but dead. Artists are much involved with things and one of the great interests in art is learning to see with the sensitivity of the artistic vision.

In their nature imagery, the Chinese developed this principle more fully than any other painters and made it a principal concern of their religious imagery. The training of a traditional Chinese painter was first training in contemplation, then training in technique. The painter was required to contemplate grass or bamboo until he was permeated by the inner spirit, the life rhythms, of grass and bamboo. The technique was strictly subordinate to this contemplation. Ideally, the technique would be so developed that its use was unconscious. The inner rhythms of things are taken in through the eyes, flow down the arm to the brush and are evoked on the paper as ink.

This inner life of things is both individual and universal. Each thing has its characteristic inner life but each is a manifestation of the universal rhythm. The painting becomes, then, an object of contemplation by means of which the spectator can commune with nature, be one with the eternal rhythms of nature. In this case, the painting is an illustration of the process;

the sage is in nature, contemplating nature. The spectator contemplates the sage contemplating nature and is thereby trained to the communion with nature, becomes in spirit one with nature by means of the painting.[7]

Both space and time are suspended. Both are certainly present by implication. Space spreads beyond the edges (or boundaries of the painting, which are not sharply enough defined to be edges); the sense is of an infinity beyond. So time is present in the same way; the man arrived where he is and will move on, earth and sky are stopped in what we know as continuous motion. Everything is stopped, suspended, held still before us, thus enforcing the necessary quiet contemplation. The rhythms of nature are quieted to require our participation in them.

It is not the obliteration of the self in the rhythmic energies of nature which we will see in Indian architecture and sculpture. In each case union with nature is the goal of religious art but the union is defined quite differently. In the one case it is absorption, in the other harmony.

Above all other arts, Chinese painting is the art of emptiness, which is the visual equivalent of silence. Nothing like it exists in any other art. The void in Chinese painting is the silence of Chinese contemplation.[8]

In his splendid book, George Rowley says this is not religious:

> Art, like religion, deals with inner reality. The artist reveals the inside of life and not the outside....
> The Chinese way of looking at life was not primarily through religion, or philosophy, or science, but through art. All their other activities seem to have been colored by their artistic sensitivity. Instead of religion, the Chinese preferred the art of living in the world; instead of rationalization, they indulged in poetic and imaginative thinking; and instead of science, they pursued the fantasies of astrology, alchemy, geomancy and fortune-telling. (Rowley, p. 3)[9]

---

[7] Given the disposition of some people to sentimentalize other cultures, it is worth noting that Chinese painting became reduced to a series of tricks that represent the appearance of this process without the discipline of contemplation. They too wrote "how-to" books.

[8] It is apt to this point to see what happens in western churches in "silent prayer". In the overwhelming majority of cases, the organ will be playing. An organ is an admirable instrument for prayer but it is certainly not silent prayer. In the few cases when there is no music, the worshipers will be expected to have words in their head. The only way to have silent prayer is to be quiet, including inside the head.

[9] Joseph Needham's great work, *Science and Civilization in China*, shows how wrong Rowley is on the matter of Chinese science.

We are back to the matter of definition. These painters did not work to the purposes of any organized religion, although they were closely connected to Taoism, Cha'an Buddhism and Confucianism. They were not religious artists in that sense. But what Rowley has described (and his is one of the best accounts I know of the essentials of Chinese painting) is the fundamental religious attitude of a great many Chinese.

Rowley speaks of "the Chinese" and that is always false. This art, this kind of religion, were products of an elite, of the cultivated, educated gentleman of leisure. It could not be otherwise; people who work for a living do not have the resources in time or money or opportunity to engage in such discipline. For all the refinement of high level Taoism, popular Taoism was a mass of superstitious activities. This does not invalidate what the few were able to accomplish by their religious thinking but it puts it in context.

The Chinese elite of this period were a highly intelligent, highly self-conscious people, articulate about their convictions and purposes. They thought about what they were doing and wrote books about it. Sherman Lee sums up much of this thinking;

> The resulting Neo-Confucianism (as it is now called) was most concerned with good government and the hierarchical but benevolent ordering of society. Yet it was also heavily tinctured by Buddhist ideals of compassion and kinship with all sentient beings and by the Buddhist/Daoist concept that the moral order was implicit in the natural order and that the two are mutually interactive...
> Visually the new landscape art offered a realism based on patient observation and conveyed through disciplined and creative brushwork. Intellectually and morally it answered to the resurgent Confucianism of the time, which considered the natural world to be a metaphor for a moral and metaphysical order. Beginning in the tenth century, most Chinese paintings of nature were interpreted in three ways: as more or less objective depictions of their subjects, as more or less subjective expressions of the painter's character and feeling, and as more or less explicit philosophical statements. (Lee 1994: 359)
> But the later (probably Han) *Zhong Yong* [*The Conduct of Life*] states a position greatly to our purpose: "Nature is vast and deep, high, intelligent, infinite, and eternal." This attributes to nature an order or principle (*li*) which is the inherent congruence of each natural thing with what Neo-Confucianism calls the Supreme Ultimate and Daoism calls the Way. The changing

variegated, visible landscape has become a map of the one, unchangeable moral and metaphysical heart of things, and therefore a fit subject for understanding. Painting a landscape, as well as observing one either real or painted, becomes an act of spiritual knowing or regeneration. (Lee 1994: 361)

Obviously, the treatment of religion here is quite unlike our own. A Chinese gentleman could be simultaneously a Confucian, a Buddhist and a Taoist (corresponding to his public life, his public worship and his private devotions). The paintings were equally congruent to all three, suggesting that the religion of the Chinese elite was not so much identified with formal algiances as with a pervasive understanding of the relation of man (*sic*) to nature, which is a fundamental religious attitude.

There is an unsolvable problem in this relation between painting and belief: which was cause and which effect? In traditional thought, conviction, in the form of verbal statement, was considered to be the cause or source of works of art. Given the powerful relation between imagery and thought, this is not so clear. I am supposing that the relation was reciprocal.

GIOVANNI BELLINI, *THE ECSTASY OF ST. FRANCIS*   Ill. 9

To move from Sung landscape painting to a fifteenth century Venetian painting is to move into a wholly different world. The Chinese painting is what it appears to be and there are few details that have to be worked out. Bellini's painting, on the other hand, is full of details, minutely represented as what they are but also saturated with meanings that are not immediately evident, at least to those who are not familiar with the Bible and Franciscan devotional literature. Everything about it, its sensuous beauty, its richness of detail, its intensity of emotion, would have made it accessible to the devout who might pray before it while the intricacy of meanings would have extended its depth for the learned.

This statement might be misunderstood by taking an exaggerated form of it. Surely many details were puzzles to the ordinary worshipper but not the principles involved. We are here dealing with a code, a system of communication, that was generally accepted: every important thing has a Biblical meaning and to look at it rightly is to absorb that meaning.

Let us look first at the form of the work.

Everything the Chinese left out, Bellini puts in. The painting is richly colored, sensual as well as sensuous in its coloring. While principal figures are placed a little away from the main axes to avoid the static symmetry of placing them on the axes, an insistent grid of vertical and horizontals affirms the axial organization of the panel and maintains the integrity of the plane surface. While the perspective construction is not as specified as it had been in the earlier, more exploratory, stages of its development, it is clearly there; everything is securely placed in depth and in its proper spatial relation to everything else. The immediate impression of deep space is much stronger than the sense of the picture plane. The painting is very much (to use a term taken from the Renaissance itself) a "window" into an imagined world which we, standing in our own world, see as other than ourselves.

Proportions are accurately adjusted to the place of objects within the established space. Each object has its distinct individuality, its contours carefully delineated by clearly defined edges, a line that defines the distinctness of things rather than their flowing together with other things. The texture of surfaces is exactly reproduced, thus enhancing the distinctness of things. The three dimensionality of things, of creatures, of the man, is clearly established by skillful modeling. The light is unmistakably that of early morning, illuminating some surfaces, leaving others in shadow. However imagined, the scene is presented as a specific place at a specific moment in time.

With some exceptions, Italian artists were more concerned with gesture as the expressive action of the human body than with the gesture of things. Bellini presents things more in terms of shape and texture and color than gesture. Interpretation of the painting depends, however, on the accurate interpretation of the gesture of the man and a study of him is instructive in understanding how we know the world.

From the cradle on, we learn the language of expressive attitudes and actions. Clearly, many of these are particular to families, to the culture of groups and of nations. Many are universal to the human race. Be that as it may, understanding that language is essential to our placement within our worlds. It is something we do so constantly that we are barely aware of doing it, yet it is a necessary part of human life. (It is also one of many counterweights to the notion that we understand the world adequately by explanatory statements about it. We understand the world by the various modes of our physical participation in it.)

Francis has walked out of his cell (his left foot is beyond the hem of his robe) and has stopped, his upper body leaning back slightly as he lifts his face to receive the rising sun. He opens his arms and hands, again to receive the glory of the morning. His mouth is open; we can presume he is praising, in prayer or song.

So far the account sets out a sense of the work as dedicated to the reproduction of appearances and encourages the standard terminology for that kind of painting: naturalism, realism, etc. Human life is lived in the immediacies of everyday life and religions must contend with its problems one way or another. Running through most religions is the strong inclination of many people to repudiate the world altogether. There are other ways. Of all the great religions, none has shown the intense concern for the dailiness of human life as some modes of Christianity and no period of Christian development has done so with the intensity of the Renaissance.[10]

The first clue is formal. The difference in scale transforms the relation; the vastness of the world is reduced to a painting that can be carried by two people. The appearance of exact reproduction of the seen world is deceptive; it is not possible to see or experience the world with this degree of precision. We see things with this precision only at the center of our visual field and close-up. To extend that precision over a vast landscape is not true to the way we experience the world. This is not "realism" but "hyper-realism". Another useful term some critics have used for Flemish painting and for certain modern painters such as Andrew Wyeth is "magic realism". It is an apt term; they share the quality of combining the precise rendering of individual appearance with a radiance of light and a precision of spacing. The effect is mesmerizing, magical, ordinary experience transfigured. The consequence is to enforce contemplation but it is a contemplation that differs from the Chinese. I am not absorbed into the harmonies of this world so much as I submit myself to the vastness and the multiplicity of the world's infinitude and specificity.

The second clue is not formal but iconographical, the kind of thing that can be known only from sources outside the work itself. Nearly every object within the painting has symbolic significance, so much so that it has taken an entire book to develop it [11] The painting weaves together scriptural allusions, traditional symbols, the biography of Francis, to generate an interpretation of Francis's mission. It would be hard to find a better example

---

[10] I should note here that the story is told of an early Greek philosopher, acting as a cook, who said to visitors, "Come on in. The gods are here too." The same story is told of Christian saints.

[11] John Fleming's *From Bonaventure to Bellini: An Essay in Franciscan Exegesis*

of the fullness and complexity of artistic thinking. Formal thought is inter-woven with literary, devotional, and theological thought to achieve a unity that is available no other way. Fleming's fine book should be inserted here in it entirety.

Fleming's summary of one issue is very much to our present point:

> Berenson's view of Bellini, at least as far as this painting is concerned, was not merely wrong but corrupting. Religious subject matter does not provide in this painting an occasion for visual "realism". Rather, wonderfully real things are the vocabulary of a privileged but coherent religious language. Nor is it satisfactory to say, with a recent critic, that the painting combines symbolism and realism. The real things are symbolic. To put this another way, real things are here the occasion of religious truth.... The fundamental guarantor of medieval literary reality was the Bible, filled with things so real that none could be realer. God, the divine Maker, was the craftsman of real things: real stones, real trees, real doves. All scriptural truth was grounded in the basis of truth, the literal sense. (Fleming, 58-59)[12]

Hyper-realism is not usual in Italy, although the sense of the significance of real things is found in different ways in other artists. Hyper-realism was most fully developed in fifteenth century Flanders: all things were created by God; therefore all things equally reveal God; the whole of nature is iconic; everything requires to be presented in the exactness of its appearance.

An Italian and Franciscan made a critical verbal statement;

> All created things of the sensible world lead the mind of the contemplator and wise man to eternal God. . . They are the shades, the resonances, the pictures of that efficient, exemplifying, and ordering art; they are the tracks, simulacra, and spectacles; they are divinely given signs set before us for the purpose of seeing God. They are examples, or rather exemplifications set before our still unrefined and sense-oriented minds, so that by the sensible things which they see they might be transferred to the intelligible which they cannot see, as if by signs to the signified. (St. Bonaventure, quoted in Freedberg 1989:165)

---

[12] The reference to Berenson is not explained in Fleming's text but assumed. It has to do with the reproduction of appearances, that the painting is merely a celebration of the seen world with no religious significance.

Both the Chinese and the Italian paintings are iconic. That is, neither contains divinity or sacrality; both are intended as instruments of transmission of sacrality, means for implanting the nature of the sacred in the sensibility of the observer. Each involves an unusually high degree of deliberate, conscious, intelligence in its making. The Bellini requires a greater degree of deliberate intelligence in its apprehension in order to grasp its complex symbolism.

The Chinese gentleman prepared himself to look at paintings by bathing, dressing in fine clothes, settling himself deliberately and quietly, using his disciplined intellect to subdue his intelligence to the quiet harmonic rhythms of the painting and thus enter into the harmony of the natural order. I have no idea what ordinary Chinese would have thought in the unlikely event that they saw the picture.

Ordinary Italians, seeing the Bellini on its altar (this painting was probably intended for a private chapel but comparable paintings were found in churches) could have delighted in its sensuous beauty, could have absorbed a truly Franciscan rejoicing in the glory of the natural order. To the limits of their varying intelligence and training, others could explore the intricate symbolism of the work, training their minds and the empathetic response of their bodies to the intricate vision of the created order presented in it.

Inevitably, this entranced search for the reproduction of appearances eventually broke loose from its religious origins and became its own purpose. It has survived in various ways, even into the twentieth century.

Note, too, Fleming's assertion that Berenson's view was not merely wrong; it was corrupting; we are in the realm of "truth". Berenson cut Bellini to his own limits and interpreted Bellini by his own commitments. Berenson did not do so knowingly but because of his limitations. It is the ultimate corruption of criticism.

We have, therefore, moved from the simple image in the cave, powerful in the directness of its effect, to an exceedingly complex image, equally powerful in its ultimate simplicity. It is both possible and appropriate to respond immediately to its effect of passionate joy in the glory of the earth. It is also possible to make the trip long way round and work out the intricate weaving of allusion, allegory, narrative and history, a complex fabric of meaning. The learning, however, is wasted if the learner does not come back to a greatly enriched awareness of the glory of the earth and its things within the creativity of God manifesting himself.

Is it possible, or useful, to attempt a summary of an already brief discussion? Such a summary may serve to emphasize what images are and how they work.

Whereas in the case of the prehistoric work we have to rely on educated guesses about the interpretation, while knowing for sure only how they work on our own sensibility, in these three cases we have verbal statements of their use and their makers understanding of their purposes. (The Navaho statement is in the poetry of their ritual. The Chinese and Italian accounts are in verbal statements that are analogous to, or paralleling the paintings.)

The paintings, however, are not creations of or illustrations of verbal statements. It would be equally true to say that the words emerge from the images. The paintings are independent statements of what their makers understand, see, as fundamental truths. Because they set out these truths in physical forms, they are accessible to those who see them and absorb them.

The Navaho painting is not simply about harmony. It is a statement of the harmony that can be absorbed by the patient who is outside harmony. It is a restoration of order in beauty.

The Chinese painting is also about harmony but in a different way. Whereas the Navaho painting is part of the ritual and requires the chanting and the ritual acts of the chanter as well as the placement of the patient on the painting, the Chinese painting works primarily through the eyes. There is less direct somatic involvement and therefore some element of aloofness, of distinction. The visual experience must permeate the quiescent body and generate a harmony of spirit that constrains the ordinarily riotous flesh.

The Venetian painting establishes a distance of the spectator from the painting by placing the seen world on the other side of the picture plane (the front surface of the seen world that coincides with the flat surface of the canvas; the "pane" of the "window".) Francis (the represented figure) is in nature but not absorbed into it. He too contemplates it and rejoices in it. At the same time, the spectator who is apart from the painting can simultaneously identify with it or, perhaps better, with its represented world, represented experience. This is a double movement of involvement. The richness of the sensuous experience, the vividness of the transfiguration of the natural order makes it possible for the receptive spectator to re-experience the glory of Creation.

The treatment of the light enhances this mode of involvement. Light is actual in architecture and sculpture and the maker must take it into account. It is actual in painting only in the sense that without it we do not see the painting. Light can be a generalized presence within a work without any indication of its source. It may also be represented specifically, as in the Bellini, where the light is plainly the rising sun of dawn. The presence or absence of represented light not only helps define representation but also places the image in time.

There is always a discontinuity in our psychic relation to an image. The light by which we see the image is something other than the light represented in the image. While it is hard (nay, impossible) to know the purposes of other people, this is probably why the Chinese painter placed so little emphasis on light, other than to presuppose its presence. He wanted to lift the image out of time to enhance its contemplative presence. In contrast, Bellini is careful to establish the character of light at a particular moment. That moment is other than where we, as spectators, are, requiring us to extend our awareness in a different manner of contemplation.

Harmony, peace and wonder. These are statements of the religions and manifestations of, incarnations of, the thing stated.

6

THE ARTLESS IMAGE

W
ho sees images? How do they see the images? What do they want from images? What do they understand the images to be doing?

Mostly we do not know the answers to such questions. Images are made by people who have their own intentions and conditions for the making. Commonly we do not know how the makers of images think and feel about what they are doing but we can know a fair amount about the purposes and the understandings of those who commissioned and used them. They were the literate ones, the ones who left records of their thoughts and feelings. Often such records are lacking but interpretations such as those in the previous chapters are made by literate people who study such things, who develop such notions as "the work of art".[1]

Images are seen by large numbers of people who do not leave written records of what they think and feel when they look at images. We may not know much about what they think and feel but we can be fairly sure most of them do not think of images as works of art. It is a problem of major importance. Intellectuals, academics, are tempted to think that their way of seeing images is the correct way, the true way, that they are the judges of quality, the authors of correct interpretation.

But the world isn't made that way. Images are made and interpreted by one class of people. They are seen, received, by other people whose responses cannot be controlled merely by the manner of the making. We must do our best to get at something of that response.

---

[1] While such modes of interpretation, both those proposed in the earlier chapters and several other possibilities, are developed by special training and experience, they are not confined to the trained people. With instruction, anyone with intelligent vision and the willingness to learn can be trained to see analytically and interpretively. Otherwise, such books as this one would be futile

All the images considered, most of those yet to be considered, have been works of art of high quality. Why is it that at all times and all over the world the tendency of image making is toward high quality? If we could answer that question we would understand something of major importance about human making.

Traditionally, a "work of art" is defined as an image of high quality. Anything else is, at best, considered folk art, primitive art, or not worthy of being considered as art at all. Few people any longer have such confidence in this definition of art and we would be seriously handicapped if we were to limit ourselves to the study of such works only.

In one sense, all images, irrespective of their quality, are works of art since all are made of a physical material shaped to human purposes of communication or expression. The fact that so many are of high artistic quality does not account entirely for the power of images. The question has to be divided properly. What is "quality"? There is as little agreement on this term as there is for "art".[2]

1. The primary location of "quality" is form. The measure of high quality is mastery of form: skill in the craft, control of the elements of the formal vocabulary, accurate judgment in their use.
2. There is also a quality of subject and of the treatment of the subject.
3. The judgment of quality is made by those trained and skilled in making judgments (not the artists who are trained and skilled in the languages of art). The judges are the educated elite[3], the ones who write the textbooks, deciding for everybody else what is to be considered "art".
4. The measure of highest quality is the eloquent and intelligent use of the formal language to re-present, interpret, the subject with power and understanding. ("Subject" includes both representational and non-representational images.)
5. The average non-trained person does not care about the judgment of quality as defined by people like me.

---

[2] Many in the art world today repudiate the term "quality" altogether. They have not, however, repudiated the same kind of judgment, since they concentrate on works produced by members of some one or another minority and repressed group. Their standard of quality is real, but political.

[3] The term "elite" is normally pejorative. It is not necessarily so. It can refer to those who are specially trained and experienced in any craft. A trained automobile mechanic is among the elite of his craft. Presumably I would belong to the class of those who are trained to make judgments in the arts. I consider the judgments made by the "elite" to be, by and large, accurate.

The problem: the power and the effectiveness of images does not depend on the presence of quality as judged by the elite. Many images function powerfully quite outside their formal involvements and many formal qualities in images have a powerful effect quite apart from the formal role they play for the elite. We must understand both of these if we are to understand images.

The ambiguity of the chapter title is deliberate. Many images are "artless" in the sense of having been made by those who cannot be called artists, the innocent and naive image. These need concern us only peripherally. More to the point are those that can be called "images outside art". This is a problem, not only for the psychology of images, not only for the judgment of quality, but also for the understanding of the morality of images. More of that anon.

In many cultures, considerable evidence shows a preference among ordinary people for works of high quality. I have been told for, example, of an African tribe content to use their local carver for ordinary images but for festive occasions, they went to the carver across the valley. Vernacular buildings, "architecture without architects", are commonly of high quality: Dogon villages, Mykonos, etc. The evidence is extensive; the question is central to this investigation.

At the same time, many images **work** despite the total lack of anything that could be called formal quality, as though quality were irrelevant, even a hindrance. The crudest example might be the graffiti drawn on the walls of public toilets. It is hard to imagine what gratifications can arise from these images but clearly there is something. More nearly to our point are the images painted in the early Christian catacombs. They Ill. 10 are quite low on any scale of quality but there is no reason to think they did not perform their appointed function, which was to be visual prayers.

Since the images necessarily have form, they have a formal "language" that can be analyzed just as any form can. For another example, the so-called "Venus" of Willendorf is of no artistic quality, unlike the paintings in the caves. Yet it has a formal character that is revelatory of formal thinking. (See Chapter 4)

The problem is the place of the "popular arts" in the study of imagery. Traditionally, historians have paid no attention to such images, since they lacked the defining characteristic of art, which was quality. This is less true today but often the study of popular images is undertaken for political reasons, rather than with a desire to understand the effectiveness of such images.

Ill. 11   **WERNER SALLMAN'S *HEAD OF CHRIST*[4]**

Several things need to be said of Sallman's *Head of Christ* before we can understand its significance for this study.

It is the most widely reproduced image in the history of imagery. There are approximately five hundred million copies in circulation.

It is undoubtedly the image loved by more people than any other image has ever been.

If they pay any attention to it at all, art historians and critics judge it to be very bad. They certainly never include it in their histories or critical studies. I consider the judgment to be correct, both artistically and theologically, but to use this judgment as an excuse not to consider the work is to falsify the understanding of images.

What are the reasons for judging it to be bad as a work of art? It is technically bad, not in the physical sense (the paint stays on the canvas without deterioration) but in its use of the "language" of art.

The act of seeing accurately is an essential act of art. Although seeing the external world is central to most of the world's art, accurately seeing and using the material and formal elements of making are equally essential, in fact the first essential; much of the world's images makes no reference to the outside world (ornament, modern non-representational art) but all images of good quality accurately see the materials and processes of the making.[5]

Sallman sees nothing accurately, neither the subject nor the materials, nor the processes of construction. The painting is assembled by formula with nothing in it either seen or felt for what it is. The anatomy is faulty; the neck unnaturally long, the chin under the beard unnaturally receding. The general construction of the painting is flabby. The drawing is flaccid. The conception of the figure is determined by advertising and the movies, not by the Biblical record (Sallman had been an advertising artist by trade): Jesus is shown as the young and handsome Hollywood leading man. He has a Nordic appearance, conventional features and auburn hair with no suggestion that he was a Jew. The whole is sentimental and conventional.

---

[4] For the information in the following section, I rely on the work of Prof. David Morgan who is heading a team of scholars working on the problem of understanding Sallman's art. The interpretations are mine, which he may or may not accept.

[5] An anecdote from a related art may illustrate the point. The great painter, Edgar Degas (who should have known better) kept plaguing his friend, the poet Mallarmé, with ideas for poems. Finally, the exasperated Mallarmé said, "Poems, my dear Degas, are not made with ideas. They are made with words."

On the other hand, according to the protocols collected by Prof. Morgan, those who love it do so because they find it inspiring, calming, comforting, bringing peace to a stressful world. For them this is a true and accurate representation of the Christ.

It might appear that the split between those who love it and condemn it is between the educated elite and the average worshipper. This is only partially true. Many people, not in the art world, detest it, but it appears that their dislike is not so much of the image itself as its associations with dull and ugly Sunday School rooms, oppressive piety, etc.

Clearly, the people who love it are not going to change because of the professional judgment. Should they? I once knew a devout and educated minister, deeply involved in the art work of his national church office, who said bluntly, "The idols must be cast out of the temple!" He considered the image to be false to the point that it inevitably degrades the understanding of the Christ. Part of me agrees with him. But a case can be made on the other side and that case bears on the understanding of images.

In the first place, those who love it are accepting the possibility, even the obligation, to love certain images. This image, and the others of the same class, are not objects of study and detached appraisal but living parts of their lives. Probably most of the art professionals love images or some images but that love plays little part in their professional work of interpretation and judgment. For them, the image is a thing, not a living presence. In their own way, those who love this image are paying images greater respect than scholars often do.

Then, in the way they use it, those who love it have recovered the sense of the icon, in the strict sense of the Eastern Orthodox church, an image as the occasion and instrument of prayer. There is no reason to think that they judge Christ to be **in** the image so it certainly should not be described as an idol. Often it is placed in a special place in the home, a place to go to for devout meditation, even for family decision making. This is normal in a devout Eastern Orthodox house.

Most little country churches in this country belong to one of the traditions originating in the Protestant Reformation with its opposition to images (iconoclasm). Now, in many such churches, this image is placed on the wall behind the pulpit, much like the traditional altarpiece of the Roman Catholic Church or the Greek iconostasis[6]; thus they recover, quite

---

[6] The iconostasis is the screen between the part of the church available to the laity and the sanctuary which was accessible only to the priest. The iconostasis is normally hung with icons for devout contemplation.

unconsciously, another ancient tradition. Is it possible they are more in touch with the fundamentals of the human religious consciousness than the elite are? It is possible.

It might be worthwhile to list these fundamentals, these recurring motifs, both as summary and as emphasis.

1. The image as living presence, not merely as object.
2. The image as icon, the means for communicating with the divine.
3. The image as object and occasion for contemplation and meditation, nourishing deep personal, subjective, emotional response.
4. The image as instruction, inculcating certain ideal features of their faith.

In short, for them the image **matters,** not simply to their minds but to their lives. The fact that my colleagues and I find nothing of this in the image and, indeed, are offended by it as cheaply sentimental, is not at all the primary issue. What is at issue is **why** there should be such a difference between equally serious people.

I am not entirely confident of my answer, but I think it can be found in the way the image functions as a sign (the study of which is semiotics). For those who love it, the image is a sign of certain emotional states and virtues: gentleness, strength, compassion, peace, etc. Since these are all meritorious, it is presumptuous to find fault with them simply because the work is a sign of quite different things for me. It is also a lesson in how signs can often function with emotional authority, not merely as inert pointers.

What, then, of my friend's conviction that this image should be thrown out as false and corrupting? Leaving aside the question of his right to dictate in such a way to other people, does he have a case?

For a long time, the elite have based much of their public claims for the significance of their work on the conviction that the arts are morally uplifting. This claim has been the justification for the inclusion of the humanities in the curriculum. This is one of many examples of the triumph of theory over evidence. In short, there is no evidence at all to suggest that good art improves morals or that bad art is corrupting.[7]

---

[7] As a member of the "elite", I have to make certain qualifications to my assertion. John Ruskin is reported to have said, "An ugly lamp post is a wicked lamppost". The only sense such a statement makes is that ugliness is inherently corrupting to perception. The defense might be that the debilitating ugliness of our cities and public spaces is corrupting. That ugliness is where a great many people have to live.

All the people I know who love the Sallman image are good people, or at least as good as people normally are. I suspect that is widely true. At the same time, great art has often been made by, supported by, collected by, loved by, some very bad people. Piero della Francesca made some of the purest, most serene images in the whole history of art. His patron, Sigismondo Malatesta, was one of the most complete scoundrels of the Renaissance, intelligent, of good taste, cruel, ruthless, utterly lacking in any kind of moral scruple. The great American art collections were assembled by or for the "robber barons" of the industrial revolution. They wanted the collections for the prestige great art brought, not for any love of art, but the prestige of art is part of the power of images. The collections had no discernible effect on the character of the people who bought them.

Many great works of religious art were made for unsavory reasons. The Parthenon, the great monument of humanistic religion, was built with stolen money for the glorification of Athens. The medieval cathedrals were built as much for the glorification of the city or the feudal nobility as for the glorification of God. The Sistine Chapel was painted as a part of the political program of the popes and to nourish their vanity.

None of this compromises the religious significance of the works, a significance made possible by their quality. The great image makers, the great artists, have the ability not only to master the "language" of art but to use that language to "say", to set out, to make manifest, meanings and understandings that are not available any other way. Certainly, many generations of ordinary people have been moved to devout contemplation by medieval churches and I feel quite sure that many ordinary Athenians were not only filled with civic pride by the Parthenon, but were uplifted by it. Great works can function as well as the poor ones.

Why, then, the difference between the current judgment of the elite and the efficacy of the image? The only answer I can propose is that, for various reasons, few artists of today can make images that serve the general need as the great images once did, so people make do with what they have[8].

---

[8] This conclusion avoids taking stand on another possible resolution, that there is a kind of Gresham's Law ("bad money drives out good") in the area of images, that most people will prefer the easy, sentimental image to the great one.

We have in all this a testimony to the power of images.

THE POWER OF IMAGES[9]

In the discussion thus far, I have mentioned several functions the image can serve. So long as we think of images as "art", it is tempting to ignore these function in the pleasures of the forms. All images, have a purpose, a function, no matter the degree of their artistic quality. It might be useful to list the functions, adapting the terminology of Alan Gowans (1981)

1. Substitute imagery
    Images made to act in the place of things, persons, or ideas for memory or some kind of action, on them or by them.
2. Illustration.
    Substitute images that tell stories or record actual or mythical events.
3. Beautification.
    Images shaped to make their functions clear to those who looked at them (for Gowans, "the more intelligible, the more 'beautiful'"). (Gowans 1981: 17) The makers added substitute images, illustrations, etc. to link them to the experience of the beholder in order to "humanize" the artifact.
4. Persuasion/Conviction.

    Historic arts deliberately "styled" artifacts so as to evoke associations with, or create metaphors of ideologies and presuppositions (convictions) which underlie all social institutions. Historic arts thus were vehicles for transmitting accepted values, ethics, belief systems, upon which ultimately depends the endurance of city, State and family. Historic architecture, especially, could be defined as the art of creating large permanent metaphors of "patterns of human interrelatedness." (Gowans 1981: 17-18)

---

[9] This title is adopted from the splendid book of David Freedberg (1989) that is devoted in great and intelligent detail to the various ways images exercise power over the imagination and activities of people.

The flood of images that submerges us distinguishes our society from all those that preceded the technology that made the flood possible. Even so, the images that surround us perform exactly these same functions. They illustrate people, places and events. They are substitutes for those absent in space or time. Images tell stories. They attempt to persuade us of many things, to buy, to believe, to act. Images can do these things whether or not they have artistic quality.

If images can do those things, they possess power of a kind nothing else has. The ability to work, however, does not exhaust the power of images. They have in themselves the power of the uncanny that accompanies the mysterious power to perform all these functions. It may be saddening to think of the poor psychic life of those who draw graffiti on toilet walls, but the act demonstrates that even the crudest image carries some sense of the possession of the pictured things; the image has the power to substitute for the presence of the thing. The snapshots in the wallet, the portrait gallery in the home, restore the past and make presence present.

Certain forms of witchcraft show this same power; the things done to the image will happen to the person represented by the image. Those who deface a political portrait are part of an ancient tradition; in Renaissance Italy, for example, city governments would order an image of criminals or traitors who had escaped. The image was then condemned and punished.

In many religions throughout history, images are dressed, offered food and otherwise cared for as though they were alive — which, for their devotees they most certainly were.

Museums have to contend with the impulse of some people to attack works of art. The form of these attacks is significant: very commonly the eyes are slashed or stabbed, that feature of living people felt to reveal the inner life and, in the painting, to exercise a strange power over the spectator. Few of us have the impulse to attack the picture but the impulse is testimony to the strange and uncanny power of images.

POWER AND QUALITY

Were it possible to separate images from art, this book could have been written as though the question of quality does not arise. I have tried to establish clearly that images have function and power, that they **work** in many different ways, without regard to their quality, without raising the ancient question, "Is it art?". Part of this case was the admission, however reluctant, that a great many people who are not of the trained "elite" are more deeply aware than the elite are of the inherent power of images, or of certain images, more responsive to them with a sense of their importance. This is not the first time that things hidden from the wise have been revealed to the naive and the simple. What, then, is the place of quality, of "art" in the study of images?

I am being overly hard on my own professional tribe; we are as capable of responding as deeply as anyone else to the power of images. I touched on the problem earlier: few among these "elite" have any sense of how to relate their emotional life to their professional work and feel it to be a professional obligation, in order to be "objective", to keep the two separate. The point is not emotional pleasure (which is an important reward for serious study in the arts) but the unwillingness of the "elite" to accept the power of images to affect, to nourish, the deeper psychic life involving commitments, desires, fears, hopes, etc. The price is a large one for it hinders the understanding of the image as a centrally important form of knowing and as a vital part of the organizing of a humane life.

If the image without quality, the image outside form, is powerfully effective, what difference does quality make? Freedberg's fine book deals at length with the many uses of images, including the religious, without making any use of the principle of quality. It would be possible to write a fuller study of the various functions of images in religion outside the problem of quality. What does a concern for quality add to the discussion?

Before we can consider what difference good quality makes to religious imagery, we must first try to consider this question of definition.

In the first place, craftsmanship. At its simplest, craftsmanship is the honest and appropriate handling of the materials, with skill and respect. Craftsmanship in the making of images is not different from craftsmanship in every other human activity, plumbing, baseball, brain surgery, or whatever. It is a matter of sensitive and understanding competence.

If we speak of the "vocabulary" and the "language" of art, then craftsmanship goes further than simple technical competence, which might be considered no more than an adequate grasp of the vocabulary. It takes a craftsman's skill to draw a line accurately but more is involved than simple accuracy. The line is an expression (of many things, including feelings) and it is also an intellectual act. It divides the surface into one side and the other side, inside and outside. Expression requires an understanding of feeling in order to express it accurately. The logic of division requires an understanding of placement, proportion, rhythm, relation. There is a craftsmanship of understanding as well as of technical proficiency.

These are **moral** qualities. If we were to speak of the "morality of art", it would have to begin with craftsmanship.[10]

Then there is what might be called a "craftsmanship of the subject". This requires an understanding of the subject (including the abstract relations that are the subject of so much modern art). No subject can be understood completely; only parts of it are accessible to any one observer and only certain aspects of it are usable in a particular culture. Thus we can expect only some of the possibilities within a subject to be present in any one work but we can expect that those possibilities are presented accurately and with understanding.

The Sallman *Head of Christ* is a sign that arouses appropriate responses among worshipers of a certain disposition and commitment. It is woefully deficient in craftsmanship, since its use of its few formal elements is glib and unfeeling. It has a grasp of certain devotional attitudes and that gives it the importance I ascribed to it earlier, but it adds nothing to the understanding of the subject. Of all the great religious figures, Jesus is the most complex, in both character and significance. Every representation is inadequate but we can rightly expect the presence of some of those aspects. This we do find in Rembrandt, in Michelangelo, on the facade of Chartres Cathedral. Such representations are very different from each other but each is constructed according to a rich and profound understanding of some aspects of the figure of Jesus.

"But so does the Sallman!", someone might reasonably object. "You just don't approve of his interpretation." Well, not quite. As I tried to show earlier, I do not object to the sentiments set out in the Sallman, which are appropriate to the subject. I do not doubt the sincerity of his feelings nor the sincerity of those who share those feelings. But the painting is still only a **sign** of those feelings, triggering similar feelings in those who are receptive to it. A better work of art is a great deal more than a sign; it is a **symbol.**

In terminological oversimplification, I am using the word "symbol" as comparable to "work of art" in ordinary speech, that is to say, a work of

---

[10] Much of the dominant forms of the contemporary art world repudiates this principle altogether. Other than this note to acknowledge the existence of this sort of thing, I shall not trouble myself with it further.

high quality or a "true" work of art. In such a work, the artist has embodied, given body to, incarnated, ideas and sentiments in forms
appropriate to them and with an eloquence sufficient to carry the work
beyond mere sentiment into meaning. This assertion has a double reference.

"...in forms appropriate to them...." The forms are the means for
presenting the subject in the fullness of the artist's conception of it.
Necessarily, the presentation involves an **interpretation** of the subject, the
presentation and the interpretation growing out of the total commitment
of the artist to the world of the subject.

It follows that the analysis of the form is the necessary instrument
for the interpretation of the work, which is itself an interpretation of the
subject. While forms have a great many pleasures for those attuned to
them, this is serendipity. Forms don't exist for their own sake but as the
necessary means for the embodiment and interpretation of the subject.

"...with an eloquence sufficient to carry the work...." Eloquence is
not a word ordinarily used with reference to art or, if it is used at all, it is
only with reference to those works clearly intended to persuade. It may
have use beyond those limits, for every work of art is an appeal to
participate in its ordering, in its structures and energies and every such
participation carries with it conviction and persuasion. This is part of the
power of images, that they are present not merely to the intelligence of the
spectators but to their bodily energies.

"...beyond mere sentiment into meaning." This assertion is full of
difficulties both because there is no accepted definition of "meaning" and
because the relations between expression of sentiment and meaning are
complex. The image "works" and its working is, in one sense, its meaning;
meaning is not exhausted by verbal statements of it. At the same time,
meaning is inseparable from understanding and the fullest, most humane
understanding is conscious (although, again, not necessarily verbal). We
might take the Apostle Paul as a guide. He did not reject speaking in
tongues, which is an act of pure emotional expression, but stated that he
would rather speak one word of sense than ten thousand in tongues.

In summary, the necessary distinctions become complex:

1. Both form and subject can function independently of each other.
There is both pleasure and significance in forms apart from their function
as representations. For many people, the subject functions, works, apart
from its formal embodiment. This is sometimes true even of the professional
elite; the great formalist critic of an earlier generation, Roger Fry, is reported

to have said of the portrait of a friend, "I can't see the painting for the likeness."

2. It follows that part of the study of images is quite apart from the study of form but is devoted to the way images as subjects work for people.

3. It follows further that the most important images and the fullest study of images are found in those who succeed in fusing subject and form. In such images, the independent significance of the form is used to interpret the subject, whose energies and shapes become part of the form. In these works neither expression (emotion) nor intelligence have independent existence but interact on and with each other.

INCARNATION AS A CRITICAL THEOLOGICAL PRINCIPLE

This example underlines a problem basic to all critical interpretation: the relation between form and content, between subject matter and content. (For a sketch of these terms, see the Appendix.) In this book, I have been concerned primarily to demonstrate the intimate interrelation of form and content. I have also proposed an interpretation of the Sallman work that treats the two as quite distinguishable. Can the two be reconciled? It is not merely a problem in the interpretation of art; it is a fundamental religious problem.

In short, it is the perennial problem of both religion and propositional thinking and, therefore, of human life: what is the relation between mind and body, of spirit and matter? Is the real to be found in one or the other? The very formulation of the problem in such dualistic terms almost compels the response as a choice of one or the other. Both religions and philosophies often define themselves in terms of one or the other.

The most thorough treatment of the principle involved here is found in Christianity. If we spell the word with a small "i" rather than capitalizing it, "incarnation" can be a key critical principle. As specific to Christianity, the doctrine of the Incarnation holds that the man Jesus somehow contained, gave body to, incarnated, the divine. It is an extremely difficult notion, impossible of precise formulation and, therefore, in much dispute. In general, Christian orthodoxy has held that the two, God and the man, are distinct and, at the same time, one.

As a general principle of the ordering of things, the principle of the incarnation holds that meanings, "truth", are embodied, given a body, in-carnated, in the material of the work. While they are distinct, neither can be grasped accurately and fully without the other, except by means of the other. While the formulation of the principle is derived from a particular religion, it is not confined to that religion.

The principle is not simple, even theologically, and the Christian theological problem is, by analogy, bound up in the critical principle. For example, in some forms of Christianity, the Incarnation is understood to mean the glorification of matter and the body. If the earth and its materials, the human body itself, are fit to receive the divine, then matter and the flesh are good, capable of glorification. On the other hand, some forms of Christianity, sometimes working under the immediate influence of a Platonism which holds that matter is either evil or an illusions or a falsification, considered the Incarnation as a humiliation, which God willingly endured for the sake of human salvation but something that did not change the fact that reality is in the realm of the spirit.

This theological problem parallels the intellectual one. To a considerable degree, intellectual work has followed the second tradition: truth is found in the realm of verbal abstractions and any discipline dealing with the concrete and material (except as explained verbally) is an illusion. It is obviously a debatable subject. In my judgment, this is no longer a viable position. Even so, my defense of the Sallman work recognizes that, functionally, there is a distinction: the painting works as an image apart from the inadequacy of the form.

I remain convinced that such a principle does not make full use of images. While the principle of incarnation is most fully stated in one religion, it is basic to all true making of images. By its inherent nature, art, the fullest making of images, is an affirmation of the inseparable union of meaning and form, spirit and matter, body and soul.

7

PLACE AND SPACE: BUILDING AS IMAGE AND INSTRUMENT

> A planned city, a monument, or even a simple dwelling can be a symbol of the cosmos. ....architecture is a key to comprehending reality. To build is a religious act, the establishment of a world in the midst of primeval disorder.
> ...Yi-Fi Tuan

C an a building be an image?[1] If it can, what is it an image **of**? Images of space which is the locus of dramatic action and a component of personality. Images of the cosmos and its ordering, which is an essential dimension of religion. Markers and interpretations of sacred places.

Religious building begins with a sense of sacred place, however that sacrality may be determined. It has a necessary function in providing a place for the liturgy of the religion but no religious people have ever been content with the utilitarian. The building is shaped to make possible its particular function but it is also shaped by the people's sense of cosmic order. It is indispensable to the study of imagery.

SACRED PLACE

We can only guess, and imagine, what it was like for our earliest ancestors to be on the earth, under the sky. We can, perhaps, read back from the things that develop later and imagine them coping technically with their world but then seeing it as more than a technical problem. It became a matter of power and of meaning. The world may be full of power,

---

[1] A few buildings have been made as images of something, representations. Mostly these are curiosities and do not constitute part of this study.

of powers, yet the power becomes located, specified, in things, in places. Rivers, hills, groves, stones, become something out of the common run of things. They are set apart, saturated with meaning. The house, the village, are themselves sacred places.

Some sacred places have a numinous quality that makes them accessible to sensitive people of other cultures. Perhaps more often, the place is designated by the interaction of myth and some lost historical event. The American Southwest is one of the great numinous landscapes, particularly in the Navaho-Hopi-Pueblo area. Their sacred mountains, however, are not notable peaks, and, in fact, even Navahos do not agree which are the "right" ones. There is a Mt. Olympus in Greece but Mt. Olympus exists in myth rather than geography. Troy is not a place in Turkey to be discovered by explorers. It is a place, a necessary place, in the Iliad and in the religious imagination of ancient Greeks.

Places are connected with each other, marking patterns on the earth. These patterns of relation are invested with meaning. At some point, in some cultures, patterns on the earth becomes a reflection of the pattern in the sky.

One of the most powerful of all religious motifs is the correspondence between heaven and earth so that earth reproduces the sacred pattern. From the earliest times, cities reproduce the sacred geometry and can be considered a representation of sacred order, an image.

We see it happen late with the marking of place by menhirs, by reproducing the pattern at Stonehenge. This may reflect an earlier mode of thought that led to the development of the great culture cities (some of which are earlier than Stonehenge). From pre-Columbian Mexico, to Egypt and Sumeria to China we have monumental cities, laid out as images of cosmic order. Equally, they were political acts, for the order of earthly rule was itself an image of cosmic order. From the Sumerians and Egyptians to the Shakers and the Mormons, building is making a sacred image.

Sacred place is designated (or discovered), then built; it is place before it is space, or place within space, defining the space. Each culture has its image of cosmic order, organized around its sacred places. Sacred place is both more than and other than architecture since it includes springs, rivers, mountains, cities, countries, home.

THE SHAPES OF PLACE AS IMAGE OF ORDER

As soon as the sacred place is marked off it has a shape. The shape of space is a foundational element in the construction of the personality of a person or of a people.[2] Space is inseparable from place. When the limits are defined by physical material, architecture has begun. Architecture is the principal representation of sacred space, its image.[3]

Since the structure of built space is culturally determined, the ordering of space is also an ordering of personality in particular patterns that are symbolically powerful. Architecture is an image of order and therefore an image of meaning.

It is common now to trace imagery to the political interests of those who were responsible for it. This is appropriate because all making, including the making of images, is rooted in the totality of our involvement with the world. This is particularly true of building because, beyond the simple buildings that users can make for themselves, building is expensive and difficult, involving many people. Inevitably, the building will reflect the interests and the imagination of those responsible for it. This does not "explain" the building because those interests are themselves built into the image of cosmic order; the divine order in the so-called Middle Ages was construed in terms of a feudal monarchy.[4]

---

[2] "Without discarding the classical psychological frame of reference, with its distinction of intellect, affectivity, will, etc., phenomenology can also use a 'categorical' frame of reference. This means that the phenomenologist attempts to reconstruct the inner world of his patients through an analysis of their manner of experiencing time, space, causality, materiality and other 'categories' (in the philosophical sense of the word). The two basic categories of inner experiences are considered to be time ('temporality') and space ('spatiality')..." Ellenberger 1958: 101)

[3] The distinction is an important one. Joel Brereton's splendid article, "Sacred Space" in the *Encyclopedia of Religion* could equally well have been called, in Brereton's own terms, "sacred places". Brereton's article should be considered required reading along with this chapter since it outlines the ways in which places become sacred. His concern is not with the specific forms of sacred buildings although he outlines the several modes of architecture as image of the body, the cosmos, the social order, the sacred narrative, etc. Equally useful as an introduction to a complex subject is J.G. Davies's article, "Architecture", which outlines the many functions of religious buildings, both practical (liturgical) and symbolic. Neither author deals very much with the principle governing this study, "form-as-image".

[4] The term "totality" needs to be stressed. The achievements of modern criticism in understanding the involvements of images with our characteristic life are of the first importance; they err only where they are exclusionist and reductionist, which is usually the case. We are involved not only in our social and political interests but in our desires,

A specific religion, developing its symbolic speech, uses the essential vocabulary of form, so religious buildings speak the common speech of building. The language (the "vocabulary" and "syntax") of architecture must be known in order to understand the specific statement of spatial symbolism. Through most of history, the decisive thinking about architectural space has been done in religious buildings; the development of architecture's language has not been primarily a matter of developments in building techniques or in an abstracted evolution of style but in terms of symbolic necessity, the building as image of symbolic order.

Architecture is the shaping of space by a physical material and is made under the conditions of the material and the necessities of structure. This is true of all building so this essential vocabulary makes all buildings accessible to those not of the community of the makers. The culturally, religiously, conditioned elements of the building are particular ways of using a general "speech".

Structural necessities and techniques are both condition and instrument; neither term is sufficient by itself. All thought, including religious thought, takes place in terms of some material and is inseparable from the nature of that material, including its function, its social and political involvements, etc. Forms exist in the mind as general conceptions but they have reality only in terms of matter.

(Words and their ordering are a material to be shaped by the imagination just as physical substances are. Words are themselves physical materials, either as sound waves produced by the motion of the body and heard by a body, or as marks on paper, stone, etc.)

In all the many forms of religious buildings, two types should be kept in mind:

1. Temple. The place set aside as the habitation of the god.
2. Church, mosque, synagogue. A place set aside for congregational worship. The church is often a combination of the two, since, in the catholic tradition it contains an altar, which is the symbolic center of a temple, as well as congregational space.

The primary form of architecture is space. The other necessity is the mass required to shape the space.

---

sexual and others, in the specific qualities of our gender identification, in a multitude of interests and concerns that have to be kept in harmony by the creative mind of the maker.

The first "architectural" space was not made but found. The mass of a cave is inchoate, endless, not apprehended from the outside. It is known only by its interior space. We have no way of knowing if an undecorated cave was ever a sacred space for early people, the cave as refuge or as something like an earth womb, or whether it acquired its sacrality and its liturgical function by the paintings of the animals. The affect is the sense of incorporation into the elemental energies of the earth.

The cave remains a prime symbolic form. The earliest built caves in the West are the dolmens of prehistoric France and England and, in historic times, the tholos tombs in Mycenaean Greece, then the early temples of Malta. All these reproduced the inchoate external mass of the true cave. The finest and most sophisticated of such caves are the later "cave temples" in the west of India (see below).

Later rooms that were psychically and symbolically caves were, necessarily, parts of more complex structures. Even some "secular" structures (many of Frank Lloyd Wright's houses) are cave-like in emphasizing hiddenness, enclosure, and shelter. The cave is an elemental, essential symbolic form.

The next spatial type was the enclosure marked by upright stones; Stonehenge is only the most famous and the most elaborate of them all. These enclosures marked out a ritual space on the surface of the earth and were oriented toward the sky. There is no reason to think the caves indicated any sense of divinities rather than unspecified energies but possibly the stone circles were intended to establish a ritual relation to sky gods or at least to the sacred shape and movements of the sky. Their symbolic function involved the center, the circle, and the vertical.

As the colonnade, the principle of the stone circles became part of the imaginative equipment of the high cultures and appears as such in some Islamic mosques in temperate regions of the Near East and north India, and (as enclosed garden) in the cloisters of European churches.[5]

The earliest built structures from the "high" cultures were the pyramids of Egypt and the ziggurats of Mesopotamia; the somewhat later   Ill. 12 "pyramids" of pre-Columbian America were never true pyramids but had several shapes and were commonly closer to the ziggurat. The same is true of the much later Buddhist temple of Borobudur on Java.

---

[5] The enclosed garden is an image, as an image of Mary, whose virginity is symbolized by the enclosure.

The Egyptian pyramids are the purest statement of architecture as the organization of external space around the vertical axis. They are the truest and most exclusively external architecture in existence; their interior spaces (tomb chambers) were inaccessible and spatially inconsequential. They are also the purest geometric form in all art, the triangle as image of the eternal and the unchanging.

Both the ziggurat and the pre-Columbian pyramid are solid masses of materials but each had a temple room at the top which was reached by another major symbolic form, the monumental stairway extending from the earth to the temple as the meeting place with the god. These are unmistakably theistic.

Stone circles, pyramids and ziggurats have a center and are a center, the end of a path, a processional way, an archetypal form.

Path and place are two basic symbolic dimensions of architecture. Davies (1987: 391) usefully sums up the defining characteristics of these two. Path requires: strong edges, continuity, directionality, recognizable landmarks, a sharp terminal and end-from-end distinction. Place requires: concentration in form with pronounced borders, a readily comprehensible shape, limited in size, a focus for gathering, capable of being experienced as an inside in contrast to a surrounding exterior, and largely non-directional. These are not always distinct. The Ottoman mosque is a place and the approach to it is of no symbolic importance but the Christian basilica, which is path, the processional way, is also very much a place.

Ill. 13   The first true constructed interior space in the West is the Pantheon in Rome. (Obviously there were interior spaces from the beginning of building, since shelter was a constant necessity, but major architectural symbolism was concentrated on the exterior.) In the Pantheon, the Romans not only introduced the interior as such but still another of the few basic symbolic forms of space: the dome. The dome is universally the embracing canopy of the sky, the image of heaven. It is a prime instrument of religion in many cultures.

The creation of interior space means the continuation of the sacred way into and through the building, thus making the edges and the doorways symbolically fundamental. The earlier forms stand as masses in the light. Now light has to be controlled by windows.

The Pantheon developed into the Byzantine Church and the Islamic mosque in the Near East, particularly in the areas of Ottoman rule that inherited the Byzantine empire and so many of its forms. Whereas the Pantheon appears to be carved out of a solid mass of stone (it is actually cast concrete faced with brick) both the Byzantine church and the mosque were primarily conceived as surfaces and the mass effects are at a minimum. The different treatments of the surface are significant and deserve to be looked at separately in comparison. The mosque has a distinctly tent-like effect, which is another symbolic motif, although a less prominent one.

The only other new structural device in Western architecture is the arch which made possible the remarkable complexities of the medieval church.[6] Chinese and Japanese temples developed elaborate forms of wooden architecture that would require separate treatment.

THE ANALYSIS OF BUILDINGS AS IMAGES

Most skills, including the analysis of works of art, can be learned only by doing them, not by watching someone else doing them. For those who cannot visit the buildings, analysis is harder to do in photographs. The experience of sculpture can be approximated in photographs. American culture makes little use of sculpture so we don't grow up accustomed to seeing much of it but we are familiar with our own bodies and with seeing the bodies of others. The photograph is necessarily reduced in scale but since most of the statues are within range of the normal proportions of the body, we can approximate the awareness of it.

Buildings are placed in space and they contain space. The only way to grasp a building is to approach it, seeing it in its setting and context, to stand in immediate relation to it and move around it, into it, through it, responding with the whole probing, receptive sensibility to its spatial complexity. Most people have to make do with what they have.

The scale of the building is so far incommensurate with the photograph that it cannot be truly felt. In the classroom, it is possible to show a series of slides and come a little closer to suggesting what the experience of the building is like. Even that, however, is only an approximation.

From the exterior, buildings require something of the same analytical procedures as sculpture: the relation of the three axes to each other and to the whole, the relation of mass to space, denial of movement or its force

---

[6] This is not strictly true. Modern times produced the cantilever, then sprayed concrete with its possibility of irregular forms and, finally, various tensile forms. The effect of these on symbolic thought is a special topic.

and direction, placement in relation to context. Since a building has an interior, there are further problems: the relation of exterior to interior, the relation of wall to openings, the treatment of the entrance and the proportioning of doors to windows, the shape and direction of interior space, the use of light and darkness.

Some of these things can be determined by careful examination of good floor plans and elevations. Their total can be imagined from photographs. They can be apprehended fully only by the direct experience of them. The only way for the student to develop the necessary skills is to make use of the buildings that are available. Probably most of them will not be the eloquent spaces of the great buildings but there are all manner of buildings available on campuses and in cities. Older campuses in particular are likely to have a variety of buildings, a pseudo-Gothic chapel, the facade of a Greek temple and some well proportioned columns. Churches in town will have many different forms and many different spaces. Movie theaters are a distinctive spatial experience. Good modern buildings are much more widespread than it used to be and, while usually quite unlike any of the historical buildings, they can do much to train the sensibility in the apprehension of spaces.

I will offer several exemplary analyses and comparisons, drawing on those I have experienced most intimately and so can account for most fully.

The Hindu Temple and the Primacy of Earth

Ill. 14   Scattered across central and western India are a number of "cave temples". The cave temple is not a true cave; it is carved into the rock of a hill. There is no technical necessity or limitation that required the use of such a form. Clearly, the technical skill of the people was sufficient to build in the usual manner.[7] They chose this form for a psychic and symbolic purpose. Since the form is unusual, it would be hard to find another example that so clearly sums up psychic need and religious purposes.

It is symbolically important that many of the forms in these temples are imitations of wooden prototypes, long since disappeared; the stone temple as image of the wooden prototype. In all religious activities, the

---

[7] In one example, the Kailasa temple at Ellora, an entire temple, inside and out, was carved from the stone of the hill.

old acquires sacrality for its own sake, and sacred forms are replicated where they are structurally beside the point.

The spatial experience is that of a true cave, the entry into the earth, the sense of being surrounded by, immersed, in the amorphous, undefined material of the earth. Unlike the prehistoric caves, these are shaped by human intelligence. As befits a monastery, there are different kinds of rooms but the worship hall has a familiar temple form, rectangular with an interior colonnade forming aisles for the procession, a rounded apse. At the end of the nave there is either a stupa, sometimes with a figure of Buddha carved on it, or a lingam in the Hindu temples.

Then there is the sound.

I was visiting one of the smaller temples. The light came through the doorway. An image of the Buddha was on the far side of a square room. I was wearing a rain hat, a hard, hollow, plastic object. Holding it carelessly, I dropped it. It hit the stone floor with a hollow thud and rolled a short distance. Intrigued by the echo, I retrieved the hat and began to hit it against the wall, a crude approximation of a rhythmic chant. The sound, multiple echoes from all parts of the room, lost all qualities that identified it in any way. It lost all sense of place; it did not originate here, echo from there, but seemed to inhabit the cave. I was inside absolute sound.

This was not merely an acoustic curiosity. The psychic effect was essential. I was being emptied out, emptied of distinctive personality, absorbed into the sound, absorbed into the space, made one with the singularity of the experience, my ego dissolved.[8]

Multiplicity was absorbed into unity but it was unity without definition, without limits or edges, pure, undefinable being. The image of order, the space carved into the infinity of the matter of the hill, was also a liturgical instrument of the highest order, bringing about what it represented.

---

[8] The experience is not private to me. It is the narrative crux in E.M. Forster's remarkable novel, *A Passage to India*. Many people in recent years have, for undefended reasons, asserted the necessity for dissolving the ego and the individual personality. I hated the effect. I saw no reason, nor do I now see any reason, why my ego should be dissolved. It is a powerful religious commitment but it is not mine. It does not represent "the immemorial wisdom of the East". It is, rather, their way of doing things, the world they have made with the instruments ready to their hands. It is necessary that we learn from others how they have coped with the common task under their conditions. It is not necessary that we accept their way as superior to ours. Multiculturalism should teach not only respect for other cultures but also our own.

TEMPLE AND COSMOS: SACRED GEOMETRY

To deal with sacred geometry in the detail it deserves would take much more space than this small book.[9] To deal with it briefly is to outline certain basic elements of all sacred building. These elements are few, whatever the variety of the forms they take.

The first is not the externals of the building but its center, which is the center of the cosmos, marked by the altar from which the building itself develops as from a seed. (The notable exceptions to this centralized altar are the Islamic mosque, the synagogue, and the Protestant church, all centered on the Book.)

From the center, by a natural logic that is also mythological logic, the four cardinal directions develop, front, back, sides, or north, south, east and west. To this is added up and down which establishes the world axis. From the altar, normally a square form, there develops by geometric progression the four sides of a square, which is the defining shape of an Indian temple.[10] A center is also the center of a circle, another basic symbolic form. The sky is circle and dome. The dome, often in the form of a canopy, is basic to sacred architecture. In India it is most often found as the Buddhist stupa.

The four directions make possible, as use makes necessary, the two principles of access and entrance in the form of avenues and entrance halls. In the Indian temple, as in the Christian church, this takes the form of one or more entrance halls along one axis, seeming to convert the temple to a longitudinal form but actually only leading to the defining central square.

This interplay of circles and squares is a symbolic form found all over the world. It is displayed and explored in the greatest intricacy in the Indian-Tibetan mandala. The mandala is an arrangement of concentric circles and squares, commonly with subordinate circles or squares. It is a cosmic diagram, the circle as earth or sky, the square as the reverse. The principal deity is placed in the center, subordinate deities around the center.[11]

---

[9] The magisterial work of Stella Kramrisch, *The Hindu Temple*, which all discussions of the subject depend on, comprises two large volumes.

[10] It is also the defining shape of the great culture cities, centered on the god-king, the Lord of the Four Quarters.

[11] The mandala principle appears in many forms in western culture but most charmingly in the game of Parchesi (which originated in India). It has the central square, the four cardinal directions as avenues of access, circles in the four quarters defined by the

KANDARIYA MAHADEO TEMPLE, KHAJURAHO   Ill. 15

All this about sacred geometry is not imagined or extrapolated. It is
made explicit in several ancient Indian manuals on the construction of
temples. The floor plan of temples is developed from the central square
with an intricacy of geometric design that cannot even be decently
summarized here. Only imagine a large checkerboard pattern with the
central square locating the ineffable core of all things. Every subordinate
part, of the temple as well as the placement of the various divinities, is
developed from that central square within the pattern of other squares.
Within the extraordinary profusion of forms on an Indian temple, the
fundamental principle of order is geometry. This is the image of the cosmos
that is basic to the religious imagination.

The dominant impression of the building is not the geometry that
prescribes the placement of the forms but the formal and symbolic authority
of the overall shape and the distinctive ordering of the profusion of forms.

There is not, as in most other buildings, a clear distinction between
supported and supporting members.[12] Such a distinction (inevitably
described as "binary") creates a structural logic of the first importance for
the imagination. Here, the visual effect is of a building not so much built
as carved from a monolith, an effect strengthened by the multiple strata of
forms which suggest the forms of natural stone in a mountain and enhance
the horizontal lines that hold the building to the earth as a base for the
upward thrust of the towers. In turn, the towers mount up from the entrance
halls to the towering peak of the principal tower over the shrine which
becomes the climactic mountain peak. The terminology asserts the mythical
form: the temple is the sacred mountain, the abode of the gods, the very
body of god.

Equally, the interior of the entrance halls is the passage way into the
inner void of the cave; we are still in the spiritual world of the cave temples.

---

avenues. Progression along the avenues is The Perilous Journey. This is not the only
example of myth and symbol being translated into a game.

[12] This could be called a consequence of, or a particular use of, the structural method
employed (the sequence of cause and effect, of interaction, in the processes of the
imagination is not obvious). The building does not make use of either of the major
methods of vaulting, the post-and-lintel system, or the arched vault, which, apparently,
they did not know. It uses a corbelled vault with its natural inclination toward the
mid-line.

At the center of the main tower is the emptiness of a small, undecorated room, significantly called the "womb-chamber", containing only the lingam, directly under the towering lingam that is the principal meaning of the temple. This chamber, the womb of forms, the seed at the center of germination, the source of all fecundity, then flowers outward in all directions into the profusion of forms on the surface.

Ill. 16   The most prominent of these forms is also the strangest to the western imagination: the erotically clothed human body, particularly the female body, and the scenes of copulation. Thematically, these figures are hard to specify accurately; we lack the necessary contextual information. Formally, they seem to be the most apparent example of the flowering of the unity at the center of the temple into the multiplicity of this world's experiences. They are comparable to the Shiva Natarajah (see Chapt. 9) in their sinuous, sensual forms, swelling out from a center rather than standing under the control of gravity. (There is a dramatic illustration of this indifference to gravity in the representation of the breasts, which do not hang in their natural shape, but are hemispheres.)

The scenes of copulation are, for so intense a theme, strangely ritualistic, almost dance like in their formality. Faces are remote, wholly without expression, as though demonstrating the rigid control of spirit over flesh.

Ill. 17   **THE PARTHENON**

All buildings are in a place. The place may not have any particular character until the building organizes the space around itself. Many times the place is already consecrated as sacred by usage and quality. The Parthenon is built on the Acropolis of Athens, the High City, once the site of the royal palace, consecrated by the sacrality of kingship. With the fall of the kings and the tyrants, it became the holy place of the Athenians.

The Acropolis, not a high hill, is lifted up above the city, under the sky, the center of the plain of Attica lying between the mountains and the sea. It is the point of focus, drawing together earth, sky, and sea, the defining center of the city. Worshippers and tourists wind their way through the city to the base of the hill, climb the path up the hill, then the steps of the Propylaea, the great entrance way, through the passage and arrives there, at the center. The pilgrimage is completed, the goal attained, on the hill, above the earth, in the sun, under the sky.

The Parthenon is a simple building, two rectangular rooms, one containing the cult image of the goddess Athena, the other the temple treasury. The whole is surrounded by a colonnade and surmounted by a sloping roof. The structural forces are equally simple, consisting of the dead weight of the superstructure on the columns (this is the "post and lintel" system).

It draws together several modes of thinking about externally oriented architecture. It had an interior space, elegantly and eloquently designed but psychically much like a cave and not really functioning in any view of the temple from the outside. The exterior is geometric mass, colonnaded enclosure and center of the geographic and symbolic space.

The great image for the Greeks was the human body. The gods were pictured in the form of the exalted human body and humans were pictured as dedicated to the gods. It is appropriate to choose the body as the designating image of the Greeks. Before the representation of the body the column was their great symbol. The column is at the center of a great act of thought. The column was born of the menhir, the image of the erect human body was born out of the column. The column is not simply the supporting member of a building. It is a symbol, an image, of things important to understanding the Greeks.

The column carries over the symbolic function of the menhir, the erect stone as the fructifying link between earth and sky, as masculine potency, as phallus.

The column is also the supporting member of a building. As such, it represents the distinctive logical workings of the mind of the Greek architect. The design problem is solved in terms of carefully adjusted proportions (of height to the human body, of diameter to height), the transitions from vertical to horizontal (in that splendid creation of the Greek intelligence, the capital), the flutings that serve ornamentally, by alternation of shadow and light, to ensure the effect of solidity against bright sunlight. The curvature of a Greek column gives it the sense of elasticity; the swelling of the column suggests the swelling of a muscle supporting a heavy weight and thereby enhances the sense of the column as a body, a sense that is made more actual in the caryatid, a column carved in the form of a human body, as seen in the nearby Erectheum, where the column is transformed, translated, into the noble, grace-ful forms of maidens.

The colonnade is only distantly related to utility. The colonnade does give shelter from the weather but cultures in climates equally intense have dispensed with such aids. Clearly it answers a deep symbolic need.

The Parthenon is not centered on the Acropolis but is set to one side. The worshiper (or the tourist) comes through the great entrance, the Propylaea, and sees the Parthenon at an angle that shows two sides. With a stately, steady rhythm the eye moves along the colonnade from column to column. Seen separately, the columns carry the eye vertically. The vertical movement is contained between the long, even lines of the superstructure and the base. The flow of horizontal movement (the dominant movement) is closed at the ends by the clear cut corners. Its three axes are clearly defined. None dominates but rather all three are held in a graceful balance.

The consequence is an extraordinarily self-sufficient building. There is no reference beyond itself, no windows, no emphasis on the doorway behind the colonnade. The appearance of rigorous geometry is a little deceptive; most of the lines of the building are slightly curved, columns are slightly inclined toward the center. The result is energy held in tension by rigorous control. It is a vital building, as full of internal movements as an organically living body, yet the rhythmically vibrating movements are controlled by a powerful skeleton of geometric order.

Both the energy and the control must be stressed. To see the building in terms of its serenity and its harmony, both dominant presences, is to miss one of its enspiriting elements. A vital dimension of Greek life and Greek religion is difficult to see on the Acropolis: the Dionysiac frenzy, the priapic worship (there were rituals that had women carrying huge images of the phallus in procession), the darkness and hiddeness of the mystery religions, the profound awareness of human passion and tragedy in the great dramas, the vulgar priapic humor of the comedies. Yet it is not altogether absent. There were shrines to the earth divinities in the side of the Acropolis. Death was a presence in the ceremonials, the altar reeking with the blood of the sacrificed animals. There is more.

Energy and order are not merely balanced in equal symmetry. Energy is so centered as to give the impression of an actual force that is just controlled by the geometric order. The effect is similar to that of a living body at rest.

The worshiper sees the building from the outside, each standing in the sunlight, under the sky. The self-sufficiency of the building confirms the independence of the worshiper, yet the encompassing forms of the great hill make both parts of the larger whole. It is hard to imagine a less "natural" building than the Parthenon, yet it is designed to function as a center and an enspiriting focus of surrounding nature.

The overwhelming effect is of harmonious wholeness, a unity that confirms the independence of each of its parts. This brief sketch of the Parthenon does a great injustice to one of its major characteristics, the integrity of each part. Every small part of the building has an independent existence and has a name, yet every part contributes to the integrity of the whole.[13]

This effect of wholeness, of completion, exists despite the fact that the actual place is a mass of ruins. The Parthenon is in good part a ruin, surrounded by the shattered stones of other destroyed structures. It is hard to reconstruct the Acropolis in the imagination as it would have looked. It has to be sufficient for us that the sense of wholeness triumphs fully over ruin. Fragments of Greek sculpture have the sense of vitality that pervades the whole. The ruined hulk of the Parthenon rises serenely above the waste and ruin of the Acropolis.

The building was not made as abstract form but to serve as the place of the goddess, containing her cult image, the place where she could meet her devotees. The character of the building is the character of the goddess, Athena, the warrior maiden, wisdom and force. The colonnade of the exterior is in the Doric order, with its ascetic strength. The colonnade of the naos was Ionic, slender, ornamental, graceful.

This chapter is supposed to be devoted to space, not mass, architecture and not sculpture. Yet the sculptural program is part of the wholeness of the building, confirming and enhancing the analysis. It is possible here to look only and briefly at the processional frieze, which goes around the top of the wall under the colonnade. It represents the greatest of the processions that came to the Parthenon. Many parts of the procession are represented; we see here a group of young men and young women, pictured at a moment of pause in the movement. Even in the low relief we see the correspondence of the body and the column; the folds of drapery fall like the flutings of the column and the rhythmic verticals carry the eye forward in a steady movement, even when the figures are standing still. Gestures are grave and graceful, action is always controlled by an easy dignity. It is worth noting that, while there is a clear and sensitive distinction between male and female bodies, both have the same bearing of graceful dignity.

Ill. 18

---

[13] The actual history of the building is far more haphazard than this description implies. The present building was built on the ruins of an earlier one and makes ingenious use of parts of the old one. Nothing of that history qualifies the effect of the building.

The kind of abstraction in the representation of the bodies is of the first importance. Proportions are humanly accurate. Facial features are fully human. At the same time, they are abstracted from the ordinary, more perfect than the human ever is. They are <u>idealized</u>.

We often use the word "ideal" as something out in front of us, a goal to strive for. That is not the Greek way. The sculptors had made the principle manifest before Plato formulated it philosophically but the verbal formulation is useful. Beds, says Plato, are not true beds but only copies of the only true and real bed, which is the essence, the idea, the form of bedness.[14]

Platonism is at the headwaters of thinking in abstractions rather than particulars but to concentrate only on the thinking does not explain the appeal of Platonism. We might assume that Plato found his bed comfortable, but, for him, his bed was radiant with the Idea that was beyond concretenss. Yet a man who marries marries a person, not the Eternal Feminine or Woman in general; if he loves her truly, she is radiant with all the richness of Womanness. (If he treats her as an abstract principle, he is making a bad mistake.)

We should again look at the gesture as the expressive attitude of the body. The actual gesture is inconsequential, the figures standing at ease while there is a pause in the procession; at other points in the frieze, figures are engaged in necessary acts but the movements are determined by the actions, not by any specific internal state (compare Bellini's St. Francis). The figures simply **are** in the grace of their being. I would be hard put to it to say I have ever seen actual people with this coherence of form and physical act, this combination of graceful dignity.

These figures do not represent our actual existence or even an ideal we can aspire to but a reality we essentially are, beneath the accidental immediacies of our daily life and our ordinary forms. It is this principle, realized most fully on the Acropolis, that lends such a singular exaltation to this representation of Greek religion. The processional frieze culminates in the representation of the gods, who are larger than humans, slightly removed but clearly continuous with them. The gods are the exalted manifestations of the human, the purest human is continuous with the divine. It is the fullest and finest realization of a religious humanism.

---

[14] It follows that art is deceptive since the image of a bed is one step further removed from the truth of the bed and it is the fulfillment of the human to rise out of involvement with the immediate and the ordinary to the vision of the true idea of things, then of beauty and truth and goodness. This is one of the most powerful ideas in the history of imagery and, in my judgment, one of the most faulty.

There is no pain, no guilt, no sin, no strain, in this representation. There is only an exalted peace.

The Parthenon as the center of the whole landscape is the image of order and the means for generating in the tumult of the soul the order that is the order of the gods. It is a representation but a representation of what? The reality of Greek life?

One of the pitfalls of historical criticism is to confuse the object of representation. To what extent was the real Greece like this?

> They were quarrelsome as friends, treacherous as neighbors, brutal as masters, faithless as servants, shallow as lovers — all of which was redeemed by their intelligence and creativity. But the core of what is most admirable and what is most "impossible" about them is a kind of grandiosity — an ability not merely to conceive, but also to <u>entertain</u>, in every sense of that term, an outrageous idea, an outlandish scheme. (Slater, 1968: 4) Nothing seemed to have meaning to the Greek unless it included the defeat of another. ... The insatiable striving for honor and prestige, and the devouring envy of the successes of others continually sapped and disrupted their collective existence and prevented the formation of an enduring social order. (p.36) "They had a maxim, 'nothing too much,' but they were in fact excessive in everything" [Russell, 1945, p. 21]. Their excessive narcissistic preoccupations kept them from understanding either themselves or their environment to the degree that their intellectual adroitness would lead one to hope.... (p.40)

It doesn't sound much like the Parthenon. As Slater grants, this is one-sided and exaggerated but not so much as we might like. There were thousands of ordinary, unsung Greeks leading ordinary, respectable, lives but this account is all too accurate for much of Athenian public life.

This disparity between actuality and representation exists in every culture. What to do with this circumstance is not a question to be settled easily but it is integral to all historical interpretation and to the understanding of a people's religion. Ancient Greece is a good example to illustrate this issue because of the strange (and significant) idolatry of Greece (or of a sentimental image of Greece) that has been so important a part of western culture, concealing the real pathologies that underlay Greek life.

Those who see only the political implication of images (and of the building as image) have no problem with the Parthenon; it was very much a part of the Periclean political program, intended to inculcate a particular sense of civic order that undoubtedly was to the benefit of the ruling classes of Athens. Even its forms emerge from the taste and the interests of those classses. This is certainly true yet not determinative; why should Pericles have a sense of a program that can be exemplified in this form of building, and not some other? The significant thing is that the taste and interests of the ruling classes could produce this kind of building. (Much as we would like to, we cannot know what the ordinary Athenian thought of the Parthenon.)

The Acropolis does not represent the reality of Greek life. It does represent, it is a true image of, a vision of reality that some Athenians generated out of anguished concern with the squalid realities of human life[15] The most profound record we have of the passion, the moral squalor, the pain, of human life in Greece is in the records of the Greeks themselves with their remorseless vision of the actualities of human experience. They also had a vision of a certain human grandeur above, beyond, the squalor.

The Acropolis represents a human possibility, or a vision of human possibility, forever incapable of full realization but noble for all of that. The Athenians were human and not gods. For a time they aspired to be as gods and what they did still has the capacity to exalt the souls of those who see it.

The Medieval Cathedral and the City of God.

The Parthenon and the medieval church do not represent successive stages in the history of architecture or of religion; they are separated by many centuries and a complex development. They serve our pedagogical purpose by representing a high point in two very different attitudes.

The Parthenon and the Indian cave temple represent two poles of "cosmo-piety", the conviction that human purpose is fulfilled by incorporation into the essential rhythms of the natural order. They are so different that they are at opposite poles but the poles are on the same continuum.

---

[15] The Parthenon itself is an illustration of this contradiction. This, the greatest statement of religious humanism, of the nobility of the divine in the human, was built with stolen money (the treasury of the Delian league, established by the Greek cities to protect Greece against the Persians).

The Indian cave temple is all interior and no exterior and the interior is the interior of the earth, the cave that absorbs all things into itself. Its effect is the absorption of the individual into the wholeness of things and the energies of the earth.

In this the Parthenon is not at the other extreme from the Indian temple; the Greeks themselves were usually at extremes but their art never is and the only architecture that is solely exterior is the pyramid. The Parthenon is primarily exterior but the naos, the interior room, is the place of the goddess, containing the cult image. It was dark, cave-like.

Yet most people saw the Parthenon only from the outside, as an exterior. It did not absorb them but enhanced who they were. The Parthenon, for all its eloquent geometry, is not understood as set apart from the earth. It is the focal point of the ordering of earth and sky. Building and earth are each serenely independent yet each gracefully, easily, with consummate dignity, takes its appropriate place within the whole. All is dignity and harmony.

Christian churches are, in purpose, interiors, made for the ritual that is enacted in the interior. There are great variations in the degree of emphasis on the exterior and the type of interpretation of the function of the exterior but all are interior spaces, meant for congregational worship. They represent separation from the world, coming apart from the world.[16]

To the Greeks, religion was a profoundly important civic function. Christians have vigorously fought each other over the various ways of relating the two themes but always there is the double principle, dramatized by the ancient doctrine of the two cities, the City of Man and the City of God. Any summary is simplistic and not really necessary for present purposes, which is the way the two are represented in architecture. Our own notion of the absolute separation between the two is one extreme. Probably the other extreme is represented by the "Caesoropapism" of the Byzantine Church which amalgamated the office of emperor and pope. Some smaller Christian bodies have rejected the world altogether but they are not significant for our purposes, since they produced no art. For the most part we are dealing with one or another attempt to respect both.

The Christian is the citizen of two cities and has opportunities and responsibilities in both. There is a realm of the state and a realm of the church, each with its legitimacy ("Render unto Caesar the things that are

---

[16] There are some contemporary churches made of clear glass and set within a natural planting. This represents a return to a form of nature worship and is not entirely compatible with Christian principles, which do not include the sacrality of nature.

Caesar's and unto God the things that are God's.") The distinction between the two realms had consequences that are best illustrated in the next chapter. The immediate concern is the form of the churches.

The medieval church is turned in both directions. It has a intricately ornamented exterior, to be seen from outside, to have its effect from the outside.[17] The doorways, the point of transition between exterior and interior, the crossing of the limit, are strongly emphasized, richly ornamented. The interior is the most important aspect of the church. Its shape and the disposition of its parts are the places of interpretive analysis. The common element among nearly all of them is this dialectic between exterior and interior.

The placement of the Christian church varies. Monastic churches are removed from built up areas, chapels associated with sacred sites might be built in isolated places. The great churches, such as the medieval cathedrals, were built in cities, not detached from the city or lifted up above it but placed in the center of civic life.[18] Medieval churches were built over sacred sites, sometimes a sacrality going back to pre-Christian times, "converted" by association with a Christian martyr.[19] The church was made into the tomb of a martyr by incorporating a relic of a martyr into the altar.

Early medieval churches (the so-called "Romanesque" period) were an architecture of walls. The mass of the building dominates both the exterior and the interior. This provides an object lesson in the interaction of technical instruments and social causation in the development of religious architecture.

---

[17] In contrast, the exterior of many Byzantine churches gives the effect of looking at the back of the scenery in a theater. It is as though they would have willingly dispensed with the exterior if anyone had figured out a way of having an interior without an exterior.

[18] The beginner should be reminded that "cathedral" is not an architectural term at all and is not synonymous with "large medieval church". It is an ecclesiastical term and designates the seat ("cathedra") of a bishop; it might be, architecturally, an insignificant building. Since medieval bishops were usually secular rulers as well, the cathedral church (the appropriate term) was normally the greatest church in the diocese.

[19] Those who chose the site did not always do so with any belief that the site was sacred. They were shrewdly aware that many people felt that it was and so they built the church over the spot in order, as it were, to "convert" it. In strict theology, there can be no truly sacred place in Christianity, including "the Holy Land"; God is everywhere. That has nothing to do with religious psychology and few Christians are aware of this requirement. They will continue to feel the sacrality of both place and space and the medieval church authorities were very much aware of that and acted accordingly.

The structural problem of all architecture is the relation of the supported to the supporting. In the Parthenon this was a simple matter of supporting the dead weight of the superstructure pressing downward. The emphasis of the Christian church on the interior, on a space containing a large number of people, meant a considerable increase in the size of the interior, far greater than can be covered over (or "vaulted") by means of stone using the "post and lintel" system of the Parthenon. Initially the necessary task of covering over a large interior space was met by wooden beams. This was effective but wood is subject to fire and is not altogether pleasing aesthetically since it makes for a clutter overhead. So the stone arch was developed.

The action of an arch is double. It is a dead weight downward but it also pushes sideways and that sideways thrust has to be supported ("buttressed"). Buttressing can be achieved in one of two ways: by heavy mass or by an equal and opposing thrust from an adjacent arch. Early medieval churches were buttressed by the mass of the walls. Hence the walls were very thick and heavy, windows and doors were small so as not to reduce the weight of the walls. Interiors were at first small and relatively dark. All this can be attributed to technological necessity and not ideological purpose.

Ill. 19

Yet there is an intimate compatibility between the form of the churches and the devotional attitude that was shaped by the social and political reality of the times. It was an insecure time. People were subject to dangers of all kinds, from outside attack, from famine and disease, from oppression by their own rulers. The churches were refuges from a dangerous, inimical world. They were often so literally; the church was commonly the only or the largest stone building in the town and when unfriendly neighbors attacked the people could take refuge in the church (Durham Cathedral, which is not small, was known proverbially as "half church of God, half castle 'gainst the Scot"). The Romanesque church is the illustration of Luther's great hymn, "A mighty fortress is our God".

In some ways, these churches represented the political and social conditions of the time. They were also and equally images of imagined order.

The doorway was strongly emphasized but the ornamental interpretation of it clearly symbolized the transition from danger to refuge. Commonly, there were grotesque beasts, representing dangers overcome, or fearsome animals guarding the doorway. Abstract ornamentation was jagged, energetic to the point of the violent. Representations of Jesus showed him as the terrible judge and the protector of the entrance.

In a process partly technical, partly psychological, technology transformed these early churches. The first step was the development of the rib vault which concentrated the weight of the vault onto the pillars and made possible Romanesque churches that were much larger and higher, lighter, without changing their emphasis on the massive weight of the walls.

Two related technological developments made the Gothic church possible. The first was the realization that the concentration of weight on the pillars meant that the vaulting had to be buttressed only at those points and not continuously along the wall. The wall between the buttresses carried no weight other than itself, so could be enlarged into one vast window. The second development was the pointed arch which gave the architect far greater freedom in manipulating the shapes of the walls and the interior space. The two developments were combined when the buttress could be moved away from the main interior pillar which was then supported by the arch of the side aisles and by that striking feature of the medieval church, the arch (the "flying buttress") that carries the thrust of the vault over to the buttress.

Ill. 20   Technological developments changed the church from massive walls to an apparently delicate framework, a series of open screens between interior and exterior. Technology became the means to a conscious purpose, not its cause. The earlier churches had to be built as they were because technology didn't permit anything else. The engineering skill of the builders was now equal to nearly anything they wanted to do. They built the buildings this way because this is what they wanted to accomplish.

They wanted two things: space, particularly high space, and light. This architectural development might be correlated with social and political developments. Political society was much more secure, society was more prosperous, government more orderly.[20] There was no longer the same compulsion to militancy, to shelter, to fear of terrible forces. Christians discovered the benign dimension of their faith.

---

[20] For a great many people (Jews and Moslems, the people of southern France who were victims of the Albigensian "crusade"), the thirteenth century, the age of faith, was one of the cruelest of all centuries. Equally, those who locate cause in the structures of society have no trouble demonstrating the correlation between the hierarchical structure of feudal society and the hierarchical ordering of the architecture.

The population was increasing, so the greater size was a necessity. But larger congregations didn't need all that space overhead. Height was symbolism and not technical necessity. The greater light was not a practical requirement but a symbolic necessity.

From the outside, the Gothic church is a complex screen. Increasingly, the wall is obscured by a proliferation of ornamental devices, some of which have a practical purpose, some a result of pure exuberance of spirit. Mass is dissolved into lightness. The great portals spread open as though in invitation, drawing the people into the interior. Instead of a heavy mass set apart from surrounding space, the mass is dissolved in a complex interpenetration of space and mass, an interlocking of exterior and interior.

The interior has a primary double movement and a proliferation of subsidiary movements. To stand at the entrance to a medieval church is to be drawn forward, down the length of the church to the altar, by the succession of pillars, by the soaring leap of the arches.[21] Simultaneously, the eye moves upward, along the lines of the pillars, the upward reach of the ribs of the arches. The three major axes are clear and distinct, yet each is accompanied by parallel and subordinate axes. While the dominant axes are forward and upward, there is also an intense consciousness of the horizontal axes sideways. There is a constant symphonic interplay of these many axes.

The psychic, symbolic, effect of the double movement is unique. It is not one of being overwhelmed, despite the great size of the buildings. It is a powerful movement forward, a powerful movement upward and the result is not exaltation, as in the Parthenon, but ecstasy (*ex stasis*, from this place), the raising up of the self outside the self.

This complex spatial action is enhanced by the imposition of movement. The Parthenon does not impose any necessity for movement to apprehend it in its wholeness. It is simply there, complete. There is no need to walk around it to see the other side, which is surely a replica of this side. Being there, it confirms me here, where I am and what I am. I am ennobled and exalted but not transformed.

No view of a medieval church is ever complete. Always, the worshiper standing in one space looks through a screen of arches to other

---

[21] The mind knows that arches do not soar; the vaulting is a heavy weight downward. Perception and emotion know that the movement is upward. This discontinuity between appearance and reality is foreign to the Parthenon which is exactly what it seems to be. The psychological distinction is profound.

spaces. With every movement, the vista changes, relations shift, the self is drawn deeper into the ecstatic wholeness of the spatial rhythms. Both the Greek temple and the medieval church are the goals of processions. The Greek procession, so vividly represented in the frieze, comes to its goal, its completion and its rest in the presence of the gods, seated on Olympus. The pilgrim in the mediaeval church is never fully at rest. Pilgrims come to the receptive arms of the portals, enter, coming apart from the world, are drawn upward, simultaneously drawn forward to the altar. The altar is the focal point of the double movement, taking the forward movement and directing it upward but giving as well as receiving. It is here, in double spiritual movement, that sacrifice offered is received, transformed and given back as sacrament. The worshiper then returns to the world outside. There is never rest or completion. There is always the reality beyond the walls. The path, the pilgrimage way, does not come to rest but only a pause.

The Gothic church is the image as transformation.

The space is transfigured by light. Here we do not have to rely on our own impressions, however clear and powerful, but on the words of one who, as much as any one person can, is the creator of the Gothic style. Suger, Abbot of the Abbey Church of St. Denis, had inscribed on his new gilded doors:

> Bright is the noble work; but, being bright, the work
> Should brighten the minds, so that they may travel,
>   through the true lights,
> To the True Light where Christ is the true door.(Panofsky
> 1946, p.47)

The gilding has disappeared but the stained glass windows of mediaeval churches still work their ecstatic transformation on the spaces of the churches. The light has nothing to do with the ordinary light of day. It is transformed by color. Nearly all effect of mass is dissolved in this colored light. The space is set apart from the world outside. The tourists who admire the beauty of the windows may not recognize that they are icons, not sacred in themselves but the means of access to the sacred.

The Parthenon is the focal point of the landscape, the center. Movement through space comes to a halt where movement and its time are suspended in pure contemplation. The worshiper stands on the hill, the exalted earth, at the center, under the light of the sun, in the air of the world. The worshiper in the cathedral comes apart from the world into the space transfigured by the ecstatic light, lifted up beyond the self, then sent back into the world. Time is not so much suspended as transfigured.

In the cathedral as in the Parthenon, the sculpture and its subject matter program are essential to the completion of the building. The sculptured figures on the Parthenon are in serene harmony with the building but have their independent existence from it while remaining a part of it. The sculptures of the cathedral are woven into its fabric, fitted into its linear pattern, an element in the whole.

There are hundreds of sculptures, each playing an appointed instructional and symbolic role. It takes a whole book to account for the sculptural program of one cathedral. Only the merest sketch is possible here.

The west front of Amiens Cathedral has the most compact version Ill. 22 of such a program, concentrating in one place subjects that, in other buildings, are scattered in several places. The central doorway is dedicated to Christ, the southern to Mary, the northern to St. Firmin, a local saint; the range of the program is from the ultimate truths to its local manifestations. The central doorway displays the Last Judgment in the tympanum above the doors; the worshiper entering the church undergoes, goes under, judgment in making the passage from the world into the City of God.[22] In the judgment, kings, popes, bishops, monks, can be found among the damned and among the redeemed; earthly office does not ensure eternal salvation.

The arches above show the multitude of the heavenly hosts. Ranged in ranks on either side of the doorway are the apostles, richly detailed in individual appearance but with the same benign serenity of expression as the Christ on the central pillar.

For grasping the breadth of this program, the medallions (quatrefoils) below are most significant. Some contain figures representing the Virtues and the Vices, those behaviors that should be encouraged, those that should

---

[22] It is not entirely beside the point to mention the angel holding the scales that are used to weigh out the souls. An angel waits on one side to receive the souls of the redeemed, a demon on the other side receives the souls of the damned. The demon has his finger hooked over the pan of the scales attempting to cheat. The dignified solemnity of the Greek temple could never allow this endearing wit, the sheer ordinariness of wickedness. I am glad to report that the cheating is in vain; the scales come down on the side of salvation.

be condemned.[23] The program is not only dedicated to displaying the ultimate truths but to teaching moral behavior.

Other quatrefoils show the Labors of the Months. Signs of the zodiac identify the month, the work of the peasant farmer shows the characteristic labor of that month. Both society and the church may have been organized on the pattern of feudal hierarchy but the ordinary work of the ordinary peasant is part of the order of God. Observation was quite precise; a work such as sowing or reaping will be represented a month earlier in the south of France than in the north. Their observation of the forms of plants is precise enough to make identification easy; the ordinariness of things and the ordinariness of human work in time are part of God's creation.[24] No other body of religious art is quite so comprehensive.

Whereas the Parthenon stands apart from the passage of time, here the rhythmic passage of time as of history is part of the order of redemption.

In the Romanesque period of medieval art, there was a profound awareness of the fearful dangers of human existence and the terrors of judgment. In the later Gothic period, there was a profound awareness of tragedy, of sin, of death; subject matter programs become obsessively preoccupied with the passion of Jesus, with terrible representations of his suffering. On the Gothic of the great cathedrals in the center of France there is little sense of pain, of tragedy. The crucifixion is sometimes eliminated altogether, or only lightly displayed. All is calm, an ecstatic serenity, a transfiguration of the earth and its sufferings, a lifting up of all things human into the peace of God.

The immediate details of interpretation of one medieval building cannot be carried over directly to others since each has its own character. If this account, however limited, is accurately done it is a display of general principles. Place, space, mass, light, supports, walls, openings, movements, rhythms, carvings, proportions, are all elements of the vocabulary of the architect and need to be attended to but not by imposing some abstract scheme on the building. Rather the building must be experienced in its immediacy, in its massive spatial presence. It determines the analysis and interpretation.

---

[23] I regret to say that the imagination of the artists was not equal to making virtue particularly interesting. The vices are more fun to look at.
[24] Emile Male points out that early medieval sculptors favored plants in bud.(Male 1913:52) The High Gothic portrayed plants in full flower whereas late Gothic represented thistles and autumn dried plants. I won't attempt to interpret this odd circumstance.

HAGIA SOPHIA AND THE OTTOMAN MOSQUES.

Ill. 23
Ill. 24

Recognizing the usual risks in this terminology, the vocabulary of architecture is the same everywhere. Each culture has its own selection from this vocabulary, and its own grammar. Each building, has its own syntactical structure and, therefore, its own content. Necessarily this means that any selection from the vast number of buildings is arbitrary. If I indulge in one more comparison it is because it has a singular lesson to teach.

The larger issue is the content of a work of art as it has to do with the specificities of a particular religion. Earlier, I pointed out that the form of the Indian cave temple was used by Hindus, Buddhists and Jains; the only way to tell them apart is by the sculptures, and that is not always a reliable guide, since one group might represent the sacred figures of another.[25] There is something in the cave temple form that meets the deepest needs of the Indian religious imagination as against the requirements of a specific cult. (Elsewhere, each group developed architectural forms specific to itself.)

Sometimes the distinction is the obviously practical one of the building's usefulness for the particular liturgical requirements of a religion. A Gothic church is hardly well suited to the sacrificial liturgy of the Greeks. There are distinctions of this kind within particular religions. The liturgies of the Catholic churches necessarily focus on the altar while the Protestant churches focus on the pulpit.[26] There is a fascinating and instructive variety of treatments of these forms.

The important issue at the moment, however, is the deeper distinction of forms whose inherent content sets out a fundamental image of cosmic

---

[25] In general, the oriental religious imagination does not make the sharp distinctions that westerners are fond of. A cultivated Chinese gentleman could be a Confucian, a Cha'an Buddhist and a Taoist according to the mode of his life at the moment. I knew an automobile driver in Bombay who was a Parsee, (a sect originating in Iran and not India) but whose devotion was directed toward a Hindu saint. Christian missionaries often found Hindus grateful to be introduced to this splendid new god, Jesus, and willing to add him to the others, which is not quite what the missionaries had in mind.
[26] Some Protestant churches have gotten themselves into a tangle with this distinction. For reasons of social fashion, they have imitated the form of the 19th century Episcopal church, itself based on a 14th century monastic prototype, and then found it quite unsuited to their own service. This event is instructive in the matter of imagery. Because the Protestant churchmen were insensitive to church buildings as images of a particular sense of spatial order and religious commitment, they made an image of a building for its social suggestion.

order. The particular comparison I have chosen shows how the same essential form can be transferred from one culture, one religion, to another with important modifications made by great architects who knew the different work they were to do.

Justinian's great church of the Holy Wisdom, Hagia Sophia, was famous all over the western and Near Eastern world for centuries. When the Ottoman Turks undertook their campaign against Constantinople their major motive was territorial and political but one explicit motive was Hagia Sophia; at the fall of the city, the sultan rode directly to Hagia Sophia to see it.

As soon as possible thereafter the building of mosques began. It is clear that the architects were, figuratively and literally, looking over their shoulders at Hagia Sophia. A great work sometimes has the effect of stifling the imagination of those who follow; it has been said that Michelangelo killed Italian sculpture for fifty years. Yet these were great and original architects. They took from Hagia Sophia what they wanted and could use but they made purely Islamic buildings.

The floor plans are almost, but significantly not quite, identical. They consist of a square with another square in its center defined by pillars supporting a dome and subsidiary domes surrounding it.

A domed building is different from an arched building but the structural forces are the same, now distributed around the full circumference of the dome. The dome is a dead weight downward but it also has the sideways thrust of the arch. The subordinate domes buttress the great central domes and carry the thrust to lesser domes and the supporting walls. The mosques have lesser domes on all four sides and Hagia Sophia has them only on the eastern and the western sides. This caused a great deal of trouble. Twice the central dome partly collapsed until they added the enormous buttresses that disfigure the outside.

Violations of structural logic of this kind indicate that the people wanted something not entirely compatible with their technology. It is not that the Ottoman architects were smarter builders. The small differences made very different spaces.

Hagia Sophia is conventionally known as a "centrally planned church", one that is equal on all sides with a dome over the center as against the "basilican" plan, which is rectangular with the entrance in the center of one short end and the altar at the other.

There are very few true centrally planned churches, which would require placing the altar in the center under the dome. (Probably there have been more churches with central altars built since the second World War than in all the earlier history of the Church, a significant shift in the church as cosmic image.) Central placement of the altar implies a relation between the priest and the congregation that has not always been acceptable in Catholic theology. (Is the church a gathered community with equality between priest and laity, or is it a militant community with the priest at the head?[27] Does the priest stand between the congregation and God or with the people as spokesman? Placement of the altar has many implications, depending in good part on the form of the building as interpretation of the placement. Thus the form of the church building is an image of the church.)

It is not so simple a matter as the placement of the altar. Many religious buildings are the object of pilgrimages and processions; few go so far as the traditional Christian church in making the processional way the decisive form of the building. The church has a complex origin that is not germane here. (Among several influences are the early, house church, the catacomb chapel and the Roman law court from which the name "basilica" derives.) The word "nave" for that part of the church containing the congregation derives from the Latin word for "ship"; the symbolic implications are obvious. The colonnade is structural but it is clear that the intent of its general design was strongly influenced by the colonnaded Mediterranean street; the church is functionally the City of God and visually the image of the City of God and the interior is the processional way leading from entrance to the altar

By not having domes on the south and north sides, the architects of Hagia Sophia have superimposed a basilican church on a central one, generating a dynamic integration and interaction between the two, one of the most remarkable dialogues in architectural history.

The dome is the dominant element, floating above the great central space. "Floating" is not entirely a figure of speech; the windows at the base of the dome create a band of light, so the dome seems to float above it; a contemporary described it as "suspended from heaven by a golden chain". The dome is always symbolically the sky, the vault of heaven, and this one is a vision of paradise. The side spaces are separated by screens of arches from the central space. To stand in them, where the laity stood during

---

[27] The conception of the Church as the gathered community is so strong in modern times that a new altar has been built in many medieval churches, placed in the crossing between the nave and the transepts, thus as central as possible in a basilican plan church.

the service, is to be apart from the principal area of the church but also to see it transfigured by light as in a vision. We can only imagine the effect on the worshipers as the great procession of the clergy moved across that space to the altar.

To stand at the entrance is to see across the central space, with vision unimpeded by screens of arches, to sense the soaring upward to the crown of the dome, the movement forward to the altar. It is an ecstatic experience comparable to that of the Gothic church but less energetic, more a light filled vision. The treatment of the interior surfaces, now much battered, would have obliterated the sense of mass, of the action of weight, which is so important to the effect of the Gothic church. Ideally, the inner surface of a Byzantine church is covered with mosaics (scenes and decorative patterns made by small cubes of colored glass set in cement), transforming the mass of the wall into a surface of colored light. Where the Gothic window opens out beyond the space of the building, the Byzantine mosaic transfigures the space itself into a vision of heaven. The Gothic church opens out beyond itself. The space of the Byzantine church is itself the vision of heaven.

The mosque, on the other hand, takes the same basic plan and changes it slightly but to great effect. There is no distinction among the sides. There is, of course, an entrance doorway. The mihrab on the opposite wall, a richly ornamented niche, marks the direction toward Mecca. The psychological importance of the mihrab is great but it does not determine the space effect. In function, the mosque is unlike the church in every aspect except being intended for the congregation. It is a prayer hall and a teaching place, not a space set apart for the presence of God.

The side areas are so clearly a part of the central area that there is no clear separation between them. The proportions of one space in relation to another are easy and harmonious. The inner surfaces are smooth plaster, often painted or tiled in geometric or floral patterns. The effect is to obliterate the weight of the wall behind, not to transform it into light as in the church, but to clarify the surface. Of all significant architectural works, these are most reminiscent of the tent; is this a symbolic memory of the Turk's nomadic past?

Throughout the building, the light is even, never emphasized, always present, a calm and calming presence. Necessarily the three axes are present but there is no emphasis on any one of them. The space exists in itself, as a single, unimpeded, unqualified whole, a unity virtually without distinctive parts. The total effect is of serene quiet, without activity or drama, an evenness of emphasis, an equality of direction. It is the fullest realization of the prime Islamic symbol, an image of the absolute unity of God.[28]

In most Christian churches, there is an experience of energy, a multiplicity of direction and emphases, a complexity of interaction among masses, spaces and light, that accords well with the more complex Christian symbolizing of the divine. The Ottoman architects felt the difference very deeply and without lessening their passionate admiration for Hagia Sophia, adapted its form for a statement of their own distinctive faith.[29]

A building is pure form without representation of anything outside itself. It is also pure image, an image of sacral order .

---

[28] While this is indeed one of the most vivid embodiments of the Islamic principle of the unity of God, it is not the only form of that idea. The hypostyle halls such as the Great Mosque of Cordoba achieves the same idea with totally different means. They are large halls full of row after row of columns. Instead of a single, uninterrupted space, there is a multitude of single units of space resolved into unity. The repetition of the spatial experience in every direction is almost mesmerizing in its effect. For various historical, geographic, social and economic reasons, every religion develops a variety of forms for the manifestation of its basic ideas.

[29] While this is the only example I know of direct influence of one of these forms on another, there are other cases of affinity of spirit, made possible by the great variety of emphases in Christianity. The equality of all worshipers represented in the mosque is not unlike the Protestant principle of the priesthood of all believers. The 17th century "City churches" in London designed by Christopher Wren and Nicholas Hawksmoor have something of the evenness of emphasis and unity of effect of the Ottoman mosques. So do some of the much simpler "meeting houses" of early New England, where the devout came to meet each other and to meet God.

8

THE BODY AS IMAGE AND
THE IMAGE OF THE BODY

SPACE AND NATURE. BODY AND ACT.

These are not separate things. When we act, we act in, with, by means of, our bodies. When we act, we act in space, the space of nature, the spaces made by people. Our lives are lived in our bodies, resting or moving through the spaces of buildings and of nature. We cannot escape the work of other people (work that is the extension of themselves by their making) and our relations with them and the things they have made. Our own making is a part of the common making. Our symbolic lives (that is, our religious or "spiritual") lives are lived within and by means of the forms given to our experiences of space and nature, body and act.

In many ways, space is the most dramatically revealing of the prime symbols of the religious imagination. For this reason I began with the forms of symbolic space. It is not, however, more basic than the other two prime symbolic forms: the representation of nature and the representation of the human body. So far we have dealt briefly with the representation of nature in the form of the great animals in the caves and the paintings of landscapes. In the last chapter, we touched on the representation of the body but only as elements of buildings. It would be well now to look at the representation of the body by a sketch of the sculptured body. Sculpture will serve the immediate purpose since (as the sketch of landscape paintings showed) paintings so often show the body in the context of nature and of narrative. Sculpture is in space and so, necessarily, it defines a relation to space which is a prime purpose of the analysis but the relation can be seen more nearly in itself than is the case with painting.

In this study, mass has two modalities: the means for the forming of space and the forms of the human body. These are sometimes separable,

127

often not (that is, the representation of the body is often part of the building and shaped according to its principles, not those of the body). It defines a relation to space which is a prime purpose of the analysis but the relation can be seen more nearly in itself than is the case with painting.[1]

At the risk of unpleasing repetition, I will summarize the character of such a chapter as this one. Our purpose is the elucidation of content, which is the fundamental commitments of a people, defining their religion. While there are as many different contents as there are images, it might be said that religious content is only one among many. This is partly true (many works have a political intention which, when successful, is their content). But even these state their immediate purpose by means of a more general structure of the imagination that can be called religious (remembering the variety of definitions of religion).

THE ELEMENTS OF THE BODY IMAGE

The defining mode of the experience of the earth is the human body. It is the instrument of the experience and a primary, primal, part of the experience. It is the aspect of the earth most immediately present to each of us. We are our bodies, we are inseparable from our bodies.

We, therefore, posses already the elemental instrument for the understanding of images. It is necessary only to be aware, fully and in detail, of the shapes and workings of our own bodies in order to use that awareness for the purpose of understanding.

It is equally true that our bodies are inseparable from the world and all their workings are a matter of interacting with the things and events of that world. We can know each only by its interacting with the other.

Which is a daunting prospect. No matter how intimately aware we are of the shapes and events of our own bodies, they are, they will remain, a mystery to us. So will the world. We use symbolic images, symbolic forms to come to an accommodation with those mysteries.

The body is the means for our interaction with the world. The body is an image of the order of that world. The body is a subject that we grasp through, by means of, its images. Yet we cannot simply make an intellectual

---

[1] This comment applies to "free-standing" sculpture which is the concern of this chapter. Relief sculpture (sculpture that is part of a background) moves toward the character of painting and commonly involves a natural setting.

place for the body nor can we simply apprehend it by means of our images, for each of us has a body-image, made up of proprioception (the perception of our own bodies), the particularities of our psychic life and experiences, and the images of the body present in our culture.

The body is the means for apprehending the images. We cannot understand the work, including the images of other people, if we do not become self-conscious about our own image of our body; otherwise, we superimpose our sense of the self on others. The problem of that image of the body is extraordinarily complex. What is the edge of the self? The surface of clothing? Our skin? Somewhere within the skin? Are the orifices of the body points of vulnerability? Is the body good or evil? What is the function of beauty? Of maiming? Such questions could go on and on.

Since the body is a basic subject of art, it is well to be conscious of the different aspects of the body and its experience.

1. Its superficial (i.e., surface) appearance. Indifference to the reproduction of the specifics of individuals can take the form of idealization (some purified, abstracted essence of the human) or generalization (a least common denominator of human forms). Fidelity to appearances is multiple; there are more aspects to appearance than can be recorded in a single work. Again, appearances are not illusory; they are part of "Reality".

2. Its anatomical structure, the structure and ordering of its skeleton and muscles, generating the external forms, the articulation of bones and muscles.

3. Its organic energy as a living form, including erotic energy and desirability.

4. Its action, movement, involvement in relation, story, narrative.

5. Its inner life, its feelings, emotions, desires, etc., which is to say, its personality. This is the most difficult of all for the artist (it is the principal concern of much poetry and music). Even the "discovery" of the inner life is problematical. It can be expressed directly, but only in general terms, in the forms of the work (expressionism), or it can be suggested by the action or attitude of the figure and is, therefore, linked to #4.

6. The body in its physical wholeness. It is bilaterally symmetrical, stands on the earth, subject to gravity. It is perceptually, emotionally, dramatically ordered among the things of the earth. It also feels pain, shame, violation, maiming.

Human life is all of these in a vital unity that is barely suggested by this listing. Consider, for example, the terrible passions, the overwhelming powers, hidden in that flaccid term, desire.

No single image can give equal attention to all of these. The selection made and the manner of their use is a prime symbol of the religion embodied in the work. One of the first acts of analysis is determining the proportioning among them and the manner of their representation.

We can assume that religion began in an interplay between myth, ritual, objects, and space. Some objects might be things with no great bulk, or mass, but clearly stones, trees and the like played a primary role in the early development. Once apprehended as sacred objects, stone and wood are available as the occasion for successive modifications that bring them into the appearances of the human body. We meet the earliest human sense of mass in the form of bodies.

Mass as bodies cannot be seen apart from space. Our own bodies experience the mass, the thingness, of the earth in space. Our postulation of the beginnings of religion should not be of a space that is general but rather space that is defined. It is defined, shaped, formed, by the substance of things, by mass. Space and mass are inseparable.

Each emerges from archetypal experiences. The first experience is the body interacting with the things and bodies of the earth. Then there is the projection of the body into certain earth forms. This sets up the origins of this image motif.

First there was the menhir. The menhir was related to the standing male body by affixing the genitals to the lower front. From that point, the thought process was continuous. Certain other features were inscribed on the surface of the stone without impairing its character as an upright stone. Gradually, these features dominated the menhir quality without destroying it; the figure remains a pillar. The menhir evolved into those fundamental structural and symbolic devices, the standing human body and the column. Each is an idea, an act of thought, therefore a means of thought.

THE IMAGE AND GEOMETRIC FORM

An image is not merely a representation. It is also a form. Such sculptures as these can be defined formally by a simple diagrammatic device.

With the exception of prehistoric works and certain modern works, sculptured images do not begin with an unformed block of material but with one that has received a preliminary shape. Why should this be so? It is not easy to say. It is a truism that all unrestricted freedom is less free than freedom within rules, within lawfulness. The unformed material does not yield to the imagination but restricts it. The material cut to a 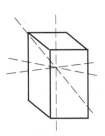 geometric block has been infused with rationality, (hence "spiritualized"), made accessible to the creative imagination. It is the starting point for the making of the image and for the imagination.

The diagram defines several things: the axes of the stereometric block of stone; the axes of the figure and how these are related to the axes of the block; the bounding planes of the work and the relation of the contained figure to these planes; the relation of the mass to space.

Two imaginary (but palpable) planes can be drawn through the vertical axis of the block of stone. One extends side to side, the other front to back. Since the spectator (or worshiper) is also a standing human body, this observing body has the same axes and the same bisecting planes. The one running side to side parallels the plane of the sculptural figure, the one front to back is the same as that of the sculptured figure. Since the sculptor can choose to be dominated by these axes and planes or to subordinate them to willed action, the diagram is a tool for defining the relation of the image to the spectator.

The diagram serves as an analytical tool for both the formal and the symbolic structure of the work. It defines the relation of the represented figure to the mass of the material and to the enveloping, containing space. It also defines the relation of the figure to the spectator, one of the prime concerns of any analysis.

It is a tool, yet more than a tool. It itself is an image, however abstract, of the relation of the body to the defined space.

This diagram, all analytical tools and principles, must be used with discretion. It is not something to impose on the work. It is a means for sensitizing the awareness to its actualities. Analysis is an active and a passive process, searching over the work and responding to it. The student should not look verbally, by formulating verbal statements to characterize the work. Be receptive and gradually the necessary words should appear in awareness.

These are not bodies, nor is any statue. Each is a mass of material organized in a particular manner by a human hand according to principles of craft directed toward a chosen end. The mass is formed to be analogous to the body and the mode of that analogy gives access to the intention and the purpose of the people who made it and made use of it.

It remains now to apply these analytical principles to particular works.

Ill. 4   THE "VENUS" OF WILLENDORF[2]

The significance of this figure (mentioned briefly in Chapter 4) lies precisely in the fact that the diagram does <u>not</u> apply to it. Why, then, not introduce it before taking up the diagram? To look at it now serves purposes that are not only pedagogical but historical: the transformation represented by the diagram is the shift from the early "prehistoric" cultures to the "high" cultures, and both the nature and the consequences of the shift need to be understood in order to apprehend the difference between the two types of religious imagination.

The figure was obviously an irregular stone modified as little as possible. It has no base, just as the cave paintings have no baseline and no frame; the diagram suggests one of the crucial inventions (or discoveries) of the religious imagination, the base.

Base and frame are not only formal devices. They are modes of orientation of the person in the world. The base and the frame establish hierarchical order; this is almost certainly not a "goddess" because divinities are normally linked to hierarchical order. The vertical and the horizontal become fundamental symbolic forms around which the symbolic world is organized. (This symbolic world determines the political world as well as being derived from it and serving its interests.) Base and frame not only "spiritualize" the figures by submitting them to the rational structures of geometry, they detach the representation from the spectator. The relation between image and spectator is radically changed, which means a transformation in the nature of religion.

---

[2] It is important to remember the point made earlier: to call such a figure "Venus" is to distort interpretation quite seriously. Venus was (is?) a goddess functioning in a specific religion, possessed of a distinct personality as a part of that religion. There is no reason at all to think this figure represents a goddess. (See Chapt 4, p. 52)

The figure is one of the oldest carved images, dating from somewhere around 30,000 BCE. There is no reason to think it represents any ideal of feminine beauty. In the absence of the face, there is clearly no interest in the individual person. The sole concern is with the enormous breasts and abdomen and the genitals, those features of the body linked to fertility. We have no way of knowing how it was used. Such figures are found in domestic, not cultic, contexts. Since the legs come to a point, they may have been stuck in the ground. It would be simple to tie a thong around the neck so it may have been worn on the body or simply carried in a pocket.

To say it is a "fertility figure" is redundancy, saying no more than that the figure is what it is. The point is the kind of image of order, process and purpose that makes such a figure possible. Equally, it doesn't help to speak of it as "magic", for the necessary issue is the image of order and process that makes the image work magically.

The key is, again, participation. The vital energy of procreation could be localized in the image and, therefore, made accessible to those who touched it or carried it or were in its presence. Their attitude could have been impersonal; the force was necessary and usable as electricity is. In such a case, the word "religious" would apply only in the most general sense: the figure as an image of reality. It may have been more specifically religious. The primal energies so prominent in the great animals are also manifest in that awesome phenomenon, the fertility of the bodies of women. Participation in that energy would, then, have a more general purpose than ensuring the immediate fertility of particular women.

Probably such distinctions are the kind of thing our minds produce without much reference to minds that did not care to detach one thing or act so clearly from another.

It was possible to say of the cave paintings that their artistic quality is of the highest. Their quality should remind us that "preliterate" people were and are as intelligent and as competent as we are, despite our temptation to assume we are superior. This figure is of low artistic quality. There are similar figures of very much higher quality while constructed on similar structural principles. I choose this one to emphasize again that many images function outside the matter of artistic quality, while, at the same time, they contain an identifiable principle of form.

This study presents a mode of analytical interpretation and not an outline of history. Nevertheless, we must recognize the fundamental transformation in the development with the birth of the "high" cultures.

Beginning around 4-3,000 BCE in Egypt and the ancient Near East, the vertical became dominant in the imagination as hierarchical order became dominant politically and religiously. This "cut" does not represent a simple before and after; the immense variety in the religious imagination during the "after" period is enough complication but there is another fundamental shift that will occupy us in a later chapter. The modern period represents a further transformation which may be of equal consequence. Beginning in the last third of the nineteenth century, the old vertical order, dominant for five millennia, began to dissolve in both painting and architecture.

Then the vertical image loses all force. The dissolving of dominant verticality is a corollary to the dissolving of the old hierarchical ordering of social and political structures. Many who were once forced to take a "lower" place— women, blacks, small nations, etc. — now refuse to do so.

For all the importance of these breaks, in both cases there is a profound continuity with what went before. So much being said by way of introduction, let us look now at two images, each governed by the principles of the diagram but using them very differently.

THE GEOMETRY OF FAITH: EGYPT AND GREECE

The diagram applies more precisely to Egyptian images than to any other in the history of the making of images. The proper use of the diagram formally and symbolically nearly exhausts the content of the figure.

The High Priest Ranofer

Ill. 25   In this figure, the High Priest Ranofer, the original block is clearly present, both in the base and in the slab in back of the figure.[3] The figure becomes one with the axes of the block. Its organic energies are subdued to the geometric order of the stone. (It would be useful to compare the

---

[3] The slab is there probably as a practical device. The stone is very hard but also breakable. Such statues have a weakness familiar to all athletes: the ankles are more susceptible to injury than any other part of the body. The slab was left as a support. Even so, most sculptors in other traditions let the figure fend for itself. They have no such symbolic need to affirm the presence of the original, geometrically defined, material. It is also worth noting, lest the diagram be thought a critical abstraction, that Egyptian sculpture reproduces it exactly. Archaeologists have excavated sculptors' studios containing unfinished statues. The block of stone has the outline of the figure drawn in on the front and sides. The image was made by connecting the outlines.

figure with a sculpture by Michelangelo. He is very nearly as respectful of the shape of the block of stone but the figure, contained within its block, struggles against its confining limits. The result is an image of dynamic energy, of a fatally imprisoned human drama.)

The proportions of the figure are within normal limits. Body parts are delineated without special emphasis. The face is conceivable as a real person but there is no stress on the individuality of features. The figure does nothing; it is simply there. While it does not act, it certainly has an attitude, lordly, confident, supremely calm. The rhythm of the figure is simple, grave, noble, subdued, with quietly undulating surfaces and large, well established forms.

The most obvious characteristic of the work is the most important element of its formal structure: the absolute dominance of the axial organization of the block and the confinement of the figure within the planes of the original surface of the block. Analysis and description are interwoven. What does this point to as suggesting the content?

Remember the original definition. Content is not "meaning", as something other than the form, contained in it as water in a pitcher. Content is inseparable from the form, communicated by means of the form. It is the form seen in its fullest and truest nature. Verbal statements are no more than helpful guides to the essential act of thinking, which is empathetic perception.

Organic life is energy, vitality. It is fertility and birth. It is transformation, growth, death, decay. That which is born must also die.

Geometry is the unchanging and eternal; a rectangle, a triangle, are exactly the same for us as they were for the Egyptians and will remain the same forever. Geometry is stability, order, control, lawfulness, the denial of time and decay, the overcoming of death.

The imaginative, symbolic structure of Egyptian religion is this profound sense of order, of the eternal, the abiding and unchanging. Action, personality, are distractions from the great unchanging order of the cosmos. It is the supreme lawfulness of the cosmos that matters. It is there and all is subject to it. It is not achieved by struggle but simply acknowledged and accepted. Even the gods are subject to this order. Death is overcome, change and transformation are denied.

Egypt is a country of unparalleled regularity. The Nile bisects the country, which lies symmetrically on either side of it. The fertile land is that part irrigated by the Nile; it is possible to stand with one foot in a fertile field and the other in the desert. There is virtually no rainfall; the sun is a constant, dependable presence. Yet there is more to this geography than simple regularity; it is the juxtaposition of life and death. The north-south axis along the river is life. To the east and west lay the terrible heat of the desert, the realm of death.

As a people, the Egyptians were as disorderly as we all are, working, desiring, copulating, fighting, loving, dying. Images do not necessarily reflect a social reality; they set out a desired ideal. In this case, they found purpose and meaning in the sense of abiding order of which this figure is a profound and exact symbol. Its strict and unwavering limits forbid participation. At the same time, the axial plane that bisects the figure front to back bisects us who stand in front of it and links us irrevocably to it. The axial plane that bisects the figure side to side lies parallel to the plane through our own figure. In attitude, the figure is quite aloof, even disdainfully aloof from the spectator (some Egyptian sculpture was made without presupposing a spectator; it was intended to be placed in the tomb as the location of the "ka" of the dead man). Nonetheless, it establishes the three dimensional grid within which both the figure and the spectator find their appointed place. As it stands proudly erect, so we stand, participating in the natural order that is above and beyond all change.

Those who wish to find an ideological statement in images certainly have no problem with this one; it so clearly serves the purposes of a hierarchical social order. Its form is as ideological as its subject. That inescapable function does not, in any degree, invalidate the other matters contained in the work. We cannot say which is cause and which effect.[4]

How much does this account tell us? If it is "true", what is it true *to*? It does not tell us, as others of their images do, that the Egyptians were a vital people, lovers of life in its organic vitality, which they recorded in their reliefs and paintings. They delighted in the nobility and sensual beauty of women, the virile energy of men. So this figure is limited. It is not all of the Egyptian imagination but it is a fundamental symbolic form that represents securely what lay beneath the rich variety of Egyptian religious thought.

---

[4] I have juxtaposed several things without implying causality. Egyptian sensibilities and, therefore, the Egyptian imagination were profoundly affected by the climate and landscape but I cannot say the landscape "caused" Egyptian religion. I do not know if the religion caused the sculpture or the sculpture caused the religion; the very question doesn't make much sense. Egyptian society was as hierarchically ordered as the sculpture. Which "caused" which? This is another question that makes little sense.

The Kouros   Ill. 26

The comparison with ancient Greece is a repetition of the comparison between Hagia Sophia and the Ottoman mosques: the later work is obviously modeled on the earlier yet makes a change that is fundamental and so emphasizes the principle involved.[5]

Ranofer dates from the Fifth Dynasty of Egypt around the 25th century BCE, the Greek from the "archaic" period in the 6th century BCE. It is a "kouros", once thought to represent Apollo but probably a votive figure dedicated as a gift to the gods in celebration and rejoicing.

Few other images in history so clearly demonstrate the power of a fundamental image of the body. This figure stands in exactly the same position as the Egyptian, with the same dependence on axial order. This is not an accident. Egypt had great prestige among the Greeks (their version of the modern "immemorial wisdom of the east"). The axial structure is the same and has the same import: geometric order as the basic structure of reality.

The images differ in the reproduction of surface appearance; the Greek is much less representational. It is not the degree of departure from representational accuracy that matters but the kind of thing that is emphasized.

At every point the Greek sculptor has emphasized those aspects of the body that enable it to move, to act. The representation is schematic, even diagrammatic, but the diagrams emphasize the knees, the shoulders, the muscles of the abdomen, the legs, the hips. Whereas the Egyptian muted all indication of organic vitality, this figure is permeated with the sense of vitality. It is tense, springy, full of the potential for movement. It doesn't act any more than the Egyptian; both simply **are**. Where the Egyptian figure is nobly static, the Greek is suffused with the potential for action. Its sculptural image is as simple as the Egyptian; its represented rhythm is the organicity of the human body. It stands in the radiant splendor of its own being.

It would be an error to stress one element against the other or to see the organic vitality as emerging from the prison of geometry. The structural

---

[5] Comparisons of this kind are the most common and, perhaps, useful device in teaching art. At the same time, there are real dangers in making such comparisons. They may unbalance the analysis by over-stressing the difference with something else. There is an even greater danger of extracting the images from their social context and treating them as though they are outside history.

issue is the extraordinary balance between the two, vitality and energy restrained by geometry, geometry enlivened by energy. Without specifics of representation, there is only the suggestion of individuality. Without revelatory action (gesture), there is no sense of personality. The figure simply **is**, as detached from the spectator as the Egyptian but imposing, by its vitality, the wonder and the harmony of human existence.

It is not clear what is represented in such figures. They may be characters from a myth but they do not illustrate the myth. They are not gods but the point is not important. They re-present divinity, because the divine is the controlled vitality of the human. Equally, within the mess that was the actuality of Greek existence, as it is of all things human, they show forth, re-present, the essentials of the human participation in the divine. The human is made numinous.

This structural principle, the distinctive harmony of energy and geometry, characterizes all significant Greek art until its dissolution. This principle accounts for the power over the imagination that Greek art continually has.

Ranofer was hidden away in the darkness of a temple, no more accessible to the average person than the portrait statues that were buried in tombs with the body of the dead. The kouros stood in the light of the sun, like the Parthenon, part of the public life, the public worship, of the city. The kouros is an early statement of the humanism of Greek religion. The gods are exalted humans and humans are elevated to a participation in the divine.[6]

SOUILLAC AND CHARTRES: THE IMAGE AND THE CHURCH.

Another comparison, this time between two figures not long separated in time (12th century) or space (central and south-western France) and representing two manifestations of the same faith.

Ill. 27   *Isaiah of Souillac*

After the beginnings of Christian art, major imagery was often part of architecture and can be fully interpreted only in terms of the dialectic

---

[6] It may be worth noting that those who look for the ideological function of images should have no more trouble with this figure than they do with the Ranofer.

tension between the statue and the building. In the Romanesque period, the first part of the so-called middle ages, there is too great a variety of treatments to make summary possible; the sculptor could submit the figure to the rigorous control of the massive wall against which it was set or play it off against the mass in various ways.

This figure is on the wall beside the entrance door of the church of Souillac in southwestern France. The wall section functions as a pillar supporting the arch of the doorway but it is not a separate, humane unit like the Greek column; it is a segment of the wall, heavy, massive, powerful, static. The wall is as powerful a symbolic form in Romanesque thought as the column was for the Greeks.

The figure is all energy and tension. It not only does not violate the wall, it affirms it by being compressed into the surface. It does not represent the body so much as allude to it by analogy. All the movements are in the horizontal plane, paralleling the plane of the wall and fixed to its surface. The only exception is the outward look of the eyes, directed toward the worshiper.

The diagram is not quite applicable to the figure; it rarely can be applied directly to relief sculpture. Nevertheless, it serves a serious analytical purpose in defining the geometric order that is as basic to this figure as to Ranofer but used very differently. The geometry is the controlling plane of the wall surface. There is no consciousness of the supporting axes of the body; the figure is not imaginable apart from its place on/in the wall. Representationally, the figure is as much an emotional state as it is a human body. It has no bones or muscles, only action; no narrative, only attitude. It represents only the highest possible state of emotional tension.

Instead of the kinds of harmony represented by the Egyptian or the Greek work, this is a forceful dissonance between mass and energy. The result is ecstatic, outside the bounds of the immediate and the mundane.

It is not easy to identify the purpose of the figure. With it, we are at the beginning of a time when sculptured figures were an integral part of the church. Later, sculptural programs were used for instruction and inspiration. There must be something of that here but primarily we are dealing with another fundamental symbolic form: the doorway. The figure cannot be understood in isolation but only in relation to its placement.

Doorways are always basic in the symbolic imagination, as the passage between inner and outer, the crossing of the limit. This is particularly true in the church. The interior of the church is the City of

God. To go from outside to inside is to pass from this world into the next; commonly in medieval churches the Last Judgment is carved above the doorway, so the worshiper undergoes, goes under, the Last Judgment in entering the church. The door is Christ, who said, "I am the door" (John 10: 9). A universal, archetypal, image is linked directly to the Christian message. The place of greatest danger is also the means of salvation. Ostensibly the figure is pedagogical and devotional, the prophet foretelling the Christ. Its psychic, symbolic, function is stronger.

Often on these doors, as at Souillac, there are images of terrible beasts, the fearful dangers of this world subdued by the power of Christ.

Ill. 28   *Kings and Queens of Judah*, West Portal, Chartres Cathedral.

If historical classifications matter, this is early Gothic. Again we have a great doorway but belonging to a different emotional and religious world. There is none of the terrible tension, the frightful energies, of Souillac.

These figures are medieval in dependence on the architecture but now it is not the mass of the wall but the vertical linear pattern of a new kind of architecture. The wall is obscured by the containing linear framework. The figures are entirely harmonious with the vertical pattern, set against the colonnettes and having the form of colonnettes themselves. They are parts of a whole larger than themselves.

There is no body beneath the drapery, no skull behind the faces. Anatomy is of no consequence; their axes are those of the vertical lines of the building, not of the body. As sculptures, the figures are necessarily objects in our space but there is no sense, as there was with both the Egyptian and the Greek, of figures occupying the same world as ourselves; they are exalted beings, visions of another world. We observe them but do not participate in a physical life as we do with the Egyptian and the Greek. Rather, we participate emotionally in what they signify.

There is an intense sense of individuality. Neither the interests of the people nor the technique of the sculptor lent themselves to the precise rendering of individual detail. Rather there is a careful delineation of separate persons, an awareness of the distinctiveness of persons. Male and female are clearly discriminated in their characteristic form but (whatever the character of their society), there is no hierarchical distinction between them. There is no distinctive personality, or rather, there is a single personality suffusing all the figures. The figures do not act beyond holding the scrolls that identified them (they probably represent the kings and queens of Judah as the royal ancestors of Christ). They have the same calm, remote, expression.

Again, I intrude a personal experience that may not be fully evident in the photographs. I have more than once come to this and other displays like it at the end of a day of travel, hot, tired, sweaty, restless and discontent. After I have been for awhile in the presence of these figures, such feelings seem unworthy, slowly drain away, replaced by peace, an exaltation of spirit.

For all their individuality, these figures do not have the distinctiveness of personality that was to come later. The individual is transfigured, taken up into the peace of God.

Donatello's *Zuccone:* the body as structure and will.   Ill. 29

We move now to the fifteenth century, the "Renaissance". The way had been prepared by Giotto and by Donatello's earlier work, not considered here. Otherwise, there is no precedent in the history of art for this figure. As much as possible in a single figure we are in the realm of narrative, a subject to be considered later.

Donatello has not invented a new formal language; the "vocabulary" of sculpture had been there from a very early time. The figure is as rigorously bound within the contours of the three dimensional block of stone as an Egyptian image (he almost certainly never saw an Egyptian work). It has the anatomical coherence and capacity for movement of Greek images and its movements are as controlled around the central vertical axis. It has the uncompromising reproduction of individual appearance of the Romans. (Donatello knew Greek sculpture, at least in small works and in its translation into Roman sculpture. He had studied Roman imagery extensively.) Its placement is in the tradition of medieval architecture, still a part of the building as it stood in its niche on the Campanile of the Cathedral of Florence.

The novelty does not appear in some eclectic combination of principles developed earlier but in the their use for a new purpose. The figure does not simply move with organic coherence; it <u>acts</u> to a determined purpose.

The figure represents an Old Testament prophet and is in the act of addressing the people. His lips are parted in speech, he is looking downward (the figure, now in the Cathedral Museum, was originally about 40 feet up). The action of his arms is directed downward. The sweep of the drapery acts as a shield, over which the action is projected. Thus the figure is acting with the greatest intensity and emotional authority toward his hearers. Part of the novelty, the creativity, of the figure is this concentration on the <u>relation</u> between image and spectator; the relation of the earlier images and the spectator was structural and emotional, not dramatic.

The relation is both formal and emotional. It depends absolutely on the presence in the stone of something never before achieved with such intensity: the sense of a living personality. Personality, the whole complex of emotions, willed actions, purposes, that make up a person, is not easy to achieve with visual imagery, although it is the very matter of poetry and fiction. It can only be suggested by the formal structure of the work and by its represented action, including the gestural expression of feelings. Donatello himself seems to have felt this overwhelming sense of personality; "Zuccone" ("big pumpkin head") is the nickname he gave the statue and he is reported to have slapped it, saying, "Speak, plague take you, speak!".

It is one of the most vivid realizations of an Old Testament prophet ever achieved. A prophet is not one who foretells the future but proclaims the word of God, which the Zuccone is most definitely doing.[7] Furthermore, it is hard to imagine such a work appearing in any culture other than one nourished for centuries by the Old Testament. It is the material embodiment of the vivid literary images of powerful personalities in the Hebrew Bible.[8]

Its religious significance goes deeper than simply the presence of personality, for the figure is genuinely epoch making. Giotto generated the basic idea of a narrative art built around the distinctiveness of personality but it was Donatello's achievement to have fused personality with individuality into an image of a more nearly complete human being than had been achieved before.

Conventional history interprets this Renaissance individuality as "secular", since it differed so markedly from the earlier work we just noted

---

[7] This sentence can be read in a way that would not represent Renaissance thinking on the subject. The Old Testament as a whole was a foretelling of Christ but less as a prediction of the future than a proclaiming of the necessary divine structure of things.
[8] One of the unfortunate aspects of this study, which touches on so many religious traditions, is the absence of any serious use of Judaism. From an early time, Judaism was opposed to the making of images. This prohibition was rarely enforce rigorously but, by the time of the making of surviving images, Jews were a minority within a dominant culture and the form of the images does not differ from the forms of the dominant culture. It is good to be able to emphasize here that the culture of the "West" is not intelligible apart from the profound involvement with the Hebrew Bible.

at Chartres. This is a mistake. Donatello's work, seen as a whole, is witness to the profoundly religious sensibility that informed this single piece. What we are seeing can be interpreted, according to theological conviction, as a dramatic re-interpretation of Christianity or (as I prefer), the most profound realization of a fundamental Christian idea: the conviction of a living, willing person in response to the saving action of God.

Renaissance art, particularly Florentine art, is profoundly incarnational, the idea that God manifested himself in the form of a man. Eastern Orthodox Christians often interpreted this as God's voluntary humiliation and sacrifice, meant to lead people above and beyond the limits of the material world. Renaissance artists regularly saw it as a sanctification of the real and the material, the substance of life on this earth. It was not a denial of the transcendent but a manifestation of the transcendent in the dramatic reality of human life, of human act and decision.

Donatello's work illustrates another important point. In all this discussion, I have assumed and hinted at, even asserted mildly, a principle of prime importance: art is a fundamental mode of theological thought. To repeat; scholars in the study of religion have understood art to be no more than illustrative of propositional theological statements (or expressive of emotional states, which they think should be kept foreign to scholarship). The relation between art and any form of propositional thinking is a complicated one. For example, the program of sculpture on a medieval church, as briefly outlined in the last chapter, was undoubtedly laid down by church officials according to a carefully articulated theological system. Nevertheless, the actual content of the works, was determined by the artist, not by a theologian.

Donatello's work forcefully illustrates the principle. Formal, propositional theology was a minor part of Florentine culture; no history of theology ever includes a Florentine. Florentine philosophy gets recognition and respect and undoubtedly had influence on later artists but not on Donatello. We need not assume that he thought it out verbally; when I speak of art as theological thought I mean that the thinking is done in the formed material of the artist rather than in words, the formed material of the theologian as traditionally defined. He was an impulsive, intuitive man, not given to propositional thought as other artists, such as Michelangelo, undoubtedly were. Rather he carried forward, in his distinctive mode of thinking, principles of human character within the divine order that had been part of Florentine thought since Dante and Giotto.

Heretofore in this account it has been possible to select a single work as an example for many, with considerable loss but not fundamental loss. This is not quite so true with Donatello. A single example shows how he went about his work but the major issue, the intensity of individual personality, can be established only by looking at the whole of his production. Counting the figures in his relief sculptures, there must be several hundred men, women and children, each set forth with a distinctiveness of appearance and of individual personality. No other artists, with the possible exception of Rembrandt, established such a wide range of vividly realized individuals and it is not equaled in any other art, except with Shakespeare and the great Russian novelists.

This principle of personality, once established by Giotto and Donatello, dominated western art for several centuries. While much of the resulting imagery remained powerfully incarnational in various modes, it also happened that the sense of personality became separated from its religious origins ("secular" critics would say "liberated"). Thus was established the modern sense of the dominance of private, subjective feelings, the governing characteristic of Romanticism, still the dominant principle in our own day.[9]

AFRICA: THE BODY IN ANOTHER MODE.

The sculptured, three-dimensional images so far considered in this chapter belong to a single, long, powerful tradition. It would be unhistorical to link the works too closely to the line of influence that connects them; each is part of a particular culture, different religions, different modes of thinking and of ordering society. Nevertheless there is a discernible connection between the styles with the earlier works identifiably influencing the later. This would be all the more dramatic if space permitted filling in all the many gaps: the Sumerian, the later Greek, the Roman, the

---

[9] Again it may be worth noting the ideological origins and functions of such works. Life in medieval and early Renaissance Italy was so much a matter of naked force that, for many individual people as well as cities, to make the wrong decision in the immediacies of situations was to end up dead or destroyed. Such circumstances encourage a keenness of perception and analysis, a power of decision, that not only makes possible but demands powerful, distinctive personalities. This made possible what the image records and serves: a bourgeois, entrepreneurial economic system as a part of an oligarchic political order. These matters indicate the conditions that made such a work possible. They do not explain the work.

Celtic and Germanic forms from the north, the many different forms of the so-called middle ages. Basically, the tradition is that of the Mediterranean cultures (omitting the Byzantine and the Moslem, both indifferent to three-dimensional images).

As powerful as this tradition is, it is not the only way to make three-dimensional images. In illustrating other traditions, we should keep in mind the incidental question: does the diagram, which works so well with Western images, help in looking at the images of another culture?

This Western development can be usefully compared with one that is notably different, revealing a set of problems and assertions that are parts of wholly different form worlds. It is not condescension that suggests the choice of the African, the current condescension that would have the work of any and every "minority" peoples be the equal in quality of any other. African sculpture is one of the world's great sculptural traditions in its own right.

There is a wide variety of African images, emanating from many different tribes and sculptural traditions. No one is typical but the one illustrated is close.   Ill. 30

Most African sculptures are wood (there is a strong tradition of bronze sculptures in Benin and many sculptures are combinations of different materials). All materials impose their character on the finished work and are part of the vocabulary and of the content. Different stones, different woods, make different statues and are different forms of thought. While some woods are dense enough to permit the recording of fine details (see, for example, the linden wood of German medieval sculpture), most have to be dealt with in broad planes. Whereas a sculptor in stone normally confronts a rectilinear block of stone as it was cut from the quarry, the sculptor in wood normally, or often, faces a cylinder cut from the trunk or the branch of a tree. Whether his material was literally a cylinder or a block, most African sculptors seem to think in terms of the cylinder. The vertical axis is dominant but the two horizontal axes are barely suggested.

The principle of abstraction is distinctive. Anatomy and the internal organization of the body have no part at all in the structure of the work. Each part of the body is treated separately, reduced to a form that is partly its essential geometry, partly expressive. The parts are discontinuous, juxtaposed to each other with only minimum transition. There is none of the organic flow that characterizes so much of the western tradition but there is a profound coherence of forms; the body forms are abstracted by the same analytical principle. The forms are related by a distinctive rhythm

Ill. 31   that is the rhythm of the characteristic African dance. It is certainly not the flowing dance of the Shiva Nataraja (see the next chapter) but the kind of abrupt, discontinuous stamping on the earth that makes up so much of African dance. Often the figures are presented with bent knees, a posture that moves the body down toward the earth.

All religious art has some function and is falsified when it is detached from its place in that function. So much of African sculpture is, in one way or another, part of the ritual dance that incorporates the sculpture and the worshiper into the primal rhythms of the earth. In the museum, where most of us see it, it is a work different from the one the Africans knew and used. Even so, it shows us vividly the form world of the Africans.

Ill. 32   **GREAT BUDDHA OF KAMAKURA**

Of all the great religions, Buddhism, although it has been immensely productive of images, is least well represented by its imagery. It is probably true to say that there is a core meaning to any religion, every religion, that can only be apprehended directly and not by any representation, visual or verbal. The life of the Buddha has been represented in many forms. But how is it possible to represent, even suggest, such a principle as Nirvana?

Thomas Merton reported somewhere that he once had a vigorous discussion, almost a debate, with a Buddhist monk, a man of keen intelligence, quite capable of maintaining such an intellectual discussion. Merton asked the Buddhist how he could describe Nirvana. A strange, distant look came over the man's face. After a moment, he said quietly, "Bliss. Bliss unspeakable".

The Nothingness of Nirvana, the emptiness, the void, can be suggested by the infinite emptiness of some Chinese landscape paintings but that is not possible in sculpture.

The Buddha of Kamakura in Japan is not intended to suggest such a thing. It is an example of the many representations of Buddha manifesting the different aspects of his nature and role. A rich repertoire of gestures would have to be mastered in approaching these figures in their completeness but the formal language, the structure, of this work goes far on its own.

The figure is absolutely symmetrical, generally pyramidal with all the stability of the pyramidal form. There is little sense of the immense weight of the figure.[10]. It seems, rather, to swell from the inside out into a curved surface. That surface is a symphony of curves, mostly downward, emphasizing the sense of absolute calm, absolute rest. The eyes are closed, or rather, we can suppose them turned inward in contemplation, remote from the exigencies of the world. There is no sense of strain. All suffering, all pain, is fully overcome. The effect is plenitude and peace.

India provides another form-world, another culture, and introduces so many issues of central importance in the understanding of images that it is best dealt with in a separate chapter.

---

[10] It is bronze and nearly fifty feet tall. The temple that once contained it burned a long time ago.

9

CARNAL SPIRITUALITY

Bodies desire. Bodies are desired. Nowhere are we less concerned with the high spiritual matters of the symbolism of space, or of anything, than we are in the state of desiring and being desired. At no time are we less concerned with the abstractions of theology or of ethics, with the obligations of time and relation. At no time or place are we more in thrall to the remorseless commands of the natural vitalities. Religions are, in good part, defined by their dealings with this situation. What does imagery have to say of it?

BODY AND SPIRIT

Again: by nature we are a part of nature; by nature we are apart from nature. This is the defining, the inescapable duality, of the human. It is reasonable that people who try to understand their situation should arrive at a dualism, a conviction that body and spirit, body and soul, body and mind, are two separable, two separate, things. Only fundamental religious or intellectual conviction determines which of these is considered the definition of the truly human. Since we think that mind and spirit separate us from the animals it is reasonable to suppose that mind and spirit, soul, are the definition of the human.[1]

Religions and philosophies are determined first of all by their disposition toward this problem. I say "disposition" rather than "conviction" because it seems a fundamental inclination rather than a reasoned position. Matter, the substance of the earth and human bodies, is

---

[1] This conviction has a striking contemporary illustration among those who consider the mind is like a computer, a software program that can work on any appropriate machine.

often considered a hindrance to be overcome, an illusion, or an evil. Our present concern is circumscribed by its nature: images, the kind of images that are the concern of this book, are material objects, matter.

Here we touch on one of the basic, perhaps the most important, elements in the opposition to images, iconoclasm. Philosophically it lies in the conviction that the human is to be found in the realm of the mind, so images are a distraction from human purpose.[2] Religiously, it lies in the conviction that all things material are either illusion or an evil and so nothing of the divine, the sacred, can be linked to matter.

The most acute problem for imagery is the treatment of the body. The most acute problem for the study of the body is its sexuality. Perhaps the most profound treatments of this problem are found in some forms of Hinduism and Renaissance Christianity.

Ill. 31   ## SHIVA NATARAJAH: A BODY FOR THE GOD

Shiva Natarajah, Shiva Lord of the Dance, was made in south India under the Chola dynasty around 1100 CE. There are a great many examples of the basic idea made over a long period of time and with some variations in detail. Most are of high quality. It is one of the most important representations, manifestations, of one of the most important gods in the pantheon of what we call Hinduism. It contains a plethora of signs and symbols. It is supported by a rich literature that enables scholars to interpret the signs and confirm the force of the symbols and determine something of how the image was used. It demonstrates the construction of a body by principles unlike any treated in the previous chapter. It introduces a basic issue mentioned only briefly before: the image as the actual body for the god. For all these reasons it deserves detailed treatment, requires a separate chapter that sets out the principle.

The Shiva Natarajah comes from a mentality and a religious culture quite unlike that of most of those who read this book. To interpret it, non-Hindus can bring from their culture only those things (the elements of form and symbolism) that are universal. Nothing in the western conception of the nature and function of a god, formed by the Hebrew God and the Greek gods, will serve to understand a Hindu god. Very little in western

---

[2] Another contemporary illustration: a college president, defending the exclusion of the arts from the Platonic curriculum of his college, said, "The arts deal with matter, hence there is a kind of darkness about them...."

modes of worship serves to understand the worship of Shiva. We are, therefore, compelled to step outside our own cultures, as far as possible outside our own presuppositions, in order to grasp something of what this work is.[3] Shivaite Hindus have a related problem in looking critically at one of their own images.

What do we see? That is not a simple problem; there is no innocent eye. We have to know many things to describe. Our eye is trained already by visual experiences that are not those of the makers of the image. We try as best we can.

First of all, the figure is bronze, cast and not carved. Cast figures are modeled in a plastic substance, normally clay, and a mold is made from the model in various ways. Thus the sculptor does not think primarily in terms of a geometric block of material containing a visualized figure brought into realization by cutting material away. He thinks in terms of adding and shaping a soft, pliable material. Inevitably, the figure will stress a center vertical; it represents the human body constructed around a vertical axis and subject to the force of gravity; the figure will topple over if it is not balanced. But the basic thinking is not around the geometric axes of the previous chapter.

A male figure, almost nude, clothed only in ornament. Four arms; one hand holds a small drum, another holds a flame, one is turned up with the palm forward, one turned down, pointing. The right leg is slightly bent and stands on a small, rather demonic looking figure. The other leg is raised and bent. The pose is that of a dance, suspended at this moment. The figure is surrounded by a circular form from which flames project outward.

This is as much identification as description; each item is an intended sign that is at the same time a symbol. (I have not listed all the signs.) From this point, description and analysis are confused. The body is male, yet the flesh is soft and rounded as though it were female. Some statues of Shiva are divided down the middle, male on one side, female on the other; in divinity sexual distinction is blurred. The external shape of bodily forms is accurately presented but there is no indication of distinct muscular shape or of the underlying skeletal structure as it might be indicated by projection on the surface. One form flows continuously into another.

---

[3] It is also worth mentioning the likeness within difference. India has always been in touch with other cultures, east and west. It has been quite simple to communicate on fundamental matters, war, commerce, friendship, argument, etc. Indians are people as we all are.

There is no indication of weight. The figure stands securely on the demon below but there is no pressure indicated on the form. Things like weight, a described skeletal structure, would have distracted from the flow of the dance. A vertical line can be dropped from top to bottom of the figure, a horizontal across the arms, but the forms weave back and forth across both of them. They are a stabilizing pattern but in no sense basic to the organization of the figure. Instead, it rotates around a central point that is also the center of the circle; the figure radiates outward from that central point rather than being built from the ground up. Similarly, the forms of flesh do not appear to be the forms of muscular structure but swell outward as though they were inflated from within or grew outward like the ripening of fruit.

The whole work is nearly symmetrical, which is a stable form. The two forward arms and the lifted left leg are all on the left, syncopated against the dominant symmetry, placing greater emphasis on their gestures. The gestures of all six limbs are, as nearly as possible in a three dimensional form, in a single plane at right angles to the spectator's line of sight. The circular form confirms this planar structure which places the figure over against the spectator who can contemplate it but is not physically involved in it. The lifted right hand is the only part of the figure that seems to address the spectator.

The gestures, the actions of the limbs and the body, are clearly neither dramatic nor expressive but are parts of the sign system of the ritual dance.[4] The circle is a motionless figure that is in eternal motion, ever returning onto itself. Except in acrobatics the human body does not move in circles around itself but the formalities of the dance can create the circular movement. The four arms are a sign but also they make possible the multiplication of movements within the circular pattern. Flames are movement and destruction; they radiate outward from the circle and move in rhythm around the circle.

The dance is a primary symbolic form and the character of the dance the purpose of the symbol, whether it affirms the human place on the earth (Africa) or seeks to escape from the limitations of the earth (classical ballet). Here the figure is delicately balanced but not even quite on the earth and

---

[4] The negatives in the account are in no sense weaknesses or omissions in this work. They are possibilities that are explored in other symbol systems. They are mentioned here only to distinguish this figure from those looked at earlier.

the circular movement is suspended before us. It is not a free or orgiastic movement but both erotic and disciplined.

The forms of the body are erotic, ambivalent since male and female are joined in one figure. Eroticism is not the purpose of the figure but is inherent in it because of the sense of organic vitality swelling outward from the harmonic rhythms of the dance.

Movement is stopped, held in suspension before the entranced gaze of the worshiper (we may be spectators but the work was made for worshipers). We do not participate in the dance but see it, absorb its motion under the discipline of its control. The flowing of organic life is disciplined by geometrical stability which, in turn, is enlivened into vital life.

The most decisive single part of the work is the head. It is distinctively human but unlike any human head we see. (Careful. It does not look like us but who might a Chola sculptor have seen?) The headdress touches the circle. The head is turned to our right, its gaze counterbalancing the greater visual weight of the gestures to our left. The gaze goes past us, in utter indifference to us. The head is lifted in superb pride. The face is wholly without expression, utterly detached from the dominant movements of the work, engaged in the movement but lifted above it, indifferently.

Every aspect of the work is rooted in the physical experience of the world yet the experience of the work carries the spectator above the physical. No one can dictate the response of someone else or even describe it. I see it as a simultaneous affirmation and negation. Both sides of contradictions are affirmed and, therefore, denied: geometry and organicity, movement and stasis, involvement and detachment, time and eternity, permanence and change, all resolved into the liberating rise above the contradictions.

I write as though I do not know the meaning of the signs that are part of the work, in order to suggest the resources of looking. I cannot say how my looking is affected by what I know (or have been taught). I have no idea how the ordinary Hindu worshiper sees the work in the sense of seeing that applies to my analysis.[5] To the Hindu, this figure does not "represent" the god. It **is** the god, immediately present, to be seen, to be presented for the adoration of the worshiper (see Eck 1981, passim). The statue is a body for the god (Waghorne 1981). To ignore the signs is to impoverish the viewing of the work.

---

[5] The exception always has to be the great critic and historian, Ananda Coomaraswamy, one of those rare people who are thoroughly trained in the languages of two cultures and able to mediate between them.

The great signs are rarely simple, certainly not in India where every sign is multivalent, forms and signs blending and interchanging.

The circle of flame (which is sometimes more arch than circle) is the cosmos. The demon dwarf from which the circle emerges is ignorance, illusion, overcome by the dancing tread of the god. The lifted leg is the defiance of gravity and all contingent limitation. The right hand is raised in the gesture of reassurance. The left hand points to the demon of ignorance and the leg's gesture of liberation. The drum is the sign of the rhythm that brings creation into being. The flame in the left hand is destruction, the end. There is both male and female ornament, the union of opposites. These are not all the signs, nor all the significations of the signs. Indian semiosis is never simple or two dimensional.

These all coalesce into the single great image, Shiva himself, who is best defined by the continuity of the signs. This completeness is vital. In popular definition, Shiva is identified as "the god of destruction", which in Indian terms is meaningless. Shiva is this. And that. And that. And so on. Shiva is the god of transformation. The "of" is misleading: Shiva **is** the process of transformation.

The signs are symbols and a lesson in how symbols have to be apprehended. The drum is the sign of creation. Indeed. But what is a drum? This one is small, delicate. Its sound would be gentle, a vibration, a delicate rhythm that begins with the hand of Shiva and penetrates throughout the cosmos, bringing it into existence. The rhythmic vibration is present in all things, uniting all things; the dance of Shiva does not merely bring it into being but sustains it. Participating in that rhythm is the escape from the illusion, dwarfish and demonic, of separate existence.

The fire has all the complexities that fire has in experience for everybody. It is heat, warmth, protection against the cold, the life-giving light and warmth of the sun, the occasion for deep reverie, the transformer of flesh into food, light against the darkness. It is equally the enemy, the terrible power, the destroyer of forests, the destroyer of cities. It is itself a dance, a rhythmic vibration in the air; transforming the matter, destroying matter into all the things fire stands for.

Shiva holds the fire in the palm of his hand; all that fire is and means is under his control to be used and dispensed. He brings all things into being, sustains them, and brings them to their end, which, in the great cosmic circle, are renewed and come into being again. Time and eternity, life and death, creation and destruction, all affirmation, all negation, unite in the one process.

The great sign\symbol of Shiva is the lingam, the phallus, the phallus-sign (lingam also means "sign"), its base surrounded by the ring of the yoni, the female sign, the organs of generation fused at the center, the source of life. Offerings are brought to the lingam, the fruits of the earth, oil, milk, fruit, consecrated and received back by the worshiper.

Erotic union (compare the Khajuraho representations of copulation) is the union of differences, the blending of one with the other, the submission to the most profound of the natural vitalities, a submission that achieves liberation.

Maleness and femaleness are equally manifestations of the divine principle; the one participates in the other and their participation is absorption into the wholeness of unity.

It would be difficult to find an illustrative example that so thoroughly fuses representation and form, sign and image, symbol and sign, into such a full statement of the comprehensives of a great faith.

TITIAN, BERNINI AND THE REPRESENTATION OF WOMEN

It should not be surprising that the question of sexuality should, in Western art, be posed in terms of the representations of women. Historically, most artists have been men. In somewhat smaller proportion, most patrons have been men. It is reasonable to expect that, during such social situations as make possible the expression of sexuality in art, the sexual interests of men would dominate imagery.

There are two classes of the images of women I propose to pass over and then proceed to what can be little more than an elementary road map to a complex problem.

The first class includes a large body of works that can inescapably be called exploitative, both pornographic and misogynist. It is an important study, an important body of images for the understanding of the human imagination and social structures. It has much to tell about the power of desire, the corruption of desire and the working of imagery. It is certainly germane to this study but it is too large to be dealt with in the limits of this book.

The second class of works is more agreeable to deal with. These representations do not set women apart from their humanity. The interpretive problem is one we have met before. A good part of the world's images do not represent individuals but types, roles, ideals. This is as true of the images of men as of women.

If, for example, we look back at the Parthenon sculptures or the representations on the facade of Chartres Cathedral, we will see no fundamental difference in the mode of representations. The female figures are clearly represented as women in their differences of size, garments, gestures, and the like, but they are not set apart otherwise. They are, as images always are, a source of information about their period; those who, quite properly, are concerned with the social history of images, will find signs of contemporary attitudes toward women in all representations but such criticisms have to be handled with care; little in the noble and graceful representations of women on the Parthenon frieze reflects the actual status of women in Greek society. There is no suggestion of an inner life but this is as true of the images of men.

A special case, one deeply rooted in religious conviction, is found in the Italian Renaissance. Many Renaissance artists were preoccupied with setting out the inner life, the kinds of motivations and personalities that created the dramatic situations that are so prominent a part of their investigation into the human condition. In this enterprise, they made no distinction in the manner of their presentation of men and women. They did not, indeed, make any sort of political statement about the nature of the female roles as some contemporary critics would require them to do but it had not occurred to them that they were responsible for 20th century political convictions.

Another type of images of women found in many of the world's cultures, is too often grouped with the first. This class includes those works, commonly representations of the female nude, that are inspired by delight in the beauty of women. In a restricted definition of this group, there is no overt reference to any religious conviction. Nonetheless, such images depend on the fundamental attitude defined in the earlier chapters: the placement and valuation of the human within the natural order.

A revival of an ascetic Puritanism rejects all such works as exploitative, assigning them to that piece of fetishized jargon, "the male gaze". They are, indeed, designed to be looked at, to give pleasure; judgment on that looking and that pleasure depends on convictions that lie outside the realm of images and cannot be debated here. Curiously, in a libertine age, many people affirm the other pole of the human duality and reject physical pleasure. Again, the issue is deeply religious. It is immersed in that paradox identified earlier: by nature we are a part of nature and apart from nature. It appears that the current rejection of our involvement in the energies and structures of nature is motivated more by politics than by the religious, even metaphysical, convictions that inspire iconoclasm. The result is the same, on an issue at the heart of religious conviction and decision, there is an impassioned rejection of the physical and its manifold pleasures.

The other commitment accepts the materiality of the world and the flesh but again we can have, very crudely put, a duality of definition. On the one hand, there are those who take delight in the materiality of the world and the sexual beauty of the body and go no further and see no more. Frequently, in the Renaissance, Biblical subjects such as Mary Magdalene or Susannah and the Elders, were chosen because they provided an excuse to show a beautiful woman with her clothes falling off.

The concern of this study is those works that place beauty and pleasure, the orderings of desire, in a larger human, even sacred, context. Such images are the ones that concern me at the moment.

All human beauty contains some element of the erotic, particularly where there is an emphasis on the body. Often, in the Renaissance, this beauty is part of the glorification of God, who created it. Often it is simply there, as one of the fundamental energies of earthly life.

Titian's Venuses, particularly *Venus and the Lute Player*, sum up many of these themes. Some feminist ascetics, although they speak of other people's motives with a confidence the evidence does not permit, are probably right in asserting that the patron's use of such paintings was voyeuristic. The woman is pictured as displaying herself to the gaze of the spectator. Another theme in contemporary use of these images is the image as an assertion of power: both the picture and the subject assert male power ("patriarchy") over the female. This is a good deal more problematical; the power relation is much more complex, which is usually the case in relations between the sexes. The erotic force of the nude female body along with its supreme beauty, constitute an undoubted power in its own right.[6]

Ill. 33

The painting is religious but the religion is not the Christianity to which Titian nominally belonged. It is pagan, or, rather, that strange dream of ancient paganism that was so powerful a part of Renaissance spirituality.

---

[6] Titian softens this power by having Venus look away from the spectator. Manet emphasized it in his famous — at the time, infamous — *Olympia*, looking directly toward the spectator and represented without Titian's idealization. I first saw the painting as a young man barely out of my teens. It was exhibited in a very narrow gallery. I found myself standing close to the opposite wall getting as far from it as possible. I was not equipped, then or now, to handle closeness to such a woman.

Venus is magnificent in the nobility and beauty of her body. "Christian shame" does not exist for the artist or the subject. Her sexuality and male awareness of it are presented with the same openness. She is placed in the context of music and the garden. Everything, the whole world of the senses, the activity of the senses and of desire, is presented glorified by the inherent beauty of the representation and of the paint. It cannot be called a world before the Fall, for the idea of a Fall is irrelevant in a pagan world. It is a world that never existed, could never exist. It is one of the great dreams of a great moment of our high culture.

Ill. 34   On the other hand, Titian's *Danae* shifts the emphasis. Danae is displayed almost as openly, certainly as beautifully, as Venus, yet now the body is transfigured (not merely glorified) by light. Her attention is not outward toward us, but inward within the painting, toward Zeus who comes to her in shower of gold. In an extraordinary transformation of the Renaissance dream of paganism, an ancient myth is transfigured into a Christianized version of the "divine-human encounter", a metaphor of the Incarnation. It is one of the supreme examples of carnal spirituality, the most intimate of the body's experiences transformed into a sacred image.

Ill. 35   Perhaps the most dramatic representation of carnal spirituality in Christian imagery is Bernini's *Ecstasy of St. Theresa*. The figure of Theresa is the central element of a large, complex work that requires a book length presentation. It is a transcription into stone of Theresa's own account of a mystical vision, in which she was lifted up on a cloud and an angel pierced her "to my very entrails" with the arrow of divine live until she swooned. Bernini constructed the work so it appears to the spectator as a vision. It is set apart in the darkness of its small church, lifted up as on a mysterious stage, lighted from above, apart from our world The arrow is obviously that strange object, a "phallic symbol", and Bernini makes explicit what is implicit in Theresa's account; her swoon is clearly the first stage of an orgasm. This has caused great embarrassment to many people, an embarrassment that I suspect would have annoyed Bernini considerably. To one who made no distinction between body and soul, it is entirely appropriate that bodily emotions should be the expression of a response to the divine.

I have no idea if Bernini would have subscribed to the sentimental theology which exalts copulation to the point of itself giving access to the divine. I strongly suspect he would not have been willing to accept intercourse as a sacrament. Bernini was sexually experienced (as Theresa certainly was not) and I suspect sexuality was for him simply part of the human experience to be dealt with ordinarily as part of the whole emotional life. At the same time it was available to him as a fundamental mode of statement, in this case a statement of the soul's communion with God, requiring the surrender to the divine presence of the whole of the person.

10

...TO TELL A STORY

THE SHAPES OF TIME

The image suspends time into stillness and contemplation. But our lives are lived in time; stillness and contemplation take us apart from the time that is the necessary setting for our lives.

Sometimes imagery has the task of representing time. Much of the history that is one dimension of our lives is no more than a blundering series of events without meaning in their succession, without control by intelligence or purpose. One of the functions of imagery is to give shape to time.

Several of the arts have the responsibility of shaping time. Religiously, the most important of these arts are ritual and myth. Music, drama and dance are a part of ritual, achieving a separate existence which never quite escapes from the ritual function; the most "aesthetic" audience participates in a high and formative ritual during the performances

Is there, as a great critic once proposed,[1] a rigid distinction between the arts of space and the arts of time? Most of us hear music only as succession, but for the musician and the trained listener, the music does not fully exist until the end when the whole can be held in consciousness. The drama, enacted in time, is not fulfilled until the end, with the whole held in memory. The painting, apparently apprehended in a moment, unfolds in time to the careful spectator.

Yet Lessing was not completely wrong: the music takes time to perform, the painting can have an immediate and instant impact. This creates a problem for the telling of a story.

---

[1] Gotthold Lessing, in the eighteenth century.

161

THE ORIGIN OF NARRATIVE

We each have a story — or should have; the life without shape, without a project, is empty, lonely, subject only to the passions and to purposeless desire. It is the function of ritual, drama, music to give shape to lives, to find a place for us in time.

It cannot be just any shape. It has to be a shape with meaning and the meaning originates in the understanding of essential meaning. The story is not simply that of the individual life but of the whole; myth is the story of the whole, the narrative that shapes individual life.

We all have our personal narratives, the story of our lives and the story we tell to give meaning to our personal story. All cultures, by their myths, their sagas, their ordinary stories, weave a narrative that accounts for their origins and their place in the world. Conversion is not a change of opinions or even emotional tone. It is a shift from one narrative to another. It is a great hurt to lose the narrative and not have another to replace it. To lose the narrative is to lose place in the structure and the flow of the world. Nothing more fully characterizes the modern world than loss of narrative. This loss is dramatic in the "primitive" cultures, those without writing to help them cope with the impact of alien cultures. The dominant "high" cultures have lost their narrative and so have lost conviction. There is no common narrative to sustain individuals within what once was something close to wholeness.

All cultures have a narrative; it is what constitutes them as a culture. Not all cultures or religions attempt to illustrate their narrative in art. Many do, in a many ways, from the most "primitive" to the most sophisticated. The Australian Bushmen have one mode, the Navaho chanters and their "dry paintings" have another.

How does the (relatively) static image recount the myth? What is the place of story in the image, the image in the story? Every religion has its myth with its shape and logic. Those with visual images as a part of the telling of their story do so in many different ways.

An elementary distinction, between illustration and narration, is necessary. "Illustrate" and "narrate" are not the same. Navaho mythical narratives are dramatic, vigorous, complex in act and motivation. Navaho dry paintings are not intelligible without the words of the chanted myth; they represent the larger Navaho narrative but they are not themselves a narrative art. They illustrate the myth by representing, schematically, the characters of the myth and their abstract relations.

A narrative, in contrast, recreates the essential principles of the story in visual form. Stories can be told in relief sculpture and in painting. The problems are much the same in each. The greatest problem is the most obvious one. Verbal narratives have many different ways of telling the story, shifts in the point of view and the identity of the narrator, a nearly infinite number of ways of unfolding the events in time, control of spacing, of descriptive detail, of tonality, etc. The pictorial narrative is confined to a single moment in time and a single point of view.[2] By its nature it cannot avoid descriptive detail, which has a drastic effect on the narration. Old Testament narration is among the greatest of the narrative forms. It is almost wholly without descriptive detail, of things, motives or affects, confining itself to the powerful, quickly paced account of the essential action, no more and no less. In picturing such a story, the pictorial narrative cannot avoid description; the choice and manner of description are keys to interpretation.

The pictorial narrative must choose one moment in a continuous action for display and the choice of moment is another key to interpretation: is it before the climax of the action, at the climax, after the climax? Even a single figure can present this problem. In representing the story of David and Goliath, Michelangelo chose the moment before the action, Bernini a moment during the action, Donatello the moment of repose and reflection after the action. Each artist could have coped with the moment chosen by the other but the choice is always significant.

A fundamental choice is represented by the portrayal of the action. The lesser narrative artists will simply illustrate the story by showing the figures in the poses essential to the statement of the action, which is to do no more than tell the story, not elucidate its narrative content. Richer narrative art presents a complex of motive, relation and effect.

Whether the story is merely recounted externally or presented in its richness, part of the significance will always rest on the narrative being represented. In that respect, the resources of modern developments in "narratology" as a part of literary criticism are essential; artists will, explicitly or implicitly, interpret the story according to those principles before or as a part of their own interpretive representation.

---

[2] Some artists have tried to cope with this problem by including separate moments of the narrative within a single frame. This is variously effective and one moment always dominates. Then there is the form we are accustomed to in the comic strip, successive moments portrayed in a series of panels. This does not alter the character of each panel.

It is too simple, and unfair, to say that most of the world's visual narratives are illustrations rather than full narratives; they can tell us too much of their culture's basic convictions to be dealt with in so summary a fashion. As an over-simplification it will have to do for the moment for my main concern is Giotto, the greatest of the narrative artists, whose work set in motion a development without equal in the understanding of personality in dramatic interrelation with others. By way of instructive contrast, I first offer another narrative within the Christian story but with a distinctive way of presenting it that has enough in common with the modes of narrative in other religions to be a help in looking at their narratives.

Ill. 36   **THE CHURCH AT DAPHNI**

The narrative here is not simply the story (which features in the lower part of the work) but the narrative of the soul's salvation, the movement from earth's history to divine stillness.

Earlier, we looked at the oldest example of mural painting, the surfaces of the cave at Lascaux. Now we will look at another, the mosaic decoration of the church at Daphni, a middle Byzantine church in the suburbs of Athens. This lets us see one of the extreme examples of imagery covering the entire interior of a building.[3]

Mosaic is an ancient art, consisting of cubes of colored stones or glass set into a cement base coating the surface of a wall or floor. It becomes, then, the surface of the wall or floor, obliterating whatever lies behind it. The Romans often used colored stones or other hard material to cover the floors of a room or of an entire villa. Stones are opaque, so a stone mosaic is a way of making a picture on the surface. Light illumines the surface; it has no role in the work itself, although the brilliance of color in later Roman mosaic anticipated the Byzantine development.

The shift to glass cubes (in early Christian churches) was a momentous one. Glass is transparent or translucent. Light enters the glass and is reflected back out. Light is not simply the means for seeing the

---

[3] In point of fact, the mosaics do not cover the entire surface of Daphni; the damage is extensive. To experience such a church to the full, it is necessary to go to other Byzantine churches such as Hosios Lukas, or the most famous of them all, San Marco in Venice. I choose Daphni because of the high quality of the images and because the remains are sufficient to show the principal aspects in a subject matter program. In a book, we can't see the whole interior anyway.

picture or a represented element in the picture; it becomes part of the material itself. Colored light is the most impalpable, immaterial, otherworldly, of all the artistic materials, and lends itself well to the emphasis on the "spiritual", the otherworldly, in Christianity.[4]

The church is small. It has the standard Byzantine floor plan, a central dome over a cross, but the emphasis has shifted from the near equality of proportions of the earlier Byzantine churches to a high cupola dome above lower side sections, thus throwing great emphasis on height. In the center of the cupola, Christ is represented as Pantokrator, Lord of the Universe. Just below are the apostles. Located around the middle level are various narratives of the life and passion of Jesus and below that a series of saints and bishops in appropriate hierarchical order. The ordering of the images establishes the hierarchical ordering of the cosmos, from the history of this world, through sacred history to the eternal. "The Byzantine church was an image of the Byzantine Cosmos, with its well-ordered hierarchy of values." (Demus 102)

The effect of mosaics is to transform the interior of a church into a light filled vision. The use of space is even more remarkable:

> This complicated symbolism was all based on a new conception of the image. According to this conception, the image, if painted in the "right manner," was a magic counterpart of its Prototype, the Holy Person or Event it represented; a magic identity existed between the image and its Prototype, and the veneration accorded to the image was considered a tribute paid to the Holy Persons themselves... So the image enclosed a part of the real, physical space; it was not separated from the beholder by the "imaginary glass plane" of the picture surface behind which an illusory picture begins to develop. The image opened into the real space in front. The interior of the church became itself the picture space of the icons, the ideal Iconostasis [An iconostasis is the screen separating the nave of an, Eastern Orthodox church, from the sanctuary. It was normally hung with icons.]. The beholder was bodily enclosed in the grand icon of the church; he was surrounded by the congregation of the Saints, he took part in the holy events he witnessed. (103)

---

[4] For what follows, I draw almost entirely on Otto Demus's magisterial essay, "The Methods of the Byzantine Artist". (Demus 1963)

[Referring to the figures at the highest level]...they did not depict, they <u>were</u> magic realities: a holy world beyond time and causality, admitting the beholder, not only to the visions, but to the magic presence of the Holy.(103)

Demus demonstrates the structural principle of the representation. Rather than representing figures as they would appear to a spectator standing on the floor, the artists represent them as though the spectator (the worshiper) were standing immediately in front of them, lifted up in space to the presence of the images. He summarizes:

The images of mid-Byzantine church decoration are related to each other and formed into a unified whole, not by theological and iconographical concepts only, but also by formal means which create an all-embracing optical unity. The optical principles used for this purpose aim, broadly, at eliminating the diminution and deformation of perspective. (104)

Byzantine perspective might be described as "negative perspective". It takes account of the space which surrounds, and is enclosed by, the image, and which intervenes between the image and the beholder; and it aims at eliminating the perspective effects of this space on the beholder's vision. The Western artist, by contrast, when he painted the ceiling of a church, subjected his figures to the laws of perspective in order to let them appear as real bodies seen from below, with all the distortions which this view brings about. He created an illusion of space, whereas the Byzantine artist aimed at eliminating the optical accidents of space. Western practice leads to a picture of reality, Byzantine practice to preserving the reality of the image.... Looking at Byzantine decoration, seeing the image undistorted, in spite of the great height at which it appears, one feels lifted up to its level, high above the ground; above the ground to which the beholder of Western decorations is firmly fixed— pressed down, as it were, by the "worm's eye view" of the <u>di sotto in su.</u> (106-7) [The last is an Italian phrase referring to the appearance of things seen "from below up".]

The whole building is an icon. The narrative is everywhere, the story of Christ and the saints around the lower levels, the story of the ascent of the soul to the Savior from bottom to top. Each episode in the whole is suspended in itself and as a stage in the narrative of the whole.

In this process, the whole presentation does not simply illustrate but narrates not only the distinct stories of the Christian history but the story of salvation. On the lower levels, closest to where the worshipper stands, the Gospel events are presented with energy and emotional intensity, the immediacies of act in time presented as a moment out of continuous history. With ascent through the successive stages, action is distilled into symbolic persons, both those of the immediate experience and those of the sacred history. All culminates in the single figure at the top. The time of passage is taken up into, transfigured, the stillness of the eternal.

THE FULFILLMENT OF NARRATIVE: GIOTTO AND THE ARENA CHAPEL

The church at Daphni tells a story. The whole arrangement of subjects tells the story of the salvation of the soul. Individual panels tell the story of the Gospel. All of it has to be arranged on the surface of the building's masses because the church is (or was when the mosaic program was complete and uninjured) a mystical vision, to transport the worshipper into another world.

But we live on the earth, in our flesh, in relation to other people, in all the ordinariness of life. Our lived narratives are not elsewhere, in a mystical vision, but here, and now. Of all the many kinds of imagery, painting is the best instrument for telling the story of the present. Some sense of that possibility began to be felt on the Gothic churches. The fullest development of narrative painting was the type generated in the Italian Renaissance. It began in fourteenth century Florence with Giotto.

There is no better instruction in visual narration than the Italian Renaissance, which took narration as one of its primary concerns and can be called the greatest, most profound, of the narrative arts.[5] One of the finest of the narrative artists was the first, Giotto, and his greatest surviving achievement, the Arena Chapel in Padua. It is like Daphni in that the whole interior of the chapel is covered with paintings and respects the surface of the walls. Its purpose is different.

In many ways, the Chapel is a study in the social involvements of art. It was built by Enrico Scrovegni as a family chapel attached to the now vanished Scrovegni palace. Enrico's father had built the family fortune by

---

[5] The argument is obviously circular: by the standard set by the Italian Renaissance, Italian Renaissance art is the finest of the narrative arts. The circularity of the argument does not refute the claim that Italian Renaissance narrative is a permanent possession of the human spirit.

usury, a great sin in those days, and the chapel was probably built as the son's attempt to expiate the sin of his father (or at least to satisfy the church). It is linked to contemporary social structures in ways worth mentioning below.

The program is still medieval: the virtues and the vices below, then a complex narrative series, and the Last Judgment over the entry. The narrative is in three levels, the life of Mary around the top, the life of Jesus in the middle and the passion of Jesus around the lower level.

Ill. 37

Any small selection of panels does damage to the full understanding of the chapel, for there are many interweavings among them, both formally and thematically. The first panel may serve as illustration of the method. The parents of Mary, Joachim and Anna, had reached old age without children. This was an obvious sign of God's displeasure, so when Joachim took his sacrifice to the temple, he was turned away; the title of the picture is "The Expulsion of Joachim from the Temple".

Giotto's principal narrative instrument is gesture. Gesture is the expressive action or attitude of anything. It is also the expressive action of the hands, arms and bodies. Gesture plays a central role in our ordinary life, one to remember when we turn to these paintings; the "language" of art is made up of the common experiences of life arranged for a deliberate purpose. We respond to the work of the artist in terms of our own experience of the world.

There are several kinds of gestures. Automatic gestures are uncontrolled responses to a stimulus; we snatch our hand away when it touches something hot. Ritual gestures are prescribed by the rules of particular institutions, the gesture of blessing of the priest, the military salute, etc. Social gestures are a kind of informal ritual and vary widely from one culture to another. Dramatic gestures are those that are part of a particular situation or action. Expressive gestures are those that set out visually an attitude, a state of feeling, an inner emotional situation that is normally an element in a dramatic interaction, a response to the situation of the world.

Obviously these overlap and interact in a wide variety of ways. The form of the military salute is carefully prescribed in army regulations but every soldier learns that it can be used in a variety of expressive ways, to communicate different attitudes: respect, contempt, indifference, etc. All gestures and their combinations are available for the artists' use, although each culture has a particular repertoire of gestures. Nearly all art has something to teach the careful observer about gesture. Not all necessarily;

Navaho dry-painting, which is a great art, is not concerned with gesture, although much African sculpture, made by a people with comparable cultural development, is often wonderfully responsive to certain kinds of gestures.

One way of distinguishing illustration from narrative in painting is the character of the portrayed gestures. Illustration merely reproduces the external form of the action with no sense of its inner motivation. This characterizes most illustrations in magazines and books. Religious illustration might show certain typical actions and attitudes such as the folded hands and uplifted eyes that are associated with prayer. In the absence of true expression, a grasp of the inner motivation through expressive gesture, the result is merely sentimental or even hypocritical.

No artist exceeds and few equal Giotto in his precise setting out of as wide a range of gestures of all types.

Giotto's concern is with people and their dramas; he eliminates everything that might diminish or distract from his narrative. In this painting, there is no indication of the church building, only the medieval choir enclosure and pulpit to identify the place. Inside the enclosure, a priest is blessing a young man with the ritual gesture. The young man is barely visible within the enclosure, received, sheltered, protected. In marked contrast, Joachim is outside the church and forcibly rejected from it. The priest's upper body is bent forward in a propulsive attitude. His left hand is pushing Joachim's back, his right hand is contemptuously inverted as it holds the robe, ejecting Joachim from the sacred enclosure.

Joachim looks back resentfully. He holds the lamb in a sheltering attitude, as one would a child, the child who will be the mother of the Lamb of God sacrificed for the sins of the world.

The right side of the painting is empty, almost the only representation of true emptiness in western painting. Such emptiness is so rare that some historians could not believe it, holding that Giotto surely had painted something, now effaced, in that space. This is not true; the emptiness is there. It is wholly unlike the emptiness of the Chinese painting, the infinite void into which the spirit can wander. It is dramatic, a vital part of the narrative. On the left side, the young man has been received into the sheltering enclosure of the church. On the right side, Joachim is thrust out into the lonely isolation of his disgrace.

All the paintings are profoundly quiet, a strange quietness since every painting is dominated by its central action. How is it achieved? What does it "mean"?

In the first place, the figures are barely individualized. This is strange, considering that medieval sculpture had achieved, a long time earlier, a remarkable individuality of form and that the profound study of individuals, central to the Renaissance tradition, developed from Giotto.

The difference lies in the sense of personality inherent in Giotto's work. Reviewing what was said earlier, individuality is the distinctiveness of the appearance of external form. Personality is the distinctiveness of the individual from others as determined by and revealed in response and action. Giotto's figures act, gravely and responsibly; their action is part of the represented drama and emerges from moral decision. They are not puppets assuming the position of represented action. Neither are they collections of instincts, acting under the force of bodily passions (later Florentine artists explored this theme, among many others). They are moral personalities choosing to act in this way, for good or evil, personalities who can be held responsible for their actions.

This is inseparable from the quietness determined by the form. Giotto is intensely conscious of the frame, the square of the picture surface. The figures are columnar, disposed in a firm and stately rhythm across the surface, the intervals determined by the relations within the story. The firm stability of this human "colonnade" is so strong that each action is felt as a departure from the vertical and acquires, in all its simplicity, a tremendous force. In the Expulsion of Joachim, the expelling priest bends forward from the waist, the force of bodily action impelling the gesture of his hands and arms.

There is never, in Giotto, a sense of capturing a momentary action, a snapshot of the transitory (again, later artists explored this theme). He chooses the most intense and revealing moment of the drama. We know, because it is a drama, that there is a before and an after, that this is a moment lifted out of time. Yet it is out of time, removed, held before us in the grid of verticals and horizontals, for deepest contemplation.

Now the absence of individuality takes on purpose. The emotion, the action, is not that of an individual who is other than ourselves. It is the action of a person, who could be ourselves. The simple power of each gesture, taking on meaning within the drama, requires a response that is more than merely telling the story. It imposes, enforces, empathy.

"Empathy" is a word commonly confused with "sympathy"; indeed, the two principles inevitably interact. The direction of the one is emotional, of the other physical, somatic. If I see a porter staggering under an enormous weight on his back, and I feel sorry for his pain and indignation at his degradation, what I feel is sympathy. If my back hurts, what I feel is empathy, a bodily identification with his experience.

Giotto's paintings require contemplation, enforce empathy. In the absence of the particularization of the other caused by the individualization of form, the spectator (worshiper) must participate in the action. This participation, in the force of empathy, means that the worshiper participates in the moral action. "Participation" was a key term in the earlier presentation of the cave paintings, of Indian sculpture, of Chinese painting. There, participation meant participating in the energies and the harmonies of the natural order. For Giotto, faithful to the Biblical enterprise, participation means a reenactment in the flesh of the bodily action of the drama.

Correspondingly, he drastically limits the feeling of sympathy. It is aroused in such extreme cases as the mourning of the women in the Lamentation and, particularly, by the painful, pitiful mound of murdered infants in the Massacre of the Innocents. Otherwise, sympathy is too easily indulgence and a distraction from the serious business of becoming human. Human dignity does not permit the public display of emotion. The little angels in various scenes can act without restraint. The most extreme human emotion is the outflung arms of Mary in the Lamentation. Otherwise, emotion is registered only in the involuntary drawing back of the corners of the mouth and the furrowing of the forehead. We are constrained to the same control as the participants and, if we do so, become one of the participants.

For us, the content of this style has a double significance. The first is internal to the work. It is a new, almost unprecedented, definition of religious imagery. I say almost unprecedented because empathy is an aspect of a very wide range of art. For example, the bent knees of so many African figures move the figure downward toward the earth in a movement characteristic of their ritual dance and is properly handled empathetically, to participate in the dance. Giotto's distinctive achievement lies in making the empathetic participation a part of moral narrative. The response, therefore, trains the body of the worshiper to the shape and the energies of the sacred story.

Giotto's work defines an epoch. It is too simple to say that the later history of western imagery well into the twentieth century is an unpacking of the possibilities inherent in the principles laid down by Giotto. It is too simple because there are aspects of German art, of Dutch, French, and

Spanish art, that are native to them and not to Italy.[6] Even among the great Italians, individual creativity achieved things that are not implicit in Giotto. Nevertheless, just as Whitehead said that all later philosophy is "a series of footnotes to Plato", so later western art is a series of footnotes to Giotto.

What Giotto achieved and his successors set out in all its range and depth, is a definition of the human as a psychophysical unity. This is a vision of the human in its wholeness. Not in its completeness for that is beyond any single purpose, but in a profound wholeness. The enterprise of western imagery has been a matter of filling in the picture that was first outlined by Giotto. There is no profounder treatment of the issues of individuality within unity and wholeness than western art since the Renaissance.

Giotto's work poses another issue of great interest, one that, for better and for worse, has become dominant in modern criticism. Giotto has been interpreted as an artist of the middle class, setting forth middle class values. This is true. He painted at a time in Italy and in Florence when the economy was sound and prosperous and the country was, relative to most of its history, reasonably peaceful. His paintings are calm and serene, the bearing of his figures is stately and dignified, their gestures controlled and disciplined. Contours are clear and distinct, forms established in their full integrity (although not in full detail). It was a world and a style of reason and order.

These are bourgeois values. Does that mean they are false? They are so only for those of different political commitments who want to impose those commitments on past cultures. Giotto's style is oblivious to many human and religious values. There is no room in it for ecstatic religion, for certain kinds of passions and tragedies and failure. Not many decades have been so peaceful. A terrible economic collapse in Florence in the 1430's, followed by the more terrible Black Death destroyed Giotto's world. It was no longer possible to think of the world as reasonable, as understandable and controllable by reason. Irrational forces dominated public affairs. Art became a very different thing.[7] Artists are people who live in particular worlds and are deeply affected by those worlds.

Have we defined Giotto's place in our study by identifying his contextual world as bourgeois and capitalist, and his style as perpetuating

---

[6] Svetlana Alpers has most notably explored the particular modes of Dutch narrative, so different from the Italian.

[7] See Millard Meiss's fine book, *Painting in Florence and Sienna after the Black Death.*

those values? Not necessarily. The inherent content of a style does not fully account for what an individual artist does with that style. The calm dignity, the quiet reasonableness, of Giotto's style seems to be incompatible with the great erotic passions and the horrors of history. This is deceptive.

A style is a baseline against which the act of the individual artist is measured. A style does not account fully for an artist; what matters is what he does with it. An age such as ours, putting a premium on expression, on passion, has a hard time with the necessary submission to Giotto's quiet. The principle involved is a simple one. A leaf that is not noticed in a forest is conspicuous lying on the beach. Loud talk that would not be heard in a cocktail party is an unwelcome intrusion in a library or a chapel.

Joachim and Anna meet after a long separation. They quietly embrace   Ill. 38
and Anna gently touches Joachim's face. Measured against the absence of the erotic in any of Giotto's predecessors and responding to the reticence of Giotto's style, there is more eroticism in Anna's caressing fingertips than in the acrobatic intertwinings that we are accustomed to seeing on film and television. In that same reticence, the Massacre of the Innocents, mild by twentieth century standards, is a horror beyond grasping.

Giotto does not exhaust the possibilities of religious imagery as interpreted in art. He does not even exhaust Christian imagery. He does set out, with nearly unequaled eloquence, one of the most profound and profoundly humane interpretations of Christianity.[8]

That statement has other implications. A periodic theme in this study has been the relation between words and images, with an emphasis on their different responsibilities. The relation is always a complex one varying from one work to another. There have been images that were dependent in many ways on theological formulations; the program, although not the form, of the medieval church was undoubtedly laid down by theologians. That is perhaps true for the Arena Chapel as well, but I know of no propositional theology that sets out verbally what is so profoundly realized in Giotto's paintings, his visual theology.

---

[8] Giotto's life raises another difficult issue: the relation between an artist's character and his art. The Arena Chapel has nasty touch of anti-Semitism. Nearly all the character portrayed are Jews but the only ones with what is thought to be the "typical" Jewish appearance are the villains. Giotto's is the most profound presentation of Franciscan simplicity and purity, yet he invested his money at 500% interest
These things cannot be evaded. They do not explain his art nor detract from his achievement, which remains despite his shortcomings. It is a useful reminder of something most religion fails to account for, that human beings are not very good and never consistent.

SECTION FOUR

RELIGION WITHOUT THE GODS

In which is considered the consequences for imagery of the dispersion of faith in the modern world and the consequences for faith of the proliferation of imagery.

11

THE END OF NARRATIVE

We do not, perhaps cannot, know why. Sometime during the nineteenth century the old narrative structure of western culture began to lose its force. The history of the twentieth century has been the slow withering away of a common narrative, and a desperate search for a narrative, an identity, in groups. These groups frantically search for a narrative, or manufacture a narrative to replace the desiccated narratives of the inheritance.

Only glibness would identify the role of imagery in this development; it is too complex in origin and in character to be other than a mystery to interpretation. We can note what took place in imagery without even hinting at causality.

Heretofore, imagery had appeared in relatively few forms and materials, within a circumscribed milieu, a complex but still limited body of subjects and purposes. With developing technology, there came an extraordinary multiplication of images, which escaped from "art" as traditionally understood, which could draw on a nearly limitless range of subjects and uses. This meant a remarkable increase in freedom with consequences we need to look at later. It also meant a loss of a center, particularly the narrative center that had been most, then part of the main body of imagery for nearly 500 years. The "modern" age had begun.

A paradox: most of what has been said so far about looking at images applies equally to the imagery of our own century; the situation of imagery in our century is wholly new. We cannot avoid looking at both terms of this paradox. This chapter will deal with the transition to the modern from the past. The next chapter will describe the new situation.

THE HUMAN IN THE FACE OF THE VOID

The complexity of the problem might be seen in the last great Renaissance painting, the first great modern painting, Picasso's *The Acrobat's Family*, painted in the early years of the century. It is a Renaissance painting because it is built on the principle of fully structured and articulated bodies in dramatic action within a three dimensional space. It is modern because each of these principles is established only to be denied. Its importance for us lies not simply in its quality, which is very high,[1] but in its embodiment of the "spiritual" situation of the modern world. It stands at a hinge of history, the turn from one epoch to another. Let us describe it as a Renaissance painting (and an accurate description comes even closer than usual to an analysis and a presentation of its content).

Ill. 39

The family, a primary example of social unity. Costume and title identify the family as part of a circus, a larger example of social unity, a microcosm. The large father is the dominant figure of the group, which includes a young man and three children. A young woman, not in costume, sits apart from the group. She is often referred to as the mother, although she seems too young for the part. It would be more convincing to speak of the father, his four children and his daughter-in-law. However passive the positions appear, the figures stand in three dimensional coherence, performing their limited action intelligibly. Only four pairs of feet are visible; they are in the position acrobats choose for the beginning of their act. Without defined action, the personalities of the figures are not clearly specified but the passivity itself generates its own psychic force. Five of the six figures could be described as beautiful. This is particularly true of the young woman, with her precisely described, utterly feminine, gesture of her graceful fingers touching her hair.

The containing space is intelligibly three dimensional, not specified as Renaissance paintings normally are. Positions are defined, the spatial relations of the figures exactly specified, their contours exactly drawn. The structure of the painting is determined by a series of verticals. The boy with the drum marks the central axis. The lower arm of the young man to

---

[1] If I had to make such a judgment, I would say this is the greatest painting of the twentieth century; its only rival would be Picasso's Guernica. Affect and subjective response do not define a work for everyone. Nevertheless, I have been able to return to this work periodically for forty-five years. I still find it a work of extraordinary beauty, evocative authority, and intellectual strength, all responses that testify to a personal sense of the presence of a supreme work of art.

the left and the head of the girl mark the beginning of the horizontal axis which extends only by implication across the painting. The balance around the central axis is a strange one but it is, nonetheless, a balance. The painting is not simply a made object to be looked at from outside; it establishes a strong relation with the spectator, requiring response and interaction.

These are the defining characteristics of a "typical" Renaissance painting (fortunately, there is no such thing as a typical Renaissance painting; these are characteristics which Renaissance paintings, in all their individuality, share). An account of the painting that stopped here would be hopelessly inadequate.

The spatial setting is a bleak and barren desert, in its spreading expanse and its beautiful, barren color. It is not truly descriptive of a desert as it has no texture other than that of the brush strokes. The visible brush strokes of desert and sky affirm the surface of the painting as a plane and the spectator is abruptly jerked back from representation to an awareness of the painting as a painting. The figures, convincingly three-dimensional, can equally be seen as flat. In several places, particularly in the representation of the bare flesh, the color is very nearly that of the desert and distinguished from it only by the clearly drawn contour. That is obscured in the skirt of the young woman, which fades into the ground she rests on.

All action is suspended, not as though it were ready to begin, for all likelihood of movement is absent. All Renaissance bodies are what they are as possessing the potentiality of movement even in stillness. There is no suggestion here of any possibility of movement. Time, so vital a part of Renaissance art, is stopped. There is no human contact. The only touch is that of the young man holding the hand of the girl; the touch is so limp, so indifferent, as to accent the absence of human relation.

The eyes, always so important in representation, are accented and denied. They are among the most psychically powerful elements of the picture but nothing of the eyes is represented; they are deep pools of darkness. In the absence of the specificity of gaze, the only way to determine direction is by the inclination of the head. No one of the figures looks at any other; they look in different directions or, as with the young woman and the two boys, in the same general direction but not at one another. The social unity of family and profession is denied, neutralized, by the isolation of each figure.

The painting is symmetrically balanced but strangely. The boy with the drum is on the central axis, so his visual weight is neutralized, leaving only two figures to our right. The two largest figures plus the little girl are to our left of the center. Two things keep the picture in balance. The young woman is further away from the center and lower down in the painting. Her visual weight plus the spatial expanse behind her tends to counter-balance the heaviness on the other side. More important to the balance is the movement.

The only movement in the painting is compositional. The first point of attention is, inevitably the little girl silhouetted against the bulk of the fat old man. The eye follows up to the young man, turns with his gaze, is jolted by the counter-gaze of the old man, follows down through the gaze and position of the boys, doubling the force of the movement by the parallel of their looks, down and to the right and out the lower quadrant. The impetus of the movement increases its force, which serves to bring the composition into balance. More important, it establishes the all-important psychic relation between spectator and painting.

That relation is already profound. The painting possesses a beauty which absorbs attention. The color harmonies are of a most unusual delicacy, the spacing between forms (both the larger and the smaller internal forms) is as precise as music. Everywhere there is the fascination and the mystery of things that just escape rational explanation: why does the young woman's hat hover so lightly above her head rather the resting on it? what is the meaning of the jar at her side, barely differentiated from the ground? what are those various hand gestures, so limp, so present but unemphatic? Then there is the intellectual involvement, the conscious or subliminal awareness that, in a great Renaissance painting, every one of its traditional devices is suspended or denied.

The gaze is one of the most important of these devices. In the Renaissance, the gaze is a powerful instrument of dramatic and psychological interaction. It is usually internal to the painting but sometimes is directed outward to the spectator. The later Renaissance (the "Baroque") deeply involves the spectator in the essential action of the picture by directing the drama and particularly the gaze outward.

The gaze of every figure except the little girl is directed out of the picture. The old man looks out to our left. The young man looks straight across parallel to the picture plane. The other three look to our right, past us, in utter indifference to us, in complete unawareness of us. We are tempted to turn and look, knowing that what we would see is — nothing.

The "we" I have been using is common among critics but it is illegitimate. It assumes that a description of the critic's own affective response has objective validity. I use it here as an invitation to share an intense personal experience of the painting, hoping that the response is given some objective validity by being directed toward its existing structural features.

"We" stand in front of the painting, confronting its beauty and barrenness, deeply aware of the discontinuities in its affirmations and denials, intrigued by its mysteries, responding to its loneliness. The network of psychic forces ranges along the lines of the gazes. None touch us. Where we stand is emptiness. We can no longer say "we" for only the detached "I", the "I" that once could stand with others as "we" in the security of institutions, beliefs, commitments, only that separate and distinct "I" can stand in the emptiness in front of this painting. I am alone with my self, with my consciousness, intensely aware of my uninvolved involvement, alone.

Can we move from the painting to the age it was made in and conclude that life was like that? Not easily. This painting was made in 1905. Europe appeared to be, was believed to be, prosperous, secure, peaceful. There had been no major (European) war for nearly a century and the catastrophes to come were not even a suspicion.

Except, perhaps, by the artists and writers. This painting could be seen, not as expressing the age, but as a profound analysis by a great and penetrating mind of his own situation and attitude, his response to the essentials of his world. Picasso began (in his so-called Blue Period) by chronicling the despair of so many of the oppressed among the poorer classes. Now, at a higher (or deeper) level, he was portraying the void.

What does this have to do with religion? Nothing directly and indirectly only in a very general sense. It possesses to a high degree the sense of the uncanny, of mysterious fascination, which is part of the numinous but it has no reference to a transcendent meaning. It sets out a world. The religious critic might say it is a world after the death of God but Picasso himself would be indifferent to such an assertion, which comes from another world. It is not an affirmation of the absence of God, for the whole idea of God is irrelevant. All the old affirmations are now sterile, empty, paralyzed. The human experience is loneliness, isolation, paralyzed quietude, discontinuity. It is an account of the world that the student of religion studies, not a religious statement in itself.

Time has been suspended, transformed into space.

Much of this makes the painting sound depressing, which is quite false, <u>for as a painting</u> it possesses to the highest degree the traditional excellencies of art. It is singularly beautiful. It manifests near perfect control, in its delicacies of color harmonies and in its tonal spacing, in the exactness of its placements, the exquisite precision of its intervals, in the consistency of its psychology, in the strength and integrity of its structure, It has a profound, deeply realized unity, an unimpeachable wholeness.

Unity and wholeness no longer belong to the external world or to the human experience of the external world. It is found only in art, achieved only by the artist. It is a final statement of the artist-as-hero.

What can be the response to this situation? Picasso's own response, one of the most singular and most powerful intellectual enterprises of the twentieth century, was to live out the career of the artist as hero. Other artists chose many different routes.

There was another response, a novelty: the artist-as-priest.

ON THE SPIRITUAL IN ART

Ill. 40   I will not linger over an analysis of Kandinsky's painting; enough has been said already to make that possible to the reader without my crutch. It may be still necessary to persuade the reader to look at the painting without prejudice for many people are still wedded to the idea that a painting must look like something else. Most paintings do but there is no law that says they must.

The elements of the painting are the same as they always have been, without the function of representing something else. Colored shapes are arranged in a certain order with respect to the edges and the axes of the painting. Both the shapes and the colors move in interlocked directions with intensity and energy. The energies of the painting are resolved into a profound unity.

To what end? In part sheer pleasure; Kandinsky's paintings are remarkably beautiful and can be enjoyed as beautiful. That is not why Kandinsky made them. For him they represented something. Therefore they are images. But primarily they are functions and it is that function we need to get at. Kandinsky himself can be our guide.

Artists talk freely and sometimes well about art. Very few artists write books. It is even rarer that an artist who was responsible for the initiation of a great style writes a book to account for what he was doing. Wassily Kandinsky was not only a great artist, he was one of the founders of the modern style. Kandinsky was not the first to make a painting without an identifiable subject matter but his book validated the idea along with the towering example of his art. He gave his fellow artists confidence.

Kandinsky's book, *Concerning the Spiritual in Art*, was first published in Germany in 1911, translated into English in 1914, and frequently republished and re-translated with editorial changes of some consequence. The book is short (54 pages in the standard English edition, including numerous illustrations) and dense. It is not easy to interpret; Kandinsky had a restless mind, impatient with logical consistency. He used words as a poet rather than a philosopher, concerned with juxtapositions and evocations rather than systematic argument. He was never content with the formulations of this book and constantly undertook to refine them, either in later editions or in other writings. Nevertheless, this is the statement that had the greatest impact.

Kandinsky uses the terms "spirit" and "soul" but they are not interchangeable.[2] In a dualism that later made Kandinsky uncomfortable, soul is "one with the body" (p. 44). Sensations, particularly color, act directly on the soul; the work of the artist is to organize, control, those sensations, again particularly color but also form (Kandinsky distinguishes between the two). This is part of the work of the spirit; ("...color harmony must rest ultimately on purposive playing upon the human soul;..")(p. 45).

The spirit appears to be the active work of the soul, an activity rather than a thing; it is not something other than the soul. Presumably all people have a soul but not all live spiritually. To borrow a term from another tradition, the spiritual life is the authentic life of the soul.

The life of the spirit is represented by a "large acute-angled triangle, divided horizontally into unequal parts". (p.27) The lower segments are occupied by the spiritually blind and inert, the upper segments by the more enlightened, although these are troubled by deep fears and misgivings. At the apex stands one man or a few men.

Artists are in each segment; not every artist is a hero. "Every segment hungers, consciously or unconsciously, for adequate spiritual satisfactions. These are offered by the artists,..."(p.27) "The whole triangle moves slowly, almost invisibly forward and upward." The heroic artist at the peak is not understood until the lower segments advance to where he once stood.

---

[2] The German words are "geist" and "seele". "Geist" is ambiguous and cannot be translated into an exact English equivalent; a standard dictionary gives thirteen English words. It contains more of the sense of mind and thought than the English word "spirit" and that is certainly important in trying to understand Kandinsky's use of it.

The true work of art is characterized by "inner necessity", one of those resonant terms that so attract the imagination, which remain almost indefinable and thus mean many different things to different people. It is not quite so ineffable for Kandinsky himself. Some passages describe a mystical union between the depths of the artist's soul and the soul of the spectator by way of the work considered simply as means. But he was a trained craftsman and a highly skilled artist. The means for the act of communion are those of the craft understood in their true nature. In his book, the emphasis lies on color almost entirely, with its almost mystic "vibrations" in the soul ("vibration" is another favorite terms; Kandinsky was quite musical and alludes frequently to music).

At times Kandinsky sounds much like a mystic who wants to escape from matter altogether to live in the life of the spirit, a strange position for an artist whose work is necessarily in matter. The balancing factor is found in his other little book, *Point and Line to Plane,* one of the richest documents in modern thought.[3]

This aesthetic has an ethic : "All means are sacred which are called for by internal necessity. All means are sinful which are not drawn from inner necessity." (p.53)

In attempting to understand what Kandinsky is getting at, we need to understand what he was developing from and struggling against. Although the modernist movement was well underway when he wrote *Concerning the Spiritual in Art*, the official art world was still dominated by nineteenth century academic painting, which was characterized by an emphasis on the anecdote and the most superficial of appearances.[4] To understand the principle of "inner necessity", it is necessary only to look at such paintings next to a Kandinsky. He was freeing himself from what he considered soulless materialism and reaffirming the values that are part of all true art (he does not make his own style normative for all art; each age has its own character, its own task, its own necessities).

The summary is inadequate, as all summaries of significant works are bound to be, but there is one characteristic of it that seems quite accurate:

---

[3] Everyone who takes *Concerning the Spiritual in Art* seriously should be required to read the other, which is a precise account of the elements of drawing and painting. Together with the great notebooks of his friend Paul Klee, this is one of the most searching investigations into the nature of art as an independent discourse.

[4] Prof. David Morgan tells me that Kandinsky spent more time in his published art criticism "attacking the success of German Impressionist and Realist painters such as Lovis Corinth", than he did the nineteenth century academics.

there is no indication of what the word "spiritual" means, other than its authentic emergence from the depths of the soul. The triangle moves "forward and upward" but moves toward <u>what</u>? There is no indication of the goal or purpose of the movement, no specification of the spiritual.

Kandinsky remained to the end of his life a member of the Russian Orthodox Church and he was undoubtedly affected deeply by the Orthodox emphasis on the third person of the Trinity. At the same time he was deeply attracted to Theosophy. He mentions with approval such names as Madame Blavatsky and Rudolph Steiner, those who "seek to approach the problem of the spirit by way of <u>inner</u> knowledge" with methods that "derive from ancient wisdom" (p. 52).

We now have the major themes that have accompanied the later use of the word "spiritual" and much thinking about religion, as well as religion and art:

1. The almost total lack of specification and definition; the spiritual is achieved and felt only within the "inner" life. There is, for Kandinsky, a profound connection between the spiritual and the formal integrity of the work of art, a connection that is demonstrable and not mystical. This connection has been almost totally discarded in later uses of the word.

2. The Romantic emphasis on the lonely hero, or small group of heroes, as an elite, leading the mass of progressively less enlightened people. The spiritual is "higher", a favorite, seductive, metaphor for most who use the word spiritual. (I shall deal later with the remarkable appeal of spatial metaphors for the spiritual life.) We have the statement of the theme of the artist as priest.

3. Inner knowledge as part of an "ancient wisdom" which has to be rediscovered in a technological, materialistic culture.

Observers will have to decide for themselves how far Kandinsky's paintings exemplify his exposition of his intentions.They can be studied in terms of the procedures that have dominated the analyses of works earlier in this book. Their vocabulary is standard: line, color, space, fictive movement, direction, interval, rhythm. The elements are masterfully combined into an image of order, an order characterized by great energy. The energy gives to his earlier works an emotional intensity that is fully expressionistic; his later, more schematic and geometric paintings are considered by many to be far less interesting, although there is certainly no inherent reason why that should be so.

These two themes, expressionism and the spiritual, have tended to dominate later discussions of the religious significance of images. They are combined in different ways. Whatever the differences, there is a common assumption of fundamental importance in the understanding of the modern mind.

With the desiccation of traditional religious practices, the need for an intermediary has been transferred to the artist, who thereby becomes a kind of priest, or a seer, or a shaman, able to enter the realm of meaning or to open the way to the realm of meaning. No one says what that realm is, what that meaning and truth are like. They only affirm that such meaning and truth exist, somewhere, and the artist is the agent of our redemption by giving us access to that realm. Paralleling this definition of the role of the artist is another theme, explicit in Kandinsky (and in the philosopher, Martin Heidegger), that the availability of this other realm is limited to the adept, to the initiates. We have here nothing less than a new gnosticism (salvation by an esoteric "knowing", which is accessible only to the initiated, not to ordinary people).

Certain artists or certain styles are considered guides to these inner mysteries, The identification of the particular body of imagery that leads to the fundamental insight varies. For Paul Tillich, it was German expressionism. For Mircea Eliade (and for many other people) it was the primitive and the oriental. For Heidegger, it was archaic Greece as mediated through German Romanticism. For others it has been the Africans, the Navaho or some other group. Lately, there is a vogue for the Neolithic. The choice is made out of the history and need of the one doing the choosing, not out of any real connection with a shared "reality".

Whatever the choices, they share the common characteristics of Romanticism. As a style of art or of thought, Romanticism cannot be identified with the precision of most styles. It is more an attitude than a style. Textbooks define Romanticism by a list of these attitudes, two of which are "a concern for the remote in time or space" and "a concern for subjectivity and the emotional life".[5]

It also places a major burden on artists, a burden no human should have to bear. Artists are people like the rest of us, as wise or as foolish, as true or as false, as great or as little, most doing as best they can within their private limits. They do a necessary work. They cannot be our redeemers.

---

[5] Labeling this movement as "Romantic" does not dispose of it; it may be true. Labeling is an unreliable guide to the study of history, disposing of great human enterprises by definitions.

How then do we deal with the problem of non-representational art if it does not give us access to an ineffable world of truth? Exemplification may be the best response.

How do we define the religion communicated by a non-representational work? Subject is not an infallible guide; Tillich is quite right in saying that there are works with a "Christian" subject that are not religious. But it does put an edge around the problem of interpretation. I can accept in principle that such and such a non-representational work is the expression of Christian joy or Buddhist resignation. How do I <u>know</u>?

It is at this point that those who are advocating an undefined "spiritual" have their field day. The spiritual has no content or definition; the paintings apparently have no definition. Therefore the paintings are available to be described as sacraments in this undefined religion. Can we define them more accurately?

For many works, the answer should be, "Why should we?". It is possible to be too solemn about too many things and not all art has to be seen in relation to the ultimate or an Ultimate. Gertrude Stein was approached by a reporter, "Miss Stein, what do you think of modern art?". "I like to look at it", was her sensible reply. Artist are not, by definition, priests; often they are having a wonderful good time making objects that are a delight, or set forth the solution of an important formal problem or record with insight some distinctive human experience.

Pleasure or instruction may not be all. There is, at times, the response felt in the presence of the numinous, the character of so many works in so many religions, the sense of something more than is immediately and physically evident, the sense of going beyond. Is this what we mean by "the spiritual"?

We are part of nature and other than nature. We are animal and human. We are matter — and spirit. Spirit and the spiritual are those things in us that are not exhausted by our natural, instinctual, life. Those so inclined are free to define this as something that reaches forward into a postulated, unprovable realm that is disconnected from matter but they are not free to make that normative for other people or other work. The humanness of the human is not detachable from the flesh or the spirit; spirit is the distinctively human way of coping with the flesh and matter.

Every successful work of art is a structure and as a structure is more than its parts. Analysis is grasping the parts. Interpretation is apprehension of the relations and, therefore, the whole as more than its parts. In modest works this can provide a distinctive delight. In the greatest works, it can inspire awe, or ecstasy, sometimes a terror ("What is beauty but the beginning of terror", said Rilke), an infinite fascination. If we try, this is not ineffable, for it is human and humans can grasp what humans do. I can be aware of the numinous in religious works outside my own commitment because they are human achievements, a revelation of the possibilities of the human, an unveiling of part of the human situation.

This is propadeutic to the problem of non-representational art but does not solve it. It will not be solved here. The issues can be determined more precisely by examining two specific cases, Mark Rothko and Barnett Newman, each an articulate man who intended his work to be seen as religious. Both are favorites with those whose concern with religious art is satisfied with "the spiritual".

The difficult problem of intention obtrudes. How seriously should we take the verbal statements of modern artists concerning their intentions to produce religious art?

These intentions take several forms. Some can be called programmatic, associated with the expressed purposes of a movement. This is usually theosophy or some related movement. The works of Mondrian and Kandinsky done under this overt intention are, in my judgment, quite trivial and undeserving of attention except as part of the work of two great artists.

Some are more generally associated with certain doctrines or attitudes of the major religions. This is usually, almost necessarily, associated with one of the oriental religions or some aspect of western religions that can be, rightly or wrongly, associated with the oriental principles. These are paintings of the Void, of that positive and generative emptiness that is Nirvana, Heidegger's comparable Nothingness or the negative spirituality, the negation that is part of both oriental and Christian mysticism. These can be handled with current critical tools, albeit with circumspection. I attempted to do so in my analysis of Picasso's "The Acrobat's Family".

Ill. 41   The problem arises with such artists as Rothko and Newman. How do we define the religious significance of such works? The critical tools are not yet sensitive enough for much confidence. They will have to develop from a precise examination of the perceptual process of apprehending and responding to the work of art. It is fruitless to act as though the work carries religious significance inherently, to be defined "objectively". Works of art are part of the transaction with the experienced world and it is the place in that transaction that matters.

Rothko was quite specific about his intentions:

> "I'm interested only in expressing basic human emotions — tragedy, ecstasy, doom, and so on— and the fact that lots of people break down and cry when confronted with my pictures shows that I communicate these basic human emotions... The people who weep before my pictures are having the same religious experience I had when I painted them, and if you, as you say, are moved only by their color relationships, then you miss the point". (Carmean and Rathbone, 250).

I do not know why people weep in front of Rothko's paintings, if, in fact, they ever do. I do not nor have I ever known anyone who does. Does that disqualify me from grasping what he was about? Or was Rothko distorting the situation? This is the problem that becomes inescapable when analysis moves from an account of the work itself to the subjective response of the spectator. Who has authority to say that any response is wrong?

What is the actual experience of a Rothko painting? They are veils of color, luminous clouds of color floating against a veil of color. Edges are soft, feathered out so they are no defined colored areas. There is no weight or substance; all is light, delicate and glowing. They can be extraordinarily beautiful, disturbing as great beauty always is; impressionable people are often moved to tears by great beauty and these paintings are beautiful. They require from the spectator no action, no specificity of response, only absorption, an entranced submission. But submission to what? There is no indication, no specification.

John Dillenberger reports in conversation that Rothko was annoyed when people found his late brown paintings to be a shift in his style toward the somber, toward death. This is very much what I felt the moment I saw them. They were imprisoning, no exit, no hope.

The Rothko chapel in Houston has become a kind of Mecca for the "art as spirituality" movement, a summary chapel of its intentions. Discussions of it are in tones of hushed reverence. It is hard to know how responsible to hold Rothko for its effects; he painted the paintings in his studio in New York, under a particular soft light. The present light, even shaded, is too bright, the room too large, too empty. I can only report my response without claiming universal validity for it. I found it one of the bleakest rooms I have ever been in, empty with no meaning to the emptiness, imprisoning, deadly. (No photograph can even approximate the affect.)

Newman's paintings are as non-representational as Rothko's. I shall confine myself to his greatest, most significant work, The Stations of the Cross.[6]

There is, in these paintings, even less incident than there is in Rothko. One theme only, the interaction of black against white, black stripes against white (actually a creamy white), white against black, sharp edged strips; some have one edge feathered out. The dialogue of black and white is complex in each painting. It becomes even more complex in the dialectic of the whole where the action of each painting is modified, enhanced, enriched, by its place in the intricacy of the whole. It (the whole series) engages both the intelligence and the sensibility of the spectator. Light does not dominate dark, nor dark light as though the dialectic were that of good and evil. They generate each other as in the primal division of light from darkness; it is not Manichean but Biblical, as though he was seeing the initial act of creation. A single painting could not have done what the series does, for now light is more prominent, now dark, and the changing relation keeps alive the generative interchange between them. In the realization of this engendering interchange, we ourselves become a part of the act. Newman's paintings require the spectator to think about them. In thought we are more than simple experiences, however spiritual. We have to mobilize our deepest individuality, an individuality that is profoundly biblical. The intelligence is too bound to a richly emotional experience to be pure enlightenment rationality. The experience is too bound to intelligent thought to be gnostic.

I have, deliberately, looked at the paintings as paintings first, postponing what Newman placed at the beginning of the series:

> Lema Sabacthani—why? Why did you forsake me? Why forsake me? To what purpose? Why?
>
> This is the Passion. This outcry of Jesus.
>
> Not the terrible walk up the Via Dolorosa, but the question that has no answer.
>
> This overwhelming question that does not complain, makes today's talk of alienation, as if alienation were a modern invention, an embarrassment.
>
> This question that has no answer has been with us so long — since Jesus — since Abraham — since Adam — the original question.

---

[6] In what follows I have made use of and sometimes quoted from my own earlier essay. (Dixon 1982)

Lema? To what purpose — is the unanswerable question of human suffering. Can the Passion be expressed by a series of anecdotes, by fourteen sentimental illustrations? Do not the Stations tell of one event? (Carmean and Rathbone:202)

This remarkable statement faces the problem of specification of non-representational art. Traditional art does so by subject matter. Some modern artists, notably Paul Klee, have done so by titles. Newman has done so by the title of his series, which might seem bizarre were it not for his prose-poem.[7] This does not impeach the self-sufficiency of the paintings as paintings, which are variations of a quite particular and specific theme. It does fasten it to the universals of human experience and raises the difficult problem of the relation of non-representational art to such universals. I quote a personal communication from Prof. David Morgan:

> The accompanying text provides a very specific field of significance in which the experience of the images is framed. The image now serves as a visual analogy of a textually transmitted meaning. Our vision is now guided, conditioned. Without the text and the title, we would be free to make the images mean anything. The text and the title limit reference, provide the image with a clear frame of reference. Without the text one might arrive at an identical interpretation of the images, but not without having to project onto the image the theological framework of suffering and redemption. We provide the text if the artist does not. Word and image cling to each other most tenaciously.

This statement poses the question and describes the solution as a modern (even "post-modern") solution, the interaction of word and image. I suggest that the words are an analogy of the images as the images are the words. We learn from this solution something of importance about our grasp of the past. Narrative images link the formal structure of a work to a particular realm of meaning. We can grasp the significance of the narrative in part by our knowledge and its involvements but in part we must rely on the text the narrative was drawn from. Newman's solution to the problem makes explicit the procedure that had been taken for granted earlier.

---

[7] Newman did not begin the series with The Stations in mind. He had painted several of them before deciding on the name.

Can the full specification be put into words? The analogy can, although the import of the paintings cannot. Leaving aside the question of whether the word "Christian" can be used adjectively, this is not a Christian painting. The title and the poem refer to Christian events and it is not beside the point that Newman's understanding of the crucifixion is deeper than most Christian homiletics: it was not the pain of it that mattered but the sense of failure and the abandonment by God.

Newman's relation to his Jewishness was complicated but very real, deeper than the tribal drawing together under external threat that informs the Jewishness of so many non-religious Jews. (Most religious affiliations are a matter of inherited tribalism.) The principle of the Messiah is a real one, the hope of a suffering people. Jesus was a Jew and held that hope and then faced, from the cross and the Way of the Cross, the final abandonment by God, the destined and inescapable suffering of the faithful people. This is Jewish humanism at its highest. Or deepest. Or most real.

And so, of course, it is Christian. Jesus was a Jew and suffered as Jews suffer and so is the cornerstone of Christian faith which can start nowhere else. Newman's vision is Judaic tragedy. It is not Greek tragedy, which gives us the word and the idea of tragedy, but it is, in its way, tragedy.

There is no Christian tragedy, even though innumerable Christians lead tragic lives, because the adjective requires that there always be hope and there is no hope in tragedy. But hope, Christian or otherwise, that is not grounded on the sense of tragedy is an empty, trivial thing. Which is why Newman could give a Christian title to a Jewish work.

This is the paradox of art. In setting forth critically the discontinuity of the modern world, the artist inevitably transcends it, for art necessarily has to do with unity and wholeness. There can be no true representation of chaos. If the work is ordered it is not an accurate representation of chaos. If it is chaotic it is not a representation of chaos but simply a mess.

So much being said, there is something more. It is both inhumane and a delusion to force on artists the role of shaman. There have been artists great enough to be spiritual guides; most are like the rest of us, doing their best to do an honest day's work. There is not something called "art" that is of its nature revelatory of a lost meaning of life. There are artists who are able, to various degrees according to their capacities, to make the physical embodiments of particular religious positions and attitudes. We need to attend to what they have done and meant, not make them instruments in our own cause.

12

THE BEGINNING IN THE END

I
n our end is our beginning. We began with the foundations, the chronological beginnings which established (or discovered) the essential vocabulary and syntax of images as a necessary way of coping with the world. We then looked thematically at various types of images, returning to chronology with the modern. This is not accidental. An essential part of the argument is that we deal with the world and each other in terms of who we are, the totality of who we are, body-mind, part of a particular time, speaking particular languages, of words, of images, of dance and mathematics and all the others.

We do not understand our own world if we do not understand the past. We do not understand the past unless we understand our own world.

The rest of this chapter will be argument, not analysis and demonstration.

We deal now with continuities and discontinuities, with paradox, with contradiction.

The first major contradiction sets off the modern period[1] from all the others. Heretofore, it was possible, necessary, to talk of images in terms of their art because that is what most of them were; images were made by artists. We could discuss them as subjects apart from their artistry but all images were works of art, even when the people who made and used them thought of them as functional objects rather than art as we know it. This is no longer true, or true in the same way.

---

[1] By "modern art", I mean "modernism", extending from the early years of the century to approximately the end of the 1950's. From then, we deal with "post-modernism". Post-modernism raises certain questions and is so entangled with the problems of French literary criticism, of partisan politics, that it cannot be dealt with adequately in a short book. It need not be quite so dominant in our attempt to understand our own world as it is among literary critics.

THE MULTIPLICATION OF IMAGES

The first, the fundamental, difference to note has nothing directly to do with religion but has everything to do with determining the context for both religion and the study of religion: the vast proliferation of images so that we, even many in the "under-developed countries", spend our lives surrounded by images. In the developed countries particularly, this means hundreds, thousands, of images, constantly displayed, shifting, moving, transforming, blurring the distinction between space and time, past and present.

Throughout most of history, images were rare and special, sometimes to the point of the magical. The rich could see more images than others. Most people saw only the images on churches or public buildings. The present proliferation of images has altered our relation to all images. By becoming habitual, images have lost much of their ancient authority. They have lost their mystery, their "aura" (Walter Benjamin). The traditional makers of images, the "artists", have been displaced to the margins. Despite their sometimes frantic efforts to attract notice, they count for little in the direct forming of the modern consciousness.[2]

Images as such have not lost their authority. While it is rare that any specific image has a general impact, the role of images in establishing imaginative order, conveying cultural information, shaping the public narrative, displaying the shapes of emotional life, has shifted to television, film, comic books, advertisements, etc. Control of images has shifted away from institutions; control of religious images has shifted away from religious institutions.[3] Churches, other religious and political institutions, have lost much of their former authority, in part because of this development.

The multiplication of images began in the late Middle Ages with the invention of the printing processes.[4] While much of its use for the wealthy was still in the realm of art, the great social change came with the proliferation of cheap prints made by carving wood blocks. This put

---

[2] There is an important exception to this statement. The ideas in use in the making of the pervasive popular images are in good part derived from the artists. Many such ideas, however, grow directly from the possibilities of new techniques.

[3] This is a little too simple; some great works of modern architecture have been done in churches and synagogues. Yet these are individual visions done for the institutions rather than emerging from any common formal imagination.

[4] As with many inventions, this one was anticipated in China and Japan by several centuries but with nothing like the consequences it had in the west.

devotional images in the hands of more and more people, including the poor and the illiterate. The development of different printing processes increased this availability of images and began to shape the modern world. The invention of printing is usually dealt with in terms of the printed book but it was equally important in the development of the printed image.

Both the multiplication of images and their character have shaped the modern world far beyond the realization of most interpreters, who are by profession wedded to the influence of words. In doing so, proliferation of images has made a world which is the context for religion and for the study of religion. Roughly speaking, a survey of that world must deal with three areas:

1. The psychic and intellectual consequences of the ubiquity of images.

2. The various uses such images can be put to, including lying and distortion.

3. The consequences of the "exactly repeatable image" and "the pictorial statement without syntax.[5]

The first two cover the subjects of most immediate concern to the study of religion but I will begin with the third, for reason I hope to make clear. Briefly: the exactly repeatable image made possible the proliferation of images; the image without syntax[6] made possible science and technology, and a fundamental possibility of the modern mind.

THE IMAGE WITHOUT SYNTAX

Ivins's book is too rich and complex to summarize adequately but certain statements are necessary to the argument. An introduction to that argument requires something that might appear painful: the abandonment of a basic premise of this book.

---

[5] The quoted phrases are taken from one of the most remarkable books of modern times, William Ivins, *Prints and Visual Communication*. Although this book has been available for more than forty years, it has had nothing like the impact it should have, probably because to take it seriously would require remaking not only our understanding of images but of philosophical thought itself and, therefore, the educational process. It is easier to ignore it. A major part of what follows in the text is adapted from Ivins' book.

[6] The "image without syntax" refers mainly to the photograph. Heretofore all images, even those made to be reproduced, were necessarily made by hand. Inevitably, their form owed much to the idiosyncrasies of personality and to the habits of recording appearances ("style") characteristic of the time. These are the "syntax" of the image. Photography has more of a syntax than Ivins allows for but it can record certain kinds of appearances with a precise accuracy hitherto unknown.

I have asserted more than once that the study of imagery is inseparable from the study of art because, necessarily, all images are works of art. They might be good art or bad art but inescapably they are all art and require analysis based on "the language of art". The problem at the moment is images that have nothing to do with art but with information.[7]

There can be no science and particularly no technology in the modern sense without the ability of scientists and engineers to communicate accurately with each other. Identification, classification, analysis and other equally essential aspects of science and technology, all depend on the creation and distribution of the accurate, exactly repeatable image. This, according to Ivins, accounts for the distinctive nature of Greek thought and its dominance over the Western intellectual imagination. They had no way of making an image except by drawing it and no way of repeating an image except by another drawing which was, inevitably, different. Consequently, as an ancient author (Pliny) recognized, they could not develop a study of a subject such as botany because the only thing they could use was verbal description, which was notoriously inaccurate.

> What was true of botany as a science of classification and recognition of plants was also true of an infinite number of other subjects of the greatest importance and interest to men. Common nouns and adjectives, which are the materials with which a verbal description is made, are after all only the names of vaguely described classes of things of the most indefinite kind and without precise concrete meanings, unless they can be exemplified by pointing to actual specimens. In the absence of actual specimens the best way (perhaps the only way) of pointing is by exhibiting properly made pictures. We can get some idea of this by trying to think what a descriptive botany or anatomy, or a book on machines or on knots and rigging, or even a sempstress's handbook, would be like in the absence of dependable illustrations. (15-16)

With their characteristic lack of interest in technological innovation (it is hard to work up an interest in technical matters when you have slaves to do all the work), the Greeks did not even attempt to develop the repeatable image. They turned, therefore, to the only devices they had that were capable of precise reproduction: words.

---

[7] To be precise they are still art but their impact on this part of the argument is not in terms of their character as art.

It is to be remembered that the only statements the ancients knew which could be exactly repeated were composed of word symbols which were mere representative members of classes. Under the circumstances, I believe, it was only natural that the ancients came to think that there was some magic in words, of such a kind that they were real and that the shifting changing phantasmagorias of sensuous awareness they described were at best composed of imitations or exemplifications of the reality that existed in the word. Plato's Ideas and Aristotle's forms, essences, and definitions, are specimens of this transference of reality from the object to the exactly repeatable and therefore seemingly permanent verbal formula. An essence, in fact, is not part of the object but part of its definition....In a funny way words and their necessary linear order forbid us to describe objects and compel us to use very poor and inadequate lists of theoretical ingredients in the manner exemplified more concretely by the ordinary cookbook recipes, (62-63)

Speaking of the similar conditions of the eighteenth century and its ideas of "the Truth of Science and of the Laws of Nature":

It did this largely because it was impossible for it to state exactly the particulars it saw in such a way that the statement could be verified. It was impossible for it to make and publish a pictorial statement that could not be challenged for its accuracy. Also it was impossible for it to make another pictorial statement about the same thing that should be like the one already made, (91)

And, a little earlier:

When it came to things and objects about which they had no immediate first-hand acquaintance and for information about which they had to rely on words and the available printed pictures... the people of the eighteenth and most of the nineteenth century could only be reasonable, for it was utterly impossible for them to be right. They had not the means available to think in particularities, which are always irrational, and they had to think in generalities. Thus it came about that they thought their generalities were true, and that when the observations did not agree with the generalities it was the observations that were wrong. (91-2) (Emphasis added.)

The underlined assertion suggests why Ivins's case has not been absorbed and taken seriously; to do so would require rethinking the structure of our intellectual life and even our educational system which is not a task to be undertaken lightly.[8] Yet it is only in the humanities and in some of the social sciences that the principle has not been taken seriously. Without any awareness of Ivins's book, the most important parts of contemporary intellectual life take the principle with absolute seriousness in the way most faithful to it: they take it for granted and proceed accordingly. As a result, at the center of modern intellectual life there is an affirmation of one of the greatest human achievement: the habit, the condition, of accuracy.

THE HABIT OF ACCURACY

There has always been the habit of accuracy in craftsmanship, which is accurate or it is a failure. Within the heritage from the Greeks, intellectuals have had no means for dealing with the kinds of accuracy that are so essential in so much of human work. What was lacking for so long was the possibility of making an accurate image, then reproducing and distributing such an image for the necessary community of work.

Without trying to go too far into formal intellectual history, I am inclined to modify Ivins's case at one point. I doubt if this development in imagery could have taken place as it has without the training in a different kind of accuracy that began with the Greeks. There is a necessary accuracy of abstract thought that is, perhaps, best developed by certain kinds of accuracy in words; this the Greeks did accomplish and, because of this achievement, we might even forgive them for the way in which they have misled us and forgive ourselves for the idolatry of the Greeks that has so obstructed the development of other serious intellectual work. Furthermore, words have their own possibilities of accuracy outside the delusions of philosophy. It is not only that we owe an immense debt to Greek poets and dramatists, as we are indebted to all the world's poetry. Some Greeks developed the habit of exact and discerning observation and synthetic analysis that enabled them to develop the first true histories and political science. Imagery would not have helped in a more accurate account of human conflict than Thuydides's *History of the Pelopennesian War,* which is the fountainhead of all serious study of history and politics. The idolatry of the Greeks has some point.

---

[8] It is somewhat more courteous to note that Ivins wrote a book about prints, not epistemology. It is likely that people outside the world of prints and of art history generally did not even know of his book. It is time they attended to it.

Another exception, that does not quite justify the Greeks. In some case, the general image serves our purposes better than the particular. A manual for the identification of birds relies more on drawings than on photographs; it is precisely those features shared by all members of a species that is important, without the interference of the idosyncracies of a particular bird. It is not a simple thing to distinguish the roles of the particular and the general. Even so, the image is a necessity; description alone would not serve.

That much being said, it is still true that the decisive condition for modern life was set by its imagery, but not by the images we commonly associate with the word. It is, rather, the images that make possible the accurate recording and transmission of essential information.

Accuracy of imagery made possible another extraordinary development: the democratization of technology. The magazine rack in the local mall is witness to this; among the sleaze and the worthy is a range of magazines making easily available a wide range of information and instruction in a remarkable number of technologies, electronics, woodworking, needlework, cooking, mechanics, etc., etc. Very large numbers of people become accustomed to images as the carriers of exact information and instruction. This is wholly unprecedented.

Thus a fundamental aspect of the modern world is a vast array of images determined by the accuracy of their reproduction of objects and processes. This body of images has its own vocabulary and syntax, extensively studied and published. Its technology becomes ever more complex with the increase in electronic equipment for the recording and transmission of vast quantities of information.

This bears directly on the study of religion because the things and actions of religions are among the vast array of objects and actions photographically available. Only special study can determine what effect this has had. My impression is that it has had very little effect on the formal study of religion. Illustrations are absent or only superficially used in the relevant publications.

But what does it do to the understanding of a religion when its sacred objects are removed from the context of their placement and use and pictured in isolation, in glowing full color, on the printed page? How can they still function as hierophanies? Can the scholar sustain any sense of the numinous, knowing that the place or the thing can appear in photographs? What sense of the sacred can survive the presentation of an image or a ritual as images on a computer screen?

Thus a decisive part of the modern world is sustained by a body of imagery unprecedented in human history. It establishes not only the information and teaching but the habit of precision and accuracy essential to serious thought. Yet that is only part of the story of the modern world.

At the other extreme from this body of images, are those that are indifferent to accuracy and precision. The technology that establishes the habit of precision and accuracy can also be used to generate images intended to deceive, manipulate, distract, entertain; advertisements can be amazingly beautiful even when I know that beauty is being used to manipulate me into thinking the product has something to do with beauty. Advertisements can be equally vulgar, manipulating other parts of our nature.

We have, therefore, a whole new image world, using the techniques developed in the technology of the first image world but using them to different purposes. Again we have a large vocabulary and a complex syntax which needs to be understood in order to understand the modern world. A distinction that was fundamental in the earlier parts of this study is equally fundamental in this one: whatever the relation between form and content in the modern image world, form and subject are clearly distinguishable and have distinct symbolic force.

The intricate, complex techniques of modern imagery are put at the service of the use of subjects as signs. Never before in human history has the context of human life been so saturated with images as signs (because never before has it been technically possible). There is a large and growing literature, both popular and professional, describing and analyzing this body of signs. Although religious signs are among those being used and manipulated, we cannot go further into them here.

The forms of these subjects have a dual symbolic role.

THE SPACE-TIME OF MODERN IMAGERY

In the first place, the techniques have made possible a wild and fascinating manipulation of relations. Whereas earlier we could speak of space and time, modern imagery makes it difficult to do so; a space-time continuum in varied forms is central to these images. Take, for a simple example, instant replay in sports. The event is seen (from a particular point of view on the other side of the screen) in "real time". It is then repeated from the side-line camera, the end zone camera, in slow motion, in a split screen. What does it do to the sensibilities of people who constantly experience this kind of inter-weaving of space and time?

It follows that full understanding of the modern mentality requires analyzing popular imagery rather than the more formal imagery of the arts. That would be a task different from the one of this book. A great deal of the vocabulary of the modern mind could be learned from watching television with the sound turned off, while leafing through a magazine.

There are original ideas in some popular imagery but most of the basic principles underlying popular imagery were already established by the artists in the early decades of the century. At the same time, some symbolic shifts are an inevitable, as a consequence of technical changes. Space travel depended on developments in physics, not imagery, but the consequences for imagery are great: it is hard to hold to the principle of the "three story universe" after seeing a photograph of the earth taken from outer space.

Many events happen only to be photographed, or happen in the way they do in order to be photographed. It is difficult to have a natural relation with nature. Road side signs announce, "Photographic overlook ahead". Many styles of art are self-consciously chosen, no longer as a matter of conviction about the way the world is but to complete a critical argument. Criticism becomes more important than art.

Almost the first sentence of Chapter 1 was, "The function of the image is the suspension of time". Any printed image suspends time and fixes it into shape, but it may be that the normative image of our time is that made possible by film, television and computers: time is movement, transition, transformation, driving in restlessness, multiple in its appearances.

These are symptoms, sometimes superficial; no one understands the fundamental reasons for the symptoms. There are only opinions.

Yet there is another mode of images, even more fundamental. Whether it is cause or effect, I do not know. Perhaps the most basic of the symbolic transformations that have taken place is common to both popular imagery and formal imagery: the dissolving of the primacy of the vertical.

THE DISSOLUTION OF THE VERTICAL

For 5,000 years or more, the "high" cultures had developed their symbolic structures around the primacy of the vertical. However great the variations, they all shared the sense of a center, of a hierarchical order of society, of government, of cosmic order. All this was manifested in the formal order of the arts: the dominance of the base and axial organization in sculpture; the dominance of the frame, the base line and the axial organization of painting; the dominance of axial organization and clear distinctions (of directions, of mass and space, of interior and exterior) in architecture.

Toward the end of the nineteenth century and the first decades of the twentieth, the dominance of the vertical as the prime cultural symbol began to weaken. In architecture, both horizontal and vertical axes began to multiply, the distinctions among interior spaces were drastically modified, the separation of interior and exterior was increasingly dissolved. In building, none of this would have been possible without certain essential technical developments, such as the steel frame, that could replace the mass of walls, reinforced concrete that made possible horizontal extension, plate glass that could fill in the spaces of the frame. These are conditions, not causes.

Other symbolic images did not require technical innovation but only a new form of symbolic thought. Many paintings and sculptures retained a vertical organization but more as a matter of convenience than of symbolism; we are still vertical bodies standing on the earth seeing many other vertical bodies. Increasingly, complete freedom of ordering was available in image making. The products of this freedom are too varied for summary other than to say that the frame and the base became conveniences rather than controlling symbolic necessities. Axial organization gave way to a dispersal of interest over the entire surface. Sculpture became permeable in both directions, penetrating the surrounding space and opening to it. Within the inescapable limitations of the frame of the screen, television images are manipulations of spatial directions and the placement of objects within the space, with a complete freedom of relation.

With collage, the distinction of reality and representation began to dissolve as real objects became incorporated into a work which was often not clearly a painting or a sculpture. The technical innovations of film and television made possible a similar manipulation of time.

Images, once rare and special as a way of comprehending the multiplicity of the world, have become so prevalent, so bewilderingly common, so technically fascinating and so often misleading, that their clamorous insistence places them outside their traditional work. So we face a void with nothing but our own consciousness to sustain us.

This is the imagery most people see, not modern art (except incidentally) but the imagery in the so-called "media". To a degree rarely equaled in art as such, subject matter and form have to be carefully distinguished in studying popular imagery; in advertising, politics, in public relations "image making", different modes of subject matter and different forms are manipulated in order to separate things that should be seen together and relate things that should be separate.

Running through all this is a key principle: <u>discontinuity</u>[9]

DISCONTINUITY

Discontinuity is part of our common experience. Nearly all of us isolate each aspect of our lives from the others, each time in our lives from what went before and comes after.

Magazines, television programs, are made up of isolated bits of things having no connection to each other. The isolated programs are broken up into isolated bits by isolated commercials having nothing to do with each other or the program. A news item on a famine in Africa might be followed by an advertisement for a luxury food.

Discontinuity penetrates into the core of scholarship itself. Semiotics thrives on taking parts away from wholes. Most modern critical methods depend on isolating one aspect of works of art from their wholeness, proving that there is no such thing as wholeness. Not only criticism, but philosophy and theology are characterized by rapid fluctuation of discontinuous loyalties; nothing is deader than last year's criticism, or philosophy, or theology, except perhaps last year's artistic styles. Art no longer develops in a cumulative fashion by the careful exploration of the potentialities of a stylistic idea. It careens from one idea to another, owing less to orderly development than it does to the market system.

Cultural analysis of this kind is unreliable, depending too much on personality, personal experience, prejudice, interest. It is almost always superficial —and unavoidable. If discontinuity is the reigning principle of modern culture, we cannot say whether imagery is cause or effect, or whether the question makes any sense. I have touched on the nature and consequences of popular imagery and its consequences for the more formal

---

[9] The most profound treatment of the theme of discontinuity in modern life is the remarkable, ignored and forgotten, book by Max Picard, *Hitler in Ourselves.*

imagery of the arts. More needs to be said, for the character of modern art is both symptom and possibility.

TRANSFORMATION OF MODERN ART

The manner of treatment must shift because the whole situation of art shifts drastically in the twentieth century.[10]

There is no unusual difficulty in understanding modern art nor any decisive shift in the way art should be understood.[11] The "vocabulary" of art remains the same, mass, space, line, color, etc. The single distinction lies in the elimination of subject matter or its considerable distortion. Since subject matter is part of the artist's material (see Appendix), to be used according to the purposes of the work, this distinction is not vital.

The great change was a shift in the origins and purposes of the work of art. Most art styles in the past began in the service of religion. The artist, therefore, worked within the structure of an established social order, sharing the purposes and pressures of that society, worked within an established style, according to public and acknowledged standards.[12]

When a work of art was ordered, the point was not the individuality of the workman but the image. Even when the patron went to Cimabue or Giotto in preference to some more limited painter, the point was to get a Madonna and Child, not "a Cimabue". The modern period began when patrons began to approach artists for "anything from your hand", as they did such artists as Michelangelo and Titian; the age of the artist as hero had begun and is not yet entirely over.

Even then, the artist worked for patrons, within an acknowledged social order, in an accepted style, however far they may have pushed its limits. The style was still that of the church; the Renaissance style even to

---

[10] Heretofore I have tried to present a program for grasping art of any culture; this section will deal only with "the west" since, for better or for worst (perhaps for better and for worst), modernism is a creation of the west.

[11] Most modern works are easier to understand than the major works of the past. A painting by Titian is a complex work requiring different critical methods. Modern artists normally choose a single idea and explore it fully. Once the idea is grasped the critical work is done. (There are exceptions to this principle, particularly in such artists as Picasso.)

[12] One of the curious features of recent debates over public support for the arts is the frequently reiterated assertion that art should protest against the principles of the social order. Before the modern period, this has almost never been true. Imagery sustained the governing principles of society.

its final stages in the so-called Baroque period, originated in the church. But the process was inexorable; the artist-as-hero could use the style for purposes that were only incidentally related to religion, that were increasingly the private vision of the artist.

Around the beginning of the nineteenth century, with the fading of the authority of the institutional church and the bankruptcy of ideas in the church, artists could work directly for the satisfaction of the prejudices of patrons or they could work for the expression of their individual views of the meaning of things. (like so many such either-or distinctions this one is too sharp. Good artists had little trouble finding support among patrons. Few important artists have spent much time starving in garrets.)

There came a split in the economy of image making. The makers of "popular" imagery took over the traditional functions of the artist: working to the order of patrons and to their social, political or economic purposes; confirming the interests of the regnant order of society; reinforcing general convictions and commitments. The "artists", apparently working to their own purposes, performed comparable functions for groups within society.

This modern "period" is not a period such as "Gothic" and "Renaissance", which have an identifiable stylistic unity. It is more an attitude than it is a period, an attitude identified as "Romanticism". It is still the attitude of our own time. Of the many aspects of this attitude, the one that matters now is the high degree of self-consciousness that is present in it.

Self-consciousness carries with it a consciousness of the other, the otherness of the world, the otherness of the art work itself, and out of that consciousness emerges an aspect of modern imagery that is not directly religious, even in the implicit sense of the word, but is the condition and context of all serious religious thinking in the modern world.

The wonderful, exhilarating, frustrating thing about modern imagery is its range and variety. Everything is available to it. Its own language is subject to its investigations. Sorting it all out, coming to terms with it, determining which parts are worth attention and which are not, is delightful, maddening, boring, endlessly instructive, exciting. Earlier, a style was a natural outgrowth of the work to be done, with changes in the style located in changing needs, changing definitions of the work and its possibilities. Now, purposes were consciously chosen and a stylistic language elaborated to accomplish those purposes.

Initially, styles developed to set out a distinctive view of the world. Even with the invention of the repeatable image that made images available to everyone, the style of their making was derived from the major styles.

Later, the chosen formal language was designed to analyze some aspect of the experienced world. Impressionism tried to find the formal equivalent of the optical experience of the world. The various forms of expressionism explored several aspects of emotional responses to the world. Surrealism probed into the fantasy life of the psyche. Some artists (usually working as isolated individuals developing their own style: Kaethe Kollwitz, Ben Shahn, etc.) turned their attention to issues of injustice, inhumanity, cruelty. Modern art has a powerful moral dimension that gets too little recognition.

Cubism, the most powerful single style of the twentieth century, represents an important transition, for here we find the attention of artists being directed toward the art work itself. Cézanne opened the way to cubism. In his work, the structure of nature is translated into the structure of the painting. Such a statement applies to most of the history of significant art but Cézanne's work is the most deliberate of them all. In traditional landscape painting, the tension between nature and the painting is subdued into a single unified image. In Cézanne the presence of both is palpably felt, each revealing the other in the intimacy of their joining. With cubism the balance was decisively shifted; the work of art was now more important than any experienced reality represented or suggested in it.

The work of art became a part of the experienced reality, itself shaping the experience of the visible world, including itself. The relation of the human psyche to its imagery decisively shifted.

Vast generalizations such as "the human psyche" are obviously pretentious; the considerable majority of the human race knew nothing about the things modern artists were doing and couldn't have cared less. It is still true that changes in imagery change all manner of things and end by having great influence among people who know nothing about the origins. Most types of modern imagery have their origin in the ideas of modern art.

In this situation, the inevitable takes place: the elementals appear. In the absence of controlling social institutions, the habits of interaction, the structures of relation, that are the substance of a culture informed by religion, the essential human characteristics appear in all their remorseless clarity. Sex and violence are ingredient to human life. Such control of them as is ever achieved is achieved only by those institutions so much under attack. If God is dead, all things are permitted.

Modern art is the more positive aspect of this reduction to elementals. Repeatedly, modern artists have defined their work as isolating some one or another aspect of inherited art (including primitive art and other art styles) and developing its possibilities. This is sometimes the human experience of the world (expressionism, surrealism, etc.), sometimes the forms of art itself; modern art is probably the most extensive and most detailed of all systematic investigations of the "language" of art. The most profound and most detailed of these investigations was that of Paul Klee, whose fundamental contributions are not yet fully absorbed.

RELIGION WITHOUT THE GODS.

One consequence of all this is the death of the gods, and God. This is the kind of statement that has been made in all seriousness by people who should know better; it is only in particular religions that gods die. As powers in the imagination and, therefore, in human experience the gods are as alive as they ever were. As to their metaphysical existence, who can say? If God is outside human knowledge, who can speak of the death of God?

The problem is, all the gods are equally alive and in the confusion we cannot know which god is God. So all the gods are equally dead, unavailable, and religion becomes a matter of tribal identification or private comfort.

Where gods are absent, gods and religions become the occasion for human making, and that making is self-conscious, deliberate and, therefore, subject to private purpose. We are in a time of the absence of religion and the proliferation of religions, of invented gods and invented rituals and invented faith.

This can be the occasion for satire but it should not be. Just as the makers of images (the "artists" and the technologists who make popular images) are being forced back into elementals, so much of this desperate and confused search is returning to the elementals of the religious experience. The whole panoply of thought and work is laid out before us.

What can we do with it? What then of the truth?

WHAT DOES IT MEAN
TO TELL THE TRUTH

In which an attempt is made to answer
an unanswerable question and to suggest
a reason for the study of the past.

13

THE SEARCH FOR TRUTH AND THE USES OF THE PAST

What of the truth? We began with Umberto Eco's assertion, that an image is anything that can be used to lie. If an image can lie, it can tell the truth. What truth can be told by the images we have been looking at?

There is no more difficult human problem than the problem of truth. I will not resolve it in this final chapter but I will make a few assertions that provide, I believe, a working foundation for the examination of the problem, and a few suggestions of ways of proceeding.

There is a truth of words, of philosophical or theological propositions but propositions do not exhaust the meaning of truth. The measure of that truth is not different from the truth of images. The first measure of truth is not an accurate description of the eternal but craftsmanship. Craftsmanship is not simply skill (which is a necessary condition: skill of hand, of thought, of imagination), but the fittingness of the instruments and the conception to the material and to the purpose as part of the requirements of the situation.

In general terms, the situation is universal, the same for all people. We begin with bodies, the primary instrument of thought and imagination, the same for all. In, as, our bodies, we inexorably face the same human situation that is widely different in its particularity: we are all born into a place and a history and a social order. The history changes with time because each act alters the historical situation so that it is constantly new. Place, geography, change more slowly but they, too, change. The nature of the human task is always the same, to live appropriately according to human needs. It is always different because the situation is always changing.

Limitations of space have prevented any full consideration between art and its geographical setting. Once or twice, I have suggested an account of images that might suggest how it works. Geography does not cause images. It is one of the generative features of the situation and at the same time a powerful influence on the imagination that must cope with the situation.

On the one hand, we have the earliest high cultures developing at the juncture of rivers and deserts, Egypt, Mesopotamia, the valleys of the Indus River and of the Yellow River. Egypt is at an extreme with the sharpness of distinction of its weather and geography giving rise to a sense of geometric order. Contrast that with a culture such as India, working out its destiny within the powerful uncertainties of its climate, the extreme contrast of ascetic deprivation in the desert of the north and the sensual fecundity of the tropical rain forest. It is hard to imagine the geometry of Khafre or Ranofer in the Indian rain forest or the sensual mobility of Shiva or the Khajuraho dancers on the banks of the Nile.

Which of these is true? Either. Neither. Both.

To judge either to be true at the expense of the other is to make a choice that is difficult to defend in all humanness. To judge neither to be true but only a cultural construct is a moral and historical relativism that I find difficult to accept. How can both be true?

If we could trace each culture back to its beginning, we would only dramatize what we can imagine, that each faced a different situation with distinctive problems and possibilities. Each worked out its destiny within those problems and possibilities and developed an imaginative, symbolic, order fulfilling the situation. Each is true because each met its situation with competence and integrity, generating both things and institutions adequate to the situation.

If we stopped there we would be guilty of both condescension and relativism. The situation is more serious than that.

Each is true because each develops a human potentiality. Geometry and fecundity are not things happening only to Egyptians or Indians but parts of human life. In these bodies of images, the themes are explored to their fullest and become, therefore, instructive about what being human is like, what possibilities are available to us. Ranofer is not likely to become a prime symbol for our culture but neither is it a dead artifact of the past.

Is there any judgment to be made of universal truth in looking at the imaginative constructs of other people? There are certain kinds of judgments: competence, integrity, adequacy to the situation, obtuseness of understanding, etc. All peoples are subject to ignorance and failure and with decent reluctance, we might make such judgments. Ranofer may be a great cultural symbol but the obsessive repetitiousness of later Egyptian image making is a weariness to the spirit.

There is a deeper problem. Within the limits of this introduction, I have had little or nothing to say about a fundamental human experience: evil, the dark and dismal corruption of the human soul, the terrifying energies that lie outside control.

Hinduism has an image of little art but startling authenticity, the goddess Kali, horrible of face, draped with a necklace of skulls, drunk on blood, dancing exultantly on the body of her consort Shiva or a decapitated demonic enemy. She cannot be understood in isolation but only as a presentation of one aspect of human experience. She is the summation of Shivaite transformation as destruction. It is difficult for me to grasp such an image, except intellectually. It is quite beyond my imagination that so fine and gentle a man as Ramakrishna could refer to her as the "Gracious Mother".

Kali may be part of symbolic wholeness and completion. But what of Xipe Totec? Xipe Totec is an Aztec image, of no great artistic quality, showing a priest wearing the skin of a sacrificed victim. This image also is true, but I mean by truth here something that would not attract an Aztec. Xipe Totec shows the depth of depravity that the human imagination can sink to, the horror that can become ingredient to a culture somewhere along the line of its generation.

The cultural relativist would reply immediately that I make such a judgment from the value system of another culture. This is undoubtedly true, nor do I have any desire to evade that judgment. The imagination that produced Xipe Totec is wholly wrong, impossible of toleration.

Tenochtitlan, the Aztec capitol, was by all accounts, one of the most beautiful cities in the world. The human imagination is complicated.

I am willing to argue the case for the judgment I make on Aztec religion but I cannot do it here. I can only invite the reader to consider the problem.

The judgment, the consideration of the problem, should be made in the context of an inescapable circumstance: Xipe Totec is not merely an Aztec horror but a dimension of ourselves.

CONCLUSION: THE USES OF HISTORY

The study so far has aimed primarily at an imaginative grasp of the world of images of past and distant peoples. If we are not to think that such a study is useful simply as a matter of historical information, something needs to be said about the contemporary use of such images. Inevitably, this takes the form of exhortation and is a matter of personal judgment.

An overly sophisticated age such as our own often yearns after a simpler, more harmonious past and vainly dreams of reconstructing it or returning to it. This dream is one of the many dreams of a golden age in the past. This yearning after such an ideal state appears to be endemic to the human mind, that there is, somewhere, an ideal society and all our troubles would be solved if we could only recover it. This is sometimes distant in time or space (archaic Greece, various oriental cultures), a future utopia (the communist withering away of the state, the Book of the Revelation), a past Golden Age (the Garden of Eden, the Founding Fathers, sometimes now the Neolithic).

In fact, the Neolithic past may have been sufficiently alive in the corporate memory of early literate people to have accounted for the myth of the Garden of Eden, which shares some of its characteristics.

It is necessary for us to be rather more sophisticated about the possibilities of such a recovery; mentalities, the technical and social orders, imaginative structures, have been completely transformed and the Neolithic is one of those homes we can't go back to again.

Which does not reduce the importance of the study of the Neolithic. They did and made what they could under the conditions of their life. Our conditions and our problems are different but we can learn from them how to do it.

All people, then and now, participate in the processes of life in the earth; we are shielded, in part, by our technologies, our intellectual and imaginative tools and our institutions that make it possible to live a life that is more than simply the primal processes. The early people are the ones who developed the first, essential, imaginative and intellectual resources for what we do. The small, intense, group of images they developed was a powerful and permanent part of the creation of the human spirit, a fundamental part of the language of religion.

We not only build on their foundations, we use their devices; all subsequent images and forms are developments and combinations of the principles they first developed. They stated the primal problem of religion, the polarities of geometric order and vital energy. They established the primal means for the symbolic expression of the experience of life, participation in the vitality of the animal, the potency of men and the fertility of women, control by geometry and the rational intelligence.

Can we know their religion by understanding their images? We cannot talk about "religion" and "art" in very ancient times; neither religion nor art had been invented. The terms and the things they signify are modern inventions, functional principles in our own symbolic systems, serving our purposes. They are necessary terms for us, necessary so long as we know what we are doing. Using them suggests that religion and art are distinct activities, done for their own purposes. Almost certainly for early peoples such activities were in no sense distinct from the rest of human life. For most of us the paintings of the animals are singularly beautiful, the finest paintings of animals ever made. We do not know if their makers even had a notion of beauty or whether beauty of representation had any part in their purpose in making the paintings.

In our symbol system, Lascaux and Stonehenge are works of art. Some others are not. This is a pointless distinction; they were all functional instruments.

The function these works performed is still a deep psychic need. If the first man and his club, or the first woman and her pot or basket, are still part of ourselves, it is even more true that these Stone Age people are parts of ourselves in a very recent past. We cannot divide ourselves from our own flesh and its workings. Neither can we divide ourselves from our past. To treat Lascaux and Stonehenge as historical mementos, curious survivals, even as aesthetically interesting, is to mistake what they are. They are present to us now. They were made for us too.

We know things those people did not know. How can we use their work in fidelity to what the works are and to what we know? Not by denying what we know; it is not my purpose to suggest that the analytical intelligence has failed us after the fashion of those who condemn "the West" with little understanding of what "the West" has accomplished. Neither should we deny the archaic in ourselves; we are a psychophysical unity.

The importance of imagery, the arts, in religion is simple and central: the arts (all the arts) and ritual (as one of the arts) are the only way to integrate the intellectual analysis and the archaic wholeness. It is a modern superstition to think that the integration requires betraying the intellect;

the making of these works was a work of high intelligence and fine craft. We can do them the courtesy of assuming that their ritual use of the works was equally intelligent. We cannot know what that ritual was nor could we participate in it truly if we knew. We can participate in the works for they represent parts of ourselves.

The images do not belong to them exclusively. If we are courteous to them, we pay as close attention as possible to the uses and the meanings the images had for them, otherwise we cannot learn from them the things they had learned about being human. Even so, the images exist now, in our world, as a part of our experiences and our structures of meaning

In studying the past, we could approach imagery only from within the confusions of our modern understanding of images, yet we could take refuge in the enterprise of understanding what imagery was to those who made it; they worked out of a conviction that their imagery corresponded to the ultimate order of things and we can try to reconstruct something of that conviction and that order. What do we do when there is no commonly accepted sense of order, when most commitments do not derive from religion and have not been incorporated into religious understanding? The problem of our own analytical and interpretive tools becomes pressing.

Much good comes from this confusion. For a culture in its prime, its sense of order is a commitment to the real; the images of another people, embodying a different sense of order, are incomprehensible. They were met, therefore, with indifference or hostility. Our own failure of nerve, our loss of confidence in our own image world, has at least made it possible for us to attend to the work of other people. We have achieved the possibility and assumed the responsibility of preserving the work of others and understanding it. Even this comes at a price and the price is too often draining the power from the works of the past. They have become too familiar from endless reproduction.[1]

With the achievement of history, we forget that the past is gone but its images and artifacts remain. The works we see are all modern works because they are present to us now. We must use them to grasp what other people did, in their own way, in their own time, to their own purposes. Only so can we be duly courteous to them. But their work is now, a part of us. Yet we treat it as a thing among other things, among the flood of images that inundate us. It becomes— oh, deadly word — interesting.

---

[1] See Benjamin, "The Work of Art in the Age of Mechanical Reproduction".

Much of the study of religion has been and is descriptive and analytical. Much has been and is interpretive, an attempt to understand what other people have stood for. In most cases, both forms of study (the second depends on the first) have been conducted as though we, the students of religion, can stand apart from other people, observing and understanding them as others, never doubting our own ability to do what we intend to do with their work.

The study of images can be and should be an important part of these interrelated modes of study. It has not been, perhaps because of the matters considered in this chapter; the conviction of the primacy of words and the diffuseness of images in our own day have combined to make it difficult to use images properly. I hope this outline of a mode of study is something of a corrective, making possible a fuller use of images in the study of religion.

At the very least, we can conclude this. Images are documents (the current term is "texts") from which we can read off acts and attitudes of other people and thereby fill out, sometimes correctly, conclusions we have reached with a more restricted range of documentation.

I am convinced, and have argued in several ways, that the use of images is much greater than that, and more fundamental.

Images are things, objects, made from a physical material. Even though, as I argued in Chapter 6, many people can use images as subject and sign apart from their physical embodiment, they are still looking at images. Images are made by a process of the intelligent and feeling body, inextricably involved in a physical material. (This is the root of the Platonic mistrust of images, ancient and modern; they are incorrigibly material. Academics, and academic study, are far more determined by Platonism than we ordinarily realize).)

This making of images, forming a physical material, is a part of our complex interaction with the physical and material world, one of the means of organizing it, one of the principal means of understanding it. Just as the making of an image is inseparable from the body's place in the world so the apprehension of images requires the awareness of the processes of our own body.

The standards of our study have been set by the rational, verbal, philosophical intelligence and we cannot proceed rightly if we violate them. It may be that we now should mistrust "objectivity" as an unattainable goal, one that wrongly assumes that we can separate ourselves from involvement with the evidence. But the ideal of objectivity enforces on us an absolute respect for the integrity of "The Other", other people who were as seriously engaged with their world as we should be with ours. Without that respect we make them into instruments of our own ambitions.

With that said, we need also to say that the students of religion can no more detach themselves from involvement with their flesh and its processes, its commitment, than those who painted the walls of the cave at Lascaux.

Those who made the images we study, made them as a way of understanding and coping with their world. When we study their work we are making, in our own forms, images of their world as a way of learning from them.

We study the work of others in order to set ourselves in motion.
— Paul Klee

APPENDIX
PROLEGOMENA TO A POSSIBLE
POETICS OF THE IMAGE
A SUPPLEMETARY ESSAY

Wherein certain matters necessary to the understanding of images and the development of skills in analysis and interpretation are set out for reference and additional reading.

Appendix
An Outline of a Possible
Poetics of the Image

(Parts of the following outline are repetitions of things already said, available here as parts of a whole. Other parts are outlines or short essays on subjects essential to the interpretation of images but not directly a part of the subject of religion.)

Part One[1]
The Image as Sign, Symbol and Subject

The Image as Sign.

The sign points to what it signifies. The important thing is the signification and not the sign itself. Once the signifying is accomplished the sign is expendable; it has no inherent value except its preserving of the signifying process for reference, teaching, continued use, etc. All cultures, all religions, have their visual codes, their body of signs that serve an essential function of communication. Since, strictly speaking, there is no inherent meaning in the sign but only a general agreement to use it in a certain way, the meaning (the reference) of a sign can be determined only by living within a culture and building up the necessary familiarity with its sign systems, or by scholarly study and codification.

The image also has significations that are not intended because they are part of those things a culture or a person takes for granted. These include matters so much of concern to current criticism, gender, class, race, etc. A grasp of both is essential to the process of interpretation.

The fatal error is treating complex works as only signs, ignoring their symbolic function and their inherent value. Another, related, flaw is assuming that a sign in another culture means what it means in our culture or what the critic has determined in advance that such signs mean. The first responsibility of the analytical critic is to determine what the sign means for those who made it.

---

[1] Parts of the following outline are repetitions of things already said, available here as parts of a whole. Other parts are outlines or short essays on subjects essential to the interpretation of images but not directly a part of the subject of religion.

The Image as Representation

Representation is a sub-category of signs but has a deeper significance. The first meaning is expected: the image looks like the subject. But "looking like" is very complicated.

The second meaning is political: in a representative democracy, the congressman represents his constituency in acting on their behalf and as their agent. In imagery, this is better stated by a hyphen; the image re-presents the subject in making the subject present. In political art, the ruler, who cannot be everywhere, sets up his image as his presence. Representation in this sense is essential to participation.

We are all involved in representation all the time. We represent ourselves to other people in that we try to present ourselves in a particular way to them. Commonly, we represent ourselves differently to different people. Tradition and often prejudice determines how we both think about and act toward other people. We are, therefore representing them in a particular way, which does not necessarily correspond to how they would like to be represented. Who has authority over representation?

Such representations are images. Images, in the sense used in this book, are a powerful means of representation, images as seen in cartoons, movies, stories, etc.

Realism and Abstraction.

The terms are not in opposition but relation. All art, all images, are realistic in that they all represent something in the experienced world, although not always things in the visible world. All art, all images, are abstract because all select, must select, some aspect of the experienced world. It is not possible and would not be desirable to represent everything. The principle of abstraction is fundamental to the analytical understanding.

THE IMAGE AS SYMBOL.

Symbols are signs that participate in as well as signify something other than themselves. This participation takes two forms:
1. An agreed emotional investment. The symbolic role is imputed to the sign. A flag, that has no inherent relation to the nation it

signifies, is transformed into a symbol; some nations assume that what is done to the flag is done to the nation. This can equally happen to the signs of a religion.

2. An inherent relation, by the nature of the symbolic image. This can be in its subject and particularly in its form. Without this natural relation, the sign is not a true symbol, since symbols function as symbols by the psychic force of this natural relation. The word "natural" does not suggest that only natural things are symbols. The products of human work are equally symbols, generated by the metaphoric relation between forms and experience.

The relations and the interweavings between signs and symbols are so intricate and various that the separation can be made only for the sake of the analysis. Only the analysis of specific images can hope to distinguish among them.

THE IMAGE AS SUBJECT

> ...the nude is not a subject
> of art, but a form of art.
> ...Kenneth Clark (25)

Since anything can be the subject of an image, no outline of subjects is possible, only certain observations.

Clark's assertion is too sweeping; the nude is also a subject to be thought about. Even so, it is basically sound and enriches the principle of form. Even while those who ordered and those who made images were thinking seriously about the nude, it was a form of thought, something to think with. Medieval people, whom we can assume were as interested in the naked body as everybody seems to be, had no need for the nude as a form of thinking about what it means to be human (it appears only when the subject requires it: Adam and Eve, the souls at the Last Judgment).

No culture draws on the full range of possible subjects; every culture has a relatively fixed range of subjects, chosen according to historical circumstance, psychic needs, basic narrative, etc. This group of subjects (the "iconography" of a culture) is only in part what the people of that culture think about, although many within the culture do that in the various modes of thinking, including images. They are, rather, the means of thinking, what the people think <u>with</u>.

Every subject functions in different modes:

1. As sign. The image signifies its subject, thereby establishing it in its psychic force.

2. As symbol, therefore as psychic energy. This includes all the traditional archetypes, the metaphoric processes that generated the basic tools of human life, the natural and the made forms of personal and corporate life, etc.

3. As form and compositional force. The subject both dictates certain forms within the representation and becomes part of the overall form. That is, a nude and a landscape have different weight and energy in the sensibilities of those who make them and those who receive them. This is not only a force in its own right, it is a determining force in any and every image. A figure running away from the center of a picture has a different formal effect from one running toward the center. The forms are also modes of interpreting the subject.

A religion should first of all be understood in terms of its repertoire of subjects, its basic narratives. It is not enough to identify and list these subjects. To understand them as forms of thought, they have to be interpreted in their full range and depth. All representations of the subject constitute such an interpretation. All religions have such a body of subjects, whether or not they are represented in visible form.

It is more common at present to use the word "representation" instead of image. Sometimes this is no more than a synonym but it does, on occasion, state another issue. The Crucifixion is not merely an image, a subject to be represented; it is itself a representation.

Visual interpretations of its subjects play a very minor role in Judaism but the subjects are central to Judaism. Many of the subject-forms generated by and generating ancient Hebraism are central modes of thought in western culture: the creating God, the Garden of Eden, the Tower of Babel, Abraham and Isaac, Job, etc.

"Religion" is the whole body of these subject-forms, interpreted in their universality. Every religion is a setting forth of forms of thought and imagination that are particular to itself and revelatory of some basic aspects of the human spirit.

PART TWO
THE IMAGE AS FORM

Postulates

1. While no image (those that concerns us in this study) exists outside the material embodiment that makes it visible to us, the study of images is not exhausted in the form of their appearance in that material.

2. Form is not merely the carrier of the image; it is the instrument for the interpretation of the image and has symbolic meaning in its own right.

3. Ultimately the image and its form are not separable, yet the separation of them is not simply a convenient tool for analysis; each has to be understood in its own right before their conjoining can be grasped.

4. The image has a life of its own as a form of thought, not merely the occasion for form's interpretation of it.

5. Each of the great subjects of art is an irreplaceable form of thought.

THE FORM OF IMAGES AND FORM AS IMAGE (SYMBOLIC FORM)[2]

Forms are two things: (1) symbolic forms; forms that are modes of thought and imagination in their own right; (2) as the embodiment of a subject, they are the modes of interpretation of that subject.

---

[2] While I owe a great debt to Cassirer's principle of symbolic form, I am here using the term in a different sense. "Symbolic forms" for Cassirer are the great inclusive modes of life — art, religion, science, etc. I am using it to refer to particular forms that function symbolically.

As symbolic form, form is itself an image. The dome is a representation, an image of the heavens above, therefore a cosmic image. There should be an inventory of such images, not only in architecture (the dome, the column, the cave, the pillar, the arch, the pyramid, etc.), but all devices whereby order, energy, distinction, union, etc. are represented, therefore made into meaning. Seen superficially, these devices are instruments of design. They should not be seen superficially.

One illustration at this point would be in order. This brief account of a simple work underlines an important distinction. Form as symbolic form is first of all those forms, such as the dome, that carry symbolic force in their own right. The "language" of forms can also be used in such a way as to state fundamental symbolic meanings. Joshua Taylor is here discussing a pair of boxes made by Indians of the Northwest coast:

> Most of Western design has been based on the interplay or opposition of two compositional principles: the proportional relationship of clearly defined forms of a relatively simple geometric sort, or a continuity of line or form in which one shape flows into the next with little concern for beginnings and endings. (27)

> This handy distinction in formal order is little help in looking at these containers from the Northwest Coast. In the first place, they seem always to be made up both of distinct formal entities arranged in nice symmetry, and of continuities. Every line is polished in contour until it moves, even when it encloses what otherwise would be a discrete and static shape. As a result the eye confronts a continuously ambivalent situation, having to choose between simply looking at a form — and many forms have the unnerving habit of looking back — and joining a rhythm that leads to something else. Which does one choose? Both, of course. It is a bit like staying in one place and going somewhere else at the same time. In art, however, the awareness of being and becoming can live quite happily together, and these active though static compositions effectively demonstrate the fact. (27)

> [The principles of Western design] all belong to a world of pragmatic values and are the product of deliberate analysis. To the Indian carver, decoration had meaning, not simply by virtue of its historical or sociological reference, although traditional mythological inferences were doubtless important, but because it effectively blurred precisely the difference between object and mind, the outer and inner, which has been so dear to the tradition of

Western thought. Furthermore, the "inner" was not simply the expression of animal spirit, as sometimes seems to be the case in what we regard as primitive art, but that which maintained a quality of mystery, of an order beyond calculation or sense. (31)

Neither Taylor nor any other competent art critic would say that this text is the equivalent of the seen image, which must be <u>seen</u> to be understood. He has provided a guide to the seeing, not only by suggesting the basic principle of design used to make the object but by pointing to the "meaning", the content, the sense of the order of things, that is contained in the form. This is truly form as symbolic form, as an image of order.

The form is symbolic form in its own right but so are the myths given body by the formed material. The life of each is present distinctly but it is their con-joining that makes the work what it is. Birds and fish were present to these Indians as they cannot be to us, a part of their communal life and so part of their communal myth. They are subjects, they are images (or representations) in their own right, to be understood in all their mythological depth. It is not only the power and eloquence of the formal design that carries significance but the materialized myth.

I assume the carver wouldn't have the faintest idea what Taylor was talking about if he read or heard that passage. His thought has been translated into another language, a philosophic debate that has gone on for hundreds of years in another culture. This does not mean any specific advantage to him or to us. We are shut off from the immediacy of participation in the natural myth that is these people's mythical home. At the same time, we can learn from them; their mythical speech can be something we hear and see, just as we can, if we will, hear many others who cannot listen to us. This is not only opportunity but trust and responsibility.

THE CONCEPT OF FORM

> Life is form and form
> is the modality of life.
> ...Henri Focillon

The concept of form has had an unfortunate history in the criticism of art. Official nineteenth century European art had become a matter of sentimental anecdotes with imitative forms. In rebellion, artists and critics began to talk of "formalism" as "art for art's sake", treating this limited definition of form as the only value in art. That delivered art to the aesthetes, the few who could "appreciate" those values closed off from the rest of the human race. By limiting their audience, it cut the artists off from the discipline of general discourse. It confused the history and the criticism of art by splitting off "formal values" from all the other values so clearly a part of the work. It impoverished the idea of form by depriving it of its necessary broader reference and involvements. It limited the idea of form to those of its elements that could be talked about in detachment; many discussions of form are primarily discussions of composition.

There was a necessary truth in the elevation of form in formalism; form is, inescapably, the controlling concept in art. The concept of form must be understood.

> In one of his political tracts, Balzac has affirmed that "everything is form, and life itself is form." Not only may every activity be comprehended and defined to the extent that it assumes form and inscribes its graph in space and time, but life itself, furthermore, is a creator of forms. Life is form and form is the modality of life. The relationships that bind forms together in nature cannot be pure chance, and what we call "natural life" is in effect a relationship between forms, so inexorable that without it this natural life could not exist. So it is with art as well. The formal relationships within a work of art and among different works of art constitute an order for, and a metaphor of, the entire universe. (Focillon: 2)

Form is not only the vehicle for the presentation of the image and, by its style, the means for interpreting the image. It itself is an image, a representation, "...an order for, and a metaphor of, the entire universe". Matter, form and content are an inseparable, intricately interacting unity.

In grasping the principle of form we can start with our own bodies, not merely as analogy but as the instrument for apprehending the form and, by projection, one of the sources of form in the image. By looking at the body we can clarify the necessary distinction between form and <u>structure</u>. Structure is the inner principle of organization of form. The form is the outward manifestation of structure. The term structure can be understood on the analogy of architecture.

THE PRINCIPLE OF STRUCTURE

Every building begins with a particular task which must be accomplished under certain conditions of the site, available materials, current technology, etc. The task may be solely functional but normally includes symbolism as well; a temple must provide for priests, worshipers, liturgical action or whatever is required by that religion. It is also a cosmic symbol.

A building is a form, a complex shape in space. This is what we see and use. But within the form there are constant forces at work. In the case of architecture, these forces are decisively determined by gravity. Whatever the form and its expressiveness, the building cannot endure unless it can withstand, control, and use the force of gravity. The method of that control is determined by the task, which is to say the specification of the size of the interior, the necessary number of entrances, etc. A temple that needs an interior only large enough for the cult image and its servitors can choose the simplest structural mode, horizontal beams laid across supports. A church needing space for a large number of worshipers must be covered over differently, by an arch, a truss, or a dome.

Whatever the symbolism of form (the cosmic image), the structural method has its own deep symbolism. The post-and-lintel system, the simplest structure, has to accommodate the dead weight of the horizontal beams pressing downward on their supports, tending to break in the middle under their own weight. This is relatively static, simple, clear. The arch system, covering over a large space, has to accommodate a number of forces working in different directions, requiring a complex series of balancing of reciprocal tensions.

Structure is the means of resolving the forces that are at work within the form. Form is the outward expression and statement of structure. Neither exists without the other except as an abstract idea. We do not understand a building by understanding either alone.

How far can we carry the principle of structure from buildings (which are images) into the study of images in the more usual sense of the word? The principles apply quite comparably to the sculptured image, with the sole exception of that decisive factor: interior space. A statue is the distribution of masses in space under the force of gravity.

Another structural principle of the sculptured image is equally applicable to architecture and dramatized in sculpture. We do not experience anything as spectators detached in space and time, seeing it from the outside. We live within the structure and processes of our own bodies, standing and moving on the earth under the force of gravity.

The form of the body is a series of concavities and convexities. Each form is the outward statement of the bones and muscles underneath. The innermost structure is the coordinated arrangement of bones into the skeleton (and the form of the bones is determined by the forces that are involved in their function). Muscles and ligaments hold the bones in their necessary relation and their form derives from their function. While the essential structural principle of the body has this correspondence to architecture, it is not the full meaning of its structure. A dead body no longer possesses the principle of human structure and its anatomical structure disintegrates. The principle of the body is life, its vitality, which is motility (the ability to perceive and move in space) and memory and anticipation (the ability to move in time)[3]. Inorganic and organic forms are determined in discernible mathematical ratios by the forces that act on them. The forms of life are not arbitrary but come about by the action of forces on material in the course of evolution and their living existence. This not only tells us a great deal about how art comes about but also certain art works as images of order. The same mathematical ratios that shape organic forms can also generate the extraordinary patterns of Islamic ornament, one of the great images of order.

The hand and the eye are principle and instrument of knowing. The body's structure is the first metaphor of order in the world. The hands and the feet are in mirror symmetry. The reciprocal symmetry of the hand controls our knowing and making.

We have, as the statue and the building do, height, width and depth, assembled around vertical and horizontal axes. These are directional; we

---

[3] As illustration of the principle of form as the modality of life, see D'Arcy Wentworth Thompson's *On Growth and Form.*

can imagine a plane bisecting our bodies from side to side, front to back. These planes extend out into the world, intersecting with the axes and planes of other forms, determining the mode of our relation to them. Our relation to other forms in our spaces is too complex for simple structures but the case of images is different. They are subject to the same axial ordering which is structurally related to our bodily ordering.

There is a structure of internal relations within both bodies and made forms and a structure of relation between and among all forms, including our own. This is an identifiable part of the physical structures with a profound symbolic and psychological significance.

So far, three-dimensional forms. What does this have to do with the customary form of images in two dimensions? It is equally applicable. Every two dimensional image is placed within the axial organization of the inscribed surface. Every shape within that axial organization has its own axial organization which has to be structured within the whole.

These are identifiable physical relations which are inextricably involved in our perceptual processes. There is more. Every image is both form and structure. Every image is also a represented subject. Every subject has its own physical and psychic ordering which is part of the forces that have to be related in structures. Every subject is also a sign. Part of its signification is determined by context and purpose, part determined by the decision of the maker of the image. These, too, are forces to be related in the structure at the expense of incoherence.

The structure is the most fundamentally symbolic aspect of any image, whatever other images may be incorporated into it. Since the structure is the organizing principle of the form, it can be known only by the analysis of the form with all its constituent elements, its signs, symbols, psychic and dramatic forces, etc.It is in these terms that structure and symbol are the crucial principles in the understanding of religious imagery.

The definition does not apply only to images and their physical, perceptual structure. It is the basic characteristic of human thought.

The ordinary experience of each one of us should suffice to show how we relate to our world and raises the question, how it could ever have been thought that decisive thinking could be done in words apart from the actualities of our common life.

All of us, all the time, experience the world in terms of images, seen things. Actually, we experience things in several sensory modes other than sight and the full experience of the world requires the coordinated activity of all the senses; the seen image is an abstraction. Nevertheless, we see things all the time, even in our dreams. Many of these things are relatively neutral and most are background for the things that hold our attention. Each thing has its own dramatic place in our lives, its own emotional resonance, its own personal and public significance. A Madonna is one thing, a tree or a machine something quite different.

We experience things by means of their shape and their sensory qualities; "form" is not merely a term used in criticism but a fundamental means for experiencing our world. Every experienced thing has its form, the sum total of its sensory qualities, its placement in relation to other things (including ourselves) its color weight, texture, its bounding surfaces, its weight, and so on.

In the making of images, the thing itself can be abstracted from many of its relations. Certain sensory elements can be abstracted for distinct presentation.

On Mykonos I experienced the white cubic form of houses, the spaces of streets and squares, placed in the brightness of the sun between the blue of the sky and the different blue of the sea. What I actually "saw" was colored films, surfaces without depth or weight. My brain-mind constructed the scene from the learned experience of forms and by the movement through spaces, around three dimensional forms, which is the reality of seeing..

The whole of the experience was saturated with emotional meaning made up of time (a momentary visitor caught up in the suspension of normal time), space (the intensity of enclosure and release), heat, the brilliance of light, the contrast with my own ordinary experience of brick or wooden houses amidst trees and grass). Each of the elements of the experience can be abstracted for separate consideration.

The images I made, for all their "realism", are at a high level of abstraction. Except in memory, much of the emotion has disappeared within the ordinariness of the context of viewing. I think I see houses and streets; actually I see colored light on a screen and construct an image from that. The image is made up of lines, surfaces and colors, each of which can be thought of separately.

This complex process constitutes the language of images. The elements of form need to be sketched in order to encourage awareness. There is no abstract scheme of questions to put to a work of art but there can be an awareness of the sorts of things to look for and respond to.

THE COMPONENTS OF THE VISUAL LANGUAGE

The image, the work of art is composed of three elements: matter, form, and content. The three terms are easy to define but each is extraordinarily complex. Matter is the physical material formed by the artist into the work of art. Form is the result of the artist's action on the material, the shape given the material by the hand and mind, the thinking hand of the artist. Content is all that is communicated through and by means of the form.

Matter:

A dominant element in the character of the image. A vital part of all true images. The true image makers think in and by means of the material of their work. This makes teaching difficult since it is done by colored ink on paper or colored light on a screen, which are different materials.

Subject matter:

As its form suggests, "subject matter" is part of the material of the work of art, not its content. This distinction is critical. Subject matter is whatever is represented by the form. In popular usage and much professional usage, an image is understood as an image of something, which is its subject matter. This is too limited a view but not wholly wrong.

Form:

The elements of form are simple but the possibilities of their use and combination are infinite. Since the represented subject is part of the material, it is part of the forming. Forming as craft or art is a basic act of thought

In reality, these distinctions are not always clear. The menhir is a form and, as a form, marks the center, which is also an element of form but equally part of an image of the cosmos and of order. The cave is a form but not in the formalist sense; it is a major symbol, and a part of the symbolic vocabulary of religion.

Content:

"Content" is often used as synonymous with the subject, which confuses understanding. Content can be pointed to and talked about but the pointing and the talking are not the content, which is integral to the work.

"Modern" criticism often dealt with images as though the only thing that mattered was the form. Since this is clearly not true, formalism fell into disrepute. Popular approaches to imagery considered only the subject. "Postmodern" criticism has returned to this view, considering primarily the political reference of the subject. Since the image is inescapably form and subject, neither formalism nor popular and postmodern criticism suffices.

Both subject and form have their own content. It is their interaction that finally determines the character of the image.

Notes on the definitions:

The problematic term is content. Matter and form have a univocal reference. "Content" is used in various ways, sometimes as "subject matter", sometimes "meaning". Neither suffices for "content". "Meaning" is inadequate for serious use. It is treated as though it were contained in the work as water is contained in the pitcher, to be verbally poured out into the mind. There is no agreed reference to the term; philosophers cannot agree on what "meaning" means and aestheticians cannot agree on what a work of art is, much less how it means.

If we use content for subject, we have two terms for one thing and none for the other. Content is not form but form is both part of and a vehicle for content.

THE IMAGE AS MATTER

Every seen image is a physical material. Before it can be seen as an image it is unformed matter. It becomes an image only by the craft of the maker. The result (when it is successful) is stillness, suspension of act before contemplation, but the result is achieved only by process. The process, the craft, is determined by the mind working within the limits and according to the possibilities of the material. The dialectic is powerful.

At one time and place, only certain materials are available, or are so dominant that the formal thought takes place in terms of that material.

Greece, for example, is a stony country. While different stones were available, during the classical period marble was decidedly the favored material. It is an intermediate material, soft enough to be easily shaped, hard enough to hold fine details, lustrous to the point of translucency.[4]

At other times, materials are chosen according to deeply felt psychic needs. Egypt had many stones. Their image makers often chose to work in such stone as diorite which is extremely hard and difficult to carve, not lending itself to fine details, but to simple masses of great endurance. It used to be said that Jan van Eyck invented oil painting. This is not true; oil as a painting medium had been known for a long time. In the fifteenth century in Flanders, there was a profound and inchoate spiritual need that was met by van Eyck's use of the luminosity of oil paints.

(This event raises important and unanswerable questions having to do with historical causation and individual creativity. The response to van Eyck's achievement indicates that there was an intellectual and spiritual need which he met. Was this a need for luminosity or was it a more generalized yearning that might have been met by some other great act of creativity? If it were a need for luminosity, does this mean that, in the absence of van Eyck, some other artist would have met the need? Is it valid to assume a "need" or did the presence of a great creative act generate a new kind of consciousness that we interpret as a need? England is amply supplied with stone. It had sculpture during the Middle Ages and then none of consequence until the twentieth century. Why? The Chinese were an inventive people with an ample variety of materials available. Why were their intellectual and spiritual needs met for so long by ink on paper or silk?)

Every material has its own character, its own possibilities and limitations. Every formal idea calls for certain materials in order for its destiny to be fulfilled. Artistic thinking is inseparable from the character of the material. The fullest study of images, therefore, can never be detached from the most sensitive awareness of the materials of their embodiment.

---

[4] Care is necessary in these formulations. Things we admire about Greek images, such as their pearly white surfaces, were at least partially obscured by paint. The Greeks also used other materials.

THE IMAGE AS FORM: A VOCABULARY

The word "vocabulary" contains a danger, as though this listing were no more than a glossary of speech. The terms should be understood as designators, signs, of realities, each of which represents a substantial human achievement. (Achievement in the sense of discovery, not making; these things are parts of the real but the discovery of them is fundamental. The particulars of their use is achievement as making.) Furthermore, the terms do not designate things that are merely part of the esoterica of imagery. Each one designates something that is part of the daily experience of every living creature.

The elements of form are not form; vocabulary and syntax are not language. The elements can, for the mind's sake, be isolated, although they do not and cannot exist in isolation from each other. There cannot even be an accurate listing of them, for all the elements are protean in themselves and in their relations. The major ones have a singular psychic, symbolic and expressive authority that sets them apart.

While they do not exist separately in the actual work, they are identifiable elements of our experience of the world. Each has a clear and distinct symbolic character and, therefore, a clear and distinct symbolic role. They are ingredient to human existence, human experience of the world. As elements of the work of art they have a tangible, perceptible existence which can be dealt with objectively. Therefore, they can figure in the textbook accounts of formal analysis and be taught to beginning students. They are properly understood only as freighted with the most fundamental meanings which are incorporated into the work of art by the creativity of the maker.

Mass

Actual or represented three dimensional form with emphasis on solidity and weight. Mass is symbolically as important as space, for it is masses that define the action of gravity in space. Human life is the action of body masses on the surface of the earth under the authority of gravity. The image of mass in space, the image as mass, is the symbolic condensation of the sense of human existence held by a particular people. Both the actual and fictive treatment of masses defines the action of gravity and thus determines the place of objects and persons in space.

A statue is not first of all a representation; it is first of all a mass in space subject to and defining the work of gravity. That symbolic act is joined with the representation to form a total image. A painting, on the other hand, is surface and holds all its forms to the surface, or it carves out a fictive space that, in its origin and its shape, sets out a vision of meaning.

Those who find it difficult to think in terms of human personality as formed, actually and religiously, around its formal involvements should remember that among the earliest human acts beyond those necessary for survival are the symbolic use of space and mass in the form of the painted cave and the menhir. Both the human mind and symbolic sexuality have their beginning in such forming which led to the establishment of architectural space, that prime symbol of a culture's religion, and the upright stone, the column, that eventually becomes the statue, the symbolic condensation of the human body.

Space

Space is one of the prime symbols in art, one of the elements that most clearly sets out the image of order and relation that informs the work, thus one of the absolutely prime religious acts. Space has both shape and direction. In its shape, determined by its bounding edges, space can be a cave, a tent, a fantasy. It can be majestic or intimate, constricting or expansive. It can be segmented into units or be one all-including unity. It can be negative and inert, simply that which exists between objects, or it can be active and positive, that which contains objects. It can be forceful and directional, the pilgrimage to a goal (most Christian churches), or it can be wandering and indirect, a path through nature (Chinese landscape painting).

Space can dissolve mass as in Gothic architecture or be dominated by mass as in Romanesque architecture, or the two can be harmoniously balanced as in Renaissance architecture. Space and mass interpenetrate in Japanese architecture, while North Indian temples have a small, cruelly compressed space within an extraordinarily dynamic and energetic mass. All these are prime symbols of their culture's meanings and are, therefore, elements of the religion of that culture.

Volume and Surface

The inseparability of the elements is most evident here. Space does not exist without bounding edges, either actual or represented. A cave, or a cave-like space hollowed into a hill, is a space within an amorphous mass of material whose inner surface establishes or is established by the space. A tent is a thin surface without mass. A Byzantine church has the necessary mass but the mass is invisible behind the surface which has been transformed by mosaics into pure depthless surface. A surface which does not simply bound space but contains it is volume. Volume is actual or represented three dimensional form with emphasis on surface and contained space.

The occasion for vision as the primary experience of the world is surface. The plane surface, flat or curved, is the location of most images. A painting, which is literally all surface, contains fictive masses and volumes in rhythmic interaction.

Color

Color is divided into <u>hue</u> (that which gives the color its name), <u>intensity</u> or <u>saturation</u> (the purity of the hue; i.e., pink is a red of lower intensity), and <u>value</u> (its relation on a scale from white to black; e.g., yellow is a higher value hue than purple.) Color can be descriptive (reproducing as closely as possible the <u>local color)</u>, or emotionally and dramatically expressive or both.

Color is the instrument of all visual perception since we do not see solid forms but colored films. This is too literal and applies only to the retinal image; we see with the mind, not only the retina. Out of remembered experience, we relate the colored films to size, placement, texture, all the instruments of identity so we see things, not the retinal image. The painter can return to the colored films ("impressionism") or use other modes of color experience. It is a primary instrument of representation. It is also one of the major instruments of expression; each color at each value level has its own characteristic resonance. Color, therefore, is one of the primary instruments in establishing the emotional tonality of the work; following Kandinsky, color is the most direct means of recreating in the spectator the "spiritual" state of the artist (see Chapter 12).

Line.

A two dimensional mark. A major instrument of expression and division. Line can more nearly have a separate existence than most of the elements since drawing is only line. This is not entirely true; line does not exist alone but on a support, paper or some other surface. The character of the line is determined in part by the character of the surface, by its color, its texture, its size and shape. The line is alive, not simply on the surface, but in the surface.

Line is a logical distinction, dividing one side from another. It divides inside from outside, defining the logic of relation between inside and outside (which is a primary and primal human experience). It divides the surface into shapes, divides the surface from the depth. It has the expressive character of personality. It can present each item in the integrity of its separate existence or dissolve distinction into the flow of the whole. A simple drawing can be a symbol of cosmic order.

Geometric Shapes

Circles, rectangles, etc. Geometric forms generated by a line enclosing a plane surface. Important as forms and as archetypes. As archetype, the circle is the eternal return, endless movement. The rotation of the sky.

Center

All forms, natural and geometric, have a center, the point of equilibrium. A basic archetype, the point from which and to which all movement is organized.

Axis

An imaginary line drawn through the center of a form. An enclosed two dimensional surface has length and height. A three dimensions form has three axes, adding depth.

Frame

A line separating a representation from its surroundings. Often literal, as in the frame of a painting. The frame partly determines the relation of the image to the spectator.

Of these elements, the frame is the only one that does not occur naturally but is a human construct. It is a basic part of most images and it is a kind of image in its own right. It isolates the image, sets it apart for contemplation. Without the frame, the image could not have the full effect of depth. The framed surface is not inert. It has its two axes controlling the energies of the surface, its four edges and four corners as boundaries.

The invention of the frame is one of the dividing lines between the "primitive" and the first "civilizations". In the modern language of images, framing, as all these elements, has become more complex. Framing in movies and television is a different matter from framing a painting. The relation of image to context or setting is new and distinctive in magazines, television, etc.

Movement

Movement can be represented or actual. Represented and fictive movement puts the idea and the direction of movement into the formal structure of the work. Fictive movement becomes actual when it involves the directed movement of the eye of the spectator around and through the work. The handling of movement is primary in the establishing of static or dynamic image.

Movement generates <u>rhythm</u>. Rhythm is primarily a musical term, but the time is past when it was possible to speak of the arts of space and the arts of time, although music will retain the primary responsibility for the symbolic shape of time in the imagination. Rhythm is so important an element that it can hardly be restricted to the movement of the eye from part to part; in a real sense, it defines the character of the work itself. Every style, every work within the style, has a characteristic rhythm that, as much as any other element, defines the distinctiveness of the work.

To speak of rhythm as so fundamental is to appeal to a process as intimate and as identifiable as our own flesh, not to mysticism. The power of the arts rests to a considerable degree on the fact that their rhythms are in good part the rhythms of the human body and the natural order, the rhythms of breathing, of the heartbeat, of desire with its tension and release, the rhythms of the seasons, of the storm, the night, the river. These rhythms are brought under the control of the rhythms of human meaning and purpose as engendered by the controlling image at the center of a religion. The failure of the churches in our own day is nowhere more evident than in their surrender of the forming of rhythm to forces that contradict what they are supposed to stand for.

Modeling

The use of light and shade or hues to give the illusion of the third dimension to forms.

Proportion

The relative size of things within a representation. Size may be determined descriptively; that is, things can be proportioned to each other according to their actual size modified by their placement in space (more distant things appear smaller than closer ones) or they can be proportioned according to their importance (kings or saints portrayed as larger than ordinary people).

Perspective

The adjustment of composition, proportion, color, etc., to give the illusion of depth in a two-dimensional painting or drawing. Linear perspective uses various geometries to define the third dimension. Aerial perspective uses a natural phenomenon, the fact that things in the far distance appear bluer, to suggest space.

Light

Light is an independent element in architecture and sculpture. In painting it is a consequence of the handling of color. Both formally and emotionally, light functions distinctively within a work, whether it be painting (where the light is fictive) or sculpture and architecture (where it can be both fictive and literal). Light is an instrument of unification or separation. It relates the work to the world of the spectator or closes it off. It is a principal instrument in the creation of a sense of transcendence and a major symbolic form in religions.

Composition

Composition includes the placement of shapes in relation to each other, the relation of figure to ground, the relation of the work to its edges or bounding context, symmetry or asymmetry, balance and tension, the relation of center, axes, and edges. It can be the rejection of all dominant ordering. Composition is the setting out of the principle of relation and is a vital feature in the analysis of the religion set out in the work. The central importance of composition and design is the reason that analyses of ornament and nonrepresentational art is as central to the investigation as the more overtly "religious" elements of represented persons and expressive forms.

Composition does not refer only to the ordering of represented forms within the work. The surface to be painted, the block to be carved, are not inert but have their own structures and energies. The axes determine direction and stability, the edges are both limits and forces.

SUBJECT MATTER.

Subject matter is also a form. Subject matter is representation, drama, etc. It is part of the material to be formed. It is form in several senses. Organic forms can be abstracted into geometrical elements, a basic act in the human search for understanding. Positions establish certain forms; a seated Madonna and Child makes a pyramid, a standing figure a column. Gestures establish direction and therefore relations. Every subject contains its own energies which are psychic forces that become elements in the composition; a seated nude is a powerful psychic and, therefore, formal energy.

THE TWO-DIMENSIONAL IMAGE

> Remember that a picture — before being a battlehorse, a nude woman, or some anecdote — is essentially a plane surface covered with colors assembled in a certain order.
>
> Maurice Denis

The most powerful, the most important, of the elements of the two dimensional image is not the representation but the plane surface. The plane surface is not merely a support for the painting. This is most evident in drawings, which are marks on a surface, but clearly the surface is a vital part even of prehistoric painting. There is not, strictly speaking, a plane surface in a cave, for the wall is irregular and the painters often painted the animal around some swelling in the wall that suggested a hip or shoulder, making it a sort of very low relief sculpture. Nonetheless, it is a surface, treated as a surface.

As the invention of the base for sculpture was a fundamental moment in the history of human thought, so the invention of the frame was equally fundamental. I do not speak of the literal frame, the one we use to support a painting hanging on the wall, although that, too, is an important part of the complete analysis. It is, rather, the defining edges of the surface of the plane. This is almost always, almost everywhere, rectilinear. Some primitives ignore such a frame altogether. Some contemporary artists use differently shaped plane surfaces. Renaissance artists sometimes used a circle, medieval paintings sometimes had a curved, arched top. But the rectangle is the dominant form, particularly in Western image making.

The shape is important, for it defines the internal forces on the picture surface. Just as a sculpture has axes, so does a painting, for it is bisected vertically and horizontally by lines that are as effective as they are invisible. They are the organizing armature of the surface. The edges are nearly as much a part of the internal forces as the axes. The crossing points at the center and at the four corners exert their own gravitational pull. The plane surface is not an inert support for the work of the painter but is a field of forces. Each stroke of ink or paint on the surface becomes an element in that field, disturbing and realigning the inherent forces. A painting has a life of its own.

The strokes of paint begin the making of a vital element: the <u>picture plane</u>. The picture plane is not the same thing as the painting's surface although necessarily, coincident with it. It is the imaginary front surface of the represented space, from which the space recedes. A basic, elemental, character of the painting is determined by whether the figures and the action are held to the picture plane and affirm its force or are turned to move into the represented space. With many forms of painting the distinction has no meaning.

Here, too, elemental descriptive matters become important to the interpretation. If the picture plane is firmly established and controls the composition, then the represented image is something other than the spectator, establishing a separate world of its own. If the action moves back into the space the spectator becomes a part of the enacted event or otherwise related to it. The variations on these preliminary distinctions are so many and so different that it takes a lifetime of study to get some sense of them.[5]

Composition is the arrangement of forms within the field of forces, the arrangements on the surface and the apparent relationships in the fictive depth. Composition is the structure of relations. When these relations are firmly established, the effect is "organic unity", a cliché of criticism.

The represented forms, the images as such, are constructed by means of line, shading, and color. Line is the instrument of distinction, of separation. If the line is used to set off separate figures in clear outlines (contours), the effect is to affirm separation and individuality. If color predominates without clear contours, or if line suggests interior forms without emphasis on contours, the effect is wholeness, the individual as a part of the whole.

Line is expressive as well as descriptive; imagine the emotional difference between a sharp, jagged line and a softly curving one. Color is also one of the chief carriers of the emotional tonality of the painting.

Understanding images requires understanding the distinctive character of imagery, not simply as subject and form, but as logic and rhetoric, for our logics and our rhetorics shape our world and shape who we are. Only a few elementary points can be developed. A full treatment of the logic and rhetoric of images requires a book.

Statues and buildings are things, objects, palpable, heavy. Both are in space, both are masses in space. Whatever their relation to their contained and containing space, they are thought out as masses under the force of gravity, required to be faithful to the forces of gravity. They are organized around the geometric axes of a space that is defined by gravity, both in the masses of the material and our own perceiving bodies, standing with weight on the earth, feeling the verticality of our own bodies as they stand and move on the earth. We live and move in the web of relations to things. When we confront something, or are confronted by it, we are, at least

---

[5] Art historians will recognize the presence in this distinction and some of the others of Heinrich Wölfflin's great book, *Principles of Art History.* Students who approach the book recognizing that it does not set out the principles of art history and that its pattern of historical development should be resolutely ignored will find it still one of the best introductions to the careful seeing of a work of art.

subliminally, aware of the multitude of lines and planes that connect our bodies and the contemplated things to all the other bodies and things.

The picture, the image as picture, is a thing to be looked at. It is there, I am here, apart from the image. The picture — painted or drawn or printed — is more than just an object, a thing, but it is likely, without preparation, to be looked at as a thing which differs from other things because it calls to mind things other than itself. Now we need to see painting as a particular kind of image, itself standing for a form-world.

To see images only as represented subjects is to miss much of the power of images, for images do more than address our contemplative minds; they mold the imagination to certain forms of the world. It is not only their emotional and their intellectual force that makes them important in the study of religion. It is the way they form the world and form the imagination by the image of that world. This process can be experienced most vividly in architecture (which we experience by involving our bodies directly in it) and by sculpture (which confronts us almost as another person entering our world). So prepared we can turn to painting as another mode of involving our selves in the image. (If the typesetter and proof reader have done their work properly, note that the statement is "our selves", a noun rather than a reflexive pronoun, "ourselves".)

Every mode of making images is a form-world, a way of thinking about the world. Every form-world, therefore, is an image of order as well as a means for interpreting the images as representation. A form-world is one of the imaginative fundamentals of cultures. It is, therefore, basic to the understanding of culture and the religion that is part of the culture. Mykonos is a form-world, intense and distinctive, a way of living in the world.

"Two dimensional imagery" includes all imagery on a flat surface. Therefore the subject is all images made by marks on a flat surface: paintings, mosaics, drawings, prints, photographs, the "graphic arts". Movies, television, computers have a logic and a rhetoric of their own which sets them a little apart from earlier imagery.

The first problem is part of the definition: the image is both a series of marks on a surface and a representation. The logic of the marks is one of distinction and classification: front-back, side-to-side, up-down. Every mark, every line, is a division of the surface, both as one side-other side, and inside-outside.

Neither the representation nor the marks that evoke it can exist without the other or be seen without some awareness of the other. There is a considerable variation between those makers of images who assert the materiality of the surface (Rembrandt's "impasto", heavy mounds of paint) and those who try to efface the surface in favor of the vividness of reproduction of appearance. Flemish painting is a salutary illustration; even under magnification it is difficult to see the brush strokes but the brilliance of the paint makes the presence of the surface insistent.

The second problem is equally inescapable: the relation between surface and depth. Any single mark on the surface generates a slight sense of depth. Any representation evokes something of the third dimension.

A painting, too, is a thing, an object in our space. It is the only object whose objecthood can disappear behind illusion. "Can". It does not have to. The first great division in painting is between those paintings that preserve or assert their objecthood and those that assert the illusion created on the surface. Like most such neat pairs, this one is much too simple; there is a nearly infinite variety of possibilities between the two extremes. The issue is partly technical; it requires certain techniques to produce the illusion, the fictive reality of the painting. Behind the technique is an issue that is more than technical, since it is a matter of placing the artist and the spectator in the world or over against a world.

Little words carry much meaning: "the" world or "a" world. In the first, the painting is an object in our own world (whatever we think that world is). In the second, the artist creates an imagined world that may or may not be like the world the rest of us experience in our ordinary living.

Most painting in most cultures during most history has been a matter of making objects in the world. In some cultures, particularly Europe and America since the early Renaissance to the end of the nineteenth century, painting is making a fictitious world on the other side of the frame. (Much of modern imagery is still the making of such a fictitious world, whereas modern art has returned to the making of objects. Many people are uncomfortable with modern art because they expect art to be an opening into an imagined world, not an object intruding into out world.)

The difference is determined by the way represented objects are placed in space or, rather, whether three dimensional space is represented at all. The "linear perspective" of the Renaissance is not the only way to represent space in painting. Placing bodies in space is an essential means for the fullest presentation of narrative.

The earliest paintings that survive are placed on the defining walls of a space. They function inseparably from the formation of the space. Mural art is a major art form, a major mode of thinking, throughout the history of art. The example chosen for treatment here was the middle Byzantine church (Daphni) with its mosaic decoration defining the space, a task normally assigned to the mass of the material. At the other extreme is the easel painting, which exists as an object in space, to be contemplated for itself alone. Even so, an easel painting is normally hung on the wall and is seen in relation to the wall. Some mosaics and other forms of inlay are on the floor. Navaho dry paintings are made on the ground (and are temporary). In between are the many paintings on portable supports: book illuminations, Chinese scrolls, Australian bark paintings, etc.

The issue is the mode of response. Vision is the primary instrument of response to every art work but architecture requires not only vision but the actual participation of the whole perceptual organism; the first kind of mural painting is a part of that response as well as fundamentally shaping it. An independent easel painting relies on vision alone and whatever empathetic response the artist wishes to arouse in the contemplating spectator.

One logic, one rhetoric, is not better than another; they do different things, represent different images of the relation of humans to the world, different understandings of the function of the image. One is not more religious than the others; they define different kinds of religion.[6]

THE THREE DIMENSIONAL IMAGE

The instruments of the analysis are, perhaps, simpler for sculpture than for painting. Subject matter is far more limited; the majority of sculptures are the single human body, clothed or nude. These bodies can represent humans or divinities. There is also much sculpture of animals, vegetative material and non-representational forms.

---

[6] In view of the inclination of many people to define "multiculturalism" as requiring the condemnation of "the West" or, at best, making all cultures equal, it is well to point out that only the Western attitude makes possible this sympathetic understanding of other religions. Western perspective, by finding a place for the spectator to stand apart from the seen world, enables the spectator to describe the thing seen more nearly in its own terms; it is improbable that a member of some other culture, untouched by the principles of Western historical study, could do for Western space representation what Otto Demus has done for the Byzantines. (See Chapter 10)) This note should make clear that technical matters such as linear perspective are not incidental to the study of images but are basic in their presentation of the worlds people inhabit, within which they work out their religious destiny.

Sculpture can use many different materials: carved stone or wood, cast bronze (molten bronze poured into a mold), terra cotta. The character of the material determines much of the impact of the statue. Marble and granite are two very different materials.

The geometry of the three dimensional image.

Nearly all known sculptured images from the beginning of the earliest "high" cultures in Mesopotamia and Egypt do not begin with unformed material, but with a material that has, first of all, been made into a geometric block, rectangular in the case of stone, cylindrical or rectangular in the case of wood (remember the quotation from Isaiah.[7]. This is not true of prehistoric sculpture (the so-called "Venus" of Willendorf).

Each body part, by definition a varied organic form, can be abstracted to a basic geometric form, which is an element in a specific kind of order. While this is a common procedure, it is most fully developed in African sculpture and early modern painting (cubism).

The historical rhetoric of masses in space can illustrate content. The epoch inaugurated around 4,000 BC was, on a varying time schedule, world-wide and built on the establishment of certain basic symbolic principles:

1. The establishment of the centralized state and the dominance of patriarchal order in a hierarchical political order.[8]

2. The dominance of the vertical. This is a concomitant of the first; a centralized state requires a ruler who is elevated "above" the subjects. In our study, the vertical is seen first in the central importance of the pyramid and the Sumerian ziggurat, each marking the vertical connection between earth and sky; the vertical as the first principle of cosmic order.

3. The birth of the gods. Where before there had been non-directional space and generalized natural energies, now there is directional space and

---

[7] The exception — a large exception — is the clay used to "model" the figures the mold for cast sculptures is made from. The distinction between carved and modeled sculpture is basic. Many modeled figures are thought out in terms established by carved figures but this would be a separate study.

[8] This is by no means a pejorative statement in the modern fashion. Hierarchy and patriarchy were essential for the organization of a complex and violent world. The world is now a very different place and there is no reason to think they are any longer necessary, at least in their inherited forms

the embodiment of the various energies in identifiable personages. It is possible that the earliest of these was "The Great Mother", the mysterious, awesome energy of fertility becoming, to varying degrees, personal.

4. The movement from the animal to the human as the primary subject of imagery, the gods seen in human form.

The succession of figures in the demonstrations in the text is drawn from the distinctive development that took place in countries bordering on the Mediterranean. It is an instructive series since each stage is demonstrably connected with those that went before, yet the variety of cultures shows, most instructively, the range of ideas that are contained within the initiating idea. Other great sculptural traditions (the Indian, the African, the pre-Columbian American, etc.) are necessarily less varied and we have a smaller body of evidence for their beginnings.

The distinctive ways of handling these common themes is the primary concern of the analyses sketched in these chapters. The major distinction or cut appears for our purposes with the change in space conception from a primacy of external to a primacy of internal space, which is the concern of the next outline. At approximately the same time there appeared in the west the fundamental transformation marked by the dominance of monotheism in Judaism, Christianity and Islam. This entailed not only a fundamental shift in the conception of God but, necessarily, in the conception of the human.

THE VOCABULARY AND SYNTAX OF SPACE

I. The elements (the "vocabulary") of architecture are few and simple. It is the manner of their composition (syntax) that is important.

  A. Structural elements

    1. Mass as enclosure: walls; undefined mass surrounding the cave.

    2. Mass as support and supported.

    Walls as supporting flat ceiling or round vault.

    Post (column) as vertical element supporting lintel (horizontal element) or arch.

    3. These exhaust the elements of traditional architecture, although the possibilities of their treatment is unlimited. Modern architecture adds the cantilever, various tensile systems.

B. Structural forces.

All building is the adjustment of masses under the force of gravity.

1. Post and lintel (Parthenon): inert weight of horizontal masses on support. Pressure and tendency of the horizontal element (lintel) to break
2. Arch and dome: inert pressure downward, active pressure sideways requiring buttresses.
3. Chinese and Japanese wooden structures, several modern systems depend on interaction of linear elements in tension.

C. Symbolic vocabulary.

1. Walls as enclosing mass and as limit.
2. Openings as practical necessities and as breaks in the bounding limits.
3. Darkness and light.
4. Space and its shapes.
   Geometric patterns: circle, square, rectangles, as single or multiple.
5. Rhythms: of light and dark, mass and space, walls and openings, succession of elements, interior and exterior.
6. Movement and stasis:

II. Symbolic forms

A. Space as cosmic image.

Space in its many shapes is the prime symbol of architecture as itself and as defining the relation of humans to the cosmos as they understand it.

B. Mass as function and symbolic form

1. Mass (material)is the essential instrument for shaping space.
2. Mass as earth (cave) and as symbolic of the earth or the physical forces of earth.

C. Ornament

1. Abstract forms, vegetable forms, human forms.
2. Defines and reveals (or obscures) the enclosing mass.

All these elements in their multiple combinations and the resulting intellectual and affective consequence make up the most complete single statement of a religion.

PART THREE
THE PRINCIPLES OF ANALYSIS
AND INTERPRETATION

Since the concern of this study is the seen image, the image as embodied in a physical material and not the "image" of the politician or advertiser, there can be no distinction between image and art. All images are works of art so the vocabulary requires the vocabulary of the study of art. People make works of art for a variety of reasons, not all relevant to this study, which is concerned with those intended for religious uses or embodying religious convictions.

Interpretation is not like scientific explanation (as understood in the older positivistic science). There is no schematic procedure to follow to a demonstrable conclusion. Neither is there any systematic analytical process. Even the hermeneutic circle does not suffice; it is more a hermeneutic web or network of interwoven processes. The most we can do is set out, by way of summary, certain principles for general guidance.

Before turning to the procedures of analysis, certain principles need to be examined.

THE PRINCIPLE OF CONTEXT

The other principles have to do with the work itself. This encompasses all the factors preceding and surrounding the work. Logically, it should precede the others. Humanly, that has dangers, if context is taken as cause.

Codes

There are many codes, the codes of representation that are available as opportunity and as limit, the various signs and codes of dress, gesture, position, etc., incorporated into the representation, the social and political codes having to do with gender, social and economic class, the corpus of possible subjects, etc., all those qualities of style that determine the corpus of forms available for immediate use.

Function and Use.

All images are made for some purpose, including the pleasure of making an image. For the most part the purpose, the use, can be determined only by historical and sociological investigation and depends heavily on the use of written documents and other types of evidence. The danger lies in ascribing to an image a purpose that is neither inherent in it nor part of its own context but is derived from some purpose alien to it. At the same time, since the image as experienced is a product of the interaction of the spectator and the image produced by the original maker, it can become a different work with a different purpose. An example is the altarpiece moved from its devotional context and purpose to a museum where it becomes part of a different symbol system.

A purpose presupposes an intention, which is complicated. There is the intention of the patron who commissioned the work and decided its purpose. There is the intention of the maker, which may coincide only in part with that of the patron. There is a gap between conscious intention and realization caused by the apparently anthropomorphic principle of the "intention of the work". Obviously works cannot have an intention (although it may seem that way to the maker). The nature of a material imposes a range of characteristics, certain possibilities and certain limitations. The chosen form has an internal logic of its own that functions as a kind of intention.

Then there are the unconscious functions of the work, that are the special concern of so much contemporary criticism, the use of the work to support the interests of this or that group, or the unconscious purposes of the maker.

Finally, discussions of context as the determining historical setting of an image (work of art) often assume that we have the context available to us. It is well to remember that context is part of history and has all the characteristics of history. History does not "exist"; we have a wide, and wild assortment of documents, reminiscences and artifacts out of which we construct, as best we can, a picture (image) of the past time. With all the wonderful achievements of historical study we should remember the confusions, the deficiencies, the imbalances in our evidence. We construct the past, the contxt, much as we make works of art.

THE PRINCIPLE OF RELATION AND RESPONSE

"Response", however, involves more than simply the sensory mode used in the perception of the image. It involves the full range of relations of the spectator to the image, not just those relations of the elements within the image. There are three distinct, interlocking sets of relations:

1. The relation of the image maker to the subject and to the things represented.
2. The relation of the maker to the image, including the signs of the handiwork of themaker or the absence of such signs.
3. The relation of the spectator to the image and, by means of the image, to the subject and to the representation.

Each of these is too complex to be summarized; they must be established in each analysis. Certain Egyptian sculptures are simple; they show no sign of the handwork of the maker and were placed in a tomb and never seen. Most images are not so simple. Furthermore, even when it is clear that the image maker intended the response to the image to be thus and so, there is no assurance that spectators will respond according to instruction. It is easy to imagine the Egyptian's astonishment to see his images in museums, being looked at "aesthetically".

THE PRINCIPLE OF STRUCTURE

This, the final act of interpretation, is not separable from the principle of relation, for it is the determining principle of relation, the thing that holds everything else together. This principle raises all sorts of analytical and philosophical, even psychological, problems.

Psychologically, it is related to the question of the person or the individual. It is not unlike the assumption that there is a central core personality that determines what a person is, a proposition widely denied today. The response may be pragmatic: some people achieve, at least to a greater degree than most of us, some integration of personality and purpose, despite the inconsistencies of act and attitude that are part of being human. Some images as works of art achieve a higher degree of integration than others.

Philosophically, it raises the question (or specter) of the essence, that has haunted our thinking since the Greeks, the notion that within appearances and physical embodiment there is an invisible essence that determines what the thing is. Structure, on the analogy and the pattern of architecture, is an identifiable principle.

The analytical problem is the procedure for identifying the structure.

PROCEDURES OF ANALYSIS.

Our purpose is understanding what an image stands for and, specifically, what religious attitudes can be apprehended by means of it. The procedure of understanding has three stages: description, analysis, interpretation.[9] To use these properly, the word "stages" needs to be taken seriously. They are not three separate acts but three stages in one continuous act.

Description

Just what the word usually means, a verbal account of all the things that can be seen by the careful observer. Every description is, inescapably a form of interpretation. In principle, any intelligent, untrained person can describe a work of art. In practice, things are not so simple. We tend to see those things we are trained to see but also we see those things we expect to see.[10] Even professionals are often chagrined to find things in well known works of art they had never noticed before. Description is a necessary first stage. We must first know what is there.

In a looser sense of the word, description includes all those things that come under the heading of necessary information about the work, both internal and external. Internally, it is necessary to know much about

---

[9] These terms are used in the General Introduction to this series. I assume they mean much the same thing there as they do here.
[10] At a conference, I met a young artist who was wearing a button stating, "I'll see it when I believe it". I told him that he had summed up a good part of my teaching.

materials and their attendant techniques; each material makes possible some things and prevents others. It is necessary to know the iconography, the subject and its details, the images in the specific sense.

Grasping the semiotic function of the image is a necessary part of the description. Its function is a part of the work; it is not its definition. All images signify many things, some consciously intended, some not consciously part of their program, some attributed by the critic. Many aspects of works of art signify the hierarchical or egalitarian order of social structures, the sense of gendered meaning as an interpretation of maleness and femaleness and their relations, and various repressed sexual desires. Whether these are truly in the work or merely attributed to the work by the modern critic as a part of a modern political program is a matter than can be determined only by the analysis of the specific work in its context.

It is necessary to know as much as can be known about a work of art, both in terms of what is to be seen (the things represented in the work, and in terms of their habitual reference.

Analysis

Analysis is not a separate act but the description carried from the surface into the structure of relations within the image. Analysis is concerned with form as the interpretation of the subject but the character of the subject, as part of the material, is also an object of the analysis.

A simple example: one sculptured figure may show a man with his arms hanging down by his sides, another with his arms or an arm extended; these are descriptive facts. They may have no large analytical or interpretive significance but merely represent different subjects. The characteristic gesture of a Roman orator was the upraised right arm, which is the concern of iconography (the study of subject matter). The representation, therefore, is no more than a descriptive record of what happened. In other statues there may be a deeper significance; one manifests a static relation to space, the other a dynamic relation, matters of great analytical importance.

Analysis must establish the character of all the formal aspects of the work and their relations to each other; relation is one of the key terms of analysis. The formal structure of the work is the force that holds everything together and gives access to the significance of the work.

While form is the primary locus of analysis, a necessary condition for analysis is the material, which is both possibility and limit for every image; much of the character of every image derives from its material.

Equally, the subject introduces its own psychic energies into the formal relations and these have to be taken into account.

"Formal values" have their own symbolic interest: the respect for material and for its necessary procedures that are part of all craft; delight in accomplishment, in the setting and resolution of problems; the resolution of complexity, simplicity, wholeness, and unity; etc.

The spectator from another culture, seeing the Great Buddha of Kamakura, sees the skillful harmonizing of long, slow, curves, rhymed, repeated, counterpointed, and can feel the same delighted admiration that is accorded a fine dancer or a splendid athlete. The delight itself, if it is to be more than dandified appreciation, has its own human significance: a complex action resolved into completion, human possibility brought to fulfillment. This is a proper part of what is required to preserve the work from reduction to mere signification. Nevertheless, for the sculptor, all that is means and not ends. The particular formal harmonies of the work state, present, show, a conception of, an image of, the Buddha and, correspondingly, of general human purpose as understood by Buddhists.

Interpretation

Again, not a separate act but analysis carried to the fullest understanding of the image.

Arms hanging down or extended is a descriptive fact. A static or a dynamic relation to space is a formal fact determined analytically. A full analysis that apprehends a static or a dynamic relation to space as an essential component in a basic interpretation of reality (i.e., religion) is interpretation. Interpretation cannot be fully defined but only grasped, apprehended.

The two trinities, matter-form-content and description-analysis-interpretation, are coordinates rather than parallels.

Accurate and complete description is the foundation of all analysis and interpretation.

Form is always the forming of matter. The arena of analysis is form. The activity of analysis is the fullest apprehension of the form in its character and relation.

The purpose of analysis is interpretation. Interpretation is the elucidation of the content. Content is everything communicated through and by means of the form. Grasping the content depends on the analysis and interpretation of the form. [11]

These three phases of understanding can be described in order; they are not always followed out in that order. A full descriptive account of Roman sculpture determines that Romans were given to describing common every day actions such as an orator's gestures, whereas their close relations, the Greeks, rarely did. We know with precision what hundreds of Romans looked like. We know very little of what Greeks really looked like. This commitment to description had an impact on the way forms were used but the account could almost be described as moving directly from historical description to interpretation. The simple descriptive fact was a fundamental part of Roman ethos (the content of this aspect of Roman style). [12]

An experienced critic works back and forth among them as the work itself and the experience of it suggests. I had taught the great church of Hagia Sophia in Istanbul for many years before I saw it. I knew immediately that I would never teach it the same way again. Having seen a fundamental principle of the church's form as I had not been able to see it in photographs, I could then go back and determine descriptively and analytically what had determined the initial response

More commonly, the procedure when confronted by a new work is to look slowly and meditatively, being actively passive or passively active, but always being receptive and not dominating. This means not imposing any analytical scheme on the work but accepting guidance from the work itself, seeing what is there, gradually searching out relations, responding to the actions within the work, until it yields its inner principle. Mediocre works display their formal principles immediately. Greater works are as difficult to know as people. Equally, just as with people, it pays not to jump too quickly to the conclusion that some simple, quiet, unpretentious

---

[11] Contemporary criticism, often denying the possibility and the use of interpretation, customarily confines itself to <u>explanation</u>, accounting for the work by some cause, usually political, dear to the critic. This is work of considerable importance but it cannot escape from a swamp of controversy and can best be left to more detailed discussion elsewhere.

[12] The distinction made here may clarify the discussion of the image as subject and the image as form. The Greeks were far less interested in resemblance to external appearance than they were in the presentation of an idealized form. Romans, in their imagery, were normally uninterested in formal eloquence and sought the most exact kind of resemblance to surface appearances ("realism"). Roman images tend to be much duller than the Greek but they certainly are more informative. Both styles reflect a particular social and political order.

work contains nothing deeper than the immediately visible or that some big, noisy, busy work is profound.

The term "interpretation" has human dangers. It can too easily be taken as condescension: I appoint myself spokesman for the original makers of the image, who are presumed not able to speak clearly enough in their own speech. Perhaps "translation" would be a better term: I put the import (the content) of the images into another language, words, in order to make it accessible (this is the pedagogical function of criticism). Since all translation is necessarily false, using the term might emphasize that, while talking <u>about</u> the work has a humane use, it is no replacement for the apprehension of the work itself.

Furthermore, both interpretation and translation presupposes that I have an accurate grasp of the work, that I "understand" it. We all want to be understood without any clear understanding of what "understanding" involves. Perhaps, in the study of images, of art, some word such as "apprehension" would be best, to indicate that we grasp and are grasped by the work as a physical object, that we respond to it by the intelligent activity of our organism. We then translate what we have apprehended into critical speech.

Concluding remarks on the use of these principles:

1. The critic is as affected by these various forces and purposes as the artist is. The critic does not stand apart from involvement in the world as a detached analyst of other human beings.

Both artists and critics are creatures in the human world and immersed in its processes, involved physically and psychologically in the intricacies of sex and gender, parts of a social and economic order with its inevitable power structures, living in a natural and a human landscape with sensibilities formed by that landscape, working out careers between the demands of private purpose and the public necessities of the market, obsessed by past experiences and public images, with imaginations formed by myth, ritual and narrative, subject to the historical and economic events bearing on personal situations; in other words, the artist and the critic are subject to every circumstance, situation and force that affects us all.

2. The great artists "know" (that is, in their own form of knowledge) these forces as well as the critic does and set themselves the task of generating the symbolic forms that enable them, and others, to live a humane life in the midst of them. The problem, therefore, is the proper

placement of the various critical acts in the whole process of critical interpretation.

As all of us are, artists are variously intelligent and competent. The less intelligent ones are passively subject to one or another of these forces (only the psychotic artists are subject to one only). The greater ones are the ones most aware of the complexity of human experience, most able to generate a symbolic form that brings a wide range of them under the control of humane purpose, to be used by others to humane purpose.

For the greater artists, these forces are not so much causes as materials. They are what the artist contend with, use, interpret, incorporate knowingly into the order of the work.

The division between making person and made object is too sharp. These various forces can be present in both. Freudianism, for example, analyzes part of the psychosexual experience of the artist and of the critic. It can also alert us to certain symbols and symbolic forms that are part of the work as subject and as formal energy.

Whatever the forces that bear on the artist and become part of the work, always the decisive thing is the work. Therefore, this introduction concentrates on the procedures for grasping and being grasped by the work. All the currently fashionably critical procedures are not only valid but essential, provided we know what we are doing when we use them.[13].

The pity of it is that these procedures are directed toward the forces that are inescapably part of the whole human experience yet, by claiming power of the critic over the artist, they are used so inhumanely. Interpretation is participation in the world of another person, another people. Critical analysis is one of the most humane of the human enterprises, for its purpose is the recovery, without judgment, of the life of other people, that life in its deepest, most fundamental aspects, its religion. Critical analysis, properly done, is itself a deeply religious act, for it is the recovery of the world of the other, which is only in relation.

Critical analysis, interpretation, done properly, is itself construction. Criticism cannot be wholly objective anymore than it can be wholly subjective. It is not an analytical dissection of a cadaver anymore than it is a description of subjective responses or an account of the way the work fits into my own scheme of things or the purposes of my group. The only

---

[13] An apocryphal saying of Jesus is apt: on seeing a man at work on the Sabbath, he is reported to have said, "Blessed are you, o man, if you know what you are doing. Cursed are you if you don't"

instrument I have to use in the analysis is my own perceptual system guided by my own sensibility and intelligence, formed by the same forces or types of force that formed the artist, as subject to critical interpretation as the work of the artist. They are elements of my own world structure. I can interpret the structured world of another only by committing my own structured world to the process of interaction. Thus I open and expand my own world to the world of another. It is dangerous, as all human commitments are dangerous.

Criticism, critical interpretation, is as much a structure, as much ingredient to the construction of the world of the critic, as the work it criticizes. The world of the critic does not sit in authority over the world of the artist. One is revealed to the other only in the receptiveness of the critical act, which is humility. Criticism is not simply an instrument of relation; it is relation, one of the structures of human community.

Art is a hermeneutic of human existence. It is a hermeneutic, an interpretation, only as it participates in the act of structuring and not power. Criticism is a hermeneutic of art, but it, too, must be an act of structuring and not power.

Criticism is, finally, an act of love.

BIBLIOGRAPHY

Benjamin, Walter — *Illuminations* New York, Harcourt, Brace and World, 1968

Clark, Kenneth — *The Nude*. New York, Doubleday Anchor Books, 1959

Demus, Otto — "The Methods of the Byzantine Artst", *The Mint*, #2, 1948. Also in *Art History*, edited by Wylie Sypher, New York, Vintage Books, 1963.

Ellenberger, Henri — "A Clinical Introduction to Psychiatric Phenomenology and Existential Analysis", in *Existence*. Edited by Rollo May. New York, Simon and Schuster, 1958.

Eck, Diana L. — *Darsan: Seeing the Divinie Image in India*. Chambersburg, PA.,Anima Books 1981

Fleming, John V. — *From Bonaventura to Bellini*. Princeton, Princeton University Press, 1982

Focillon, Henri — *The Life of Forms in Art*. trans by Charles Hogan and George Kubler. New York, George Wittenborn, Inc. 1948

Freedberg, David — *The Power of Images*. Chicago, The University of Chicago Press, 1989.

Gombrich, E.H. — *Meditations on a Hobby Horse*, London, Phaidon Press, 1969

Gowans, Alan — *Learning to Look*. Bowling Green, Ohio, Bowling Green University Popular Press, 1981

Johnson, Mark	*The Body in the Mind.* Chicago, The University of Chicago Press, 1987
Kandinsky, Wassily	*Concerning the Spiritual in Art*, New York, George Wittenborn, 1947.
Kramrisch, Stella	*The Hindu Temple.* Delhi, Motilal Banarsides, 1976.
Lee, Sherman	*History of Far Eastern Art* New York, Harry N. Abrams, 1994
Levy, Gertrude Rachel	*Religious Conceptions of the Stone Age*, New York, Harper Torchbooks, 1963.
Mâle, Émile	*Religious Art in France: XIII Century* London, J.M. Dent & Sons, 1913.
Meiss, Millard	*Painting in Florence and Siena after the Black Death.* Princeton, Princeton University Press, 1951.
Needham, Joseph	*Science and Civilization in China.* University Press, 1955.
Newcomb, Franc J. and Reichard, Gladys A.	*Sandpaintings of the Navaho Shooting Chant*, New York, Dover Publications, 1975.
Panofsky, Erwin	*Abbot Suger on the Abbey Church of St. Denis and its Art Treasures,* Princeton, Princeton University Press, 1946
Rowley, George	*Principles of Chinese Painting* Princeton, Princeton University Press, 1947.
Slater, Philip E.	*The Glory of Hera*, Boston, Beacon Press, 1968
Smith, Quentin	*The Felt Meanings of the World.* West Lafayette, IN, Purdue University Press, 1986
Thompson, D'Arcy Wentworth	*On Growth and Form.* Abridged edition ed. by J.T. Bonner, Cambridge, Cambridge University Press, 1961.
Tuan, Yi-Fu	*Space and Place.* Minneapolis, University of Minnesota Press, 1977
Waghorne, Joann	*Gods of Flesh, Gods of Stone* Chambersburg, PA, Anima Books, 1985
Wölfflin, Heinrich	*The Principles of Art History.* New York, Dover Publications, n.d.

ILLUSTRATIONS

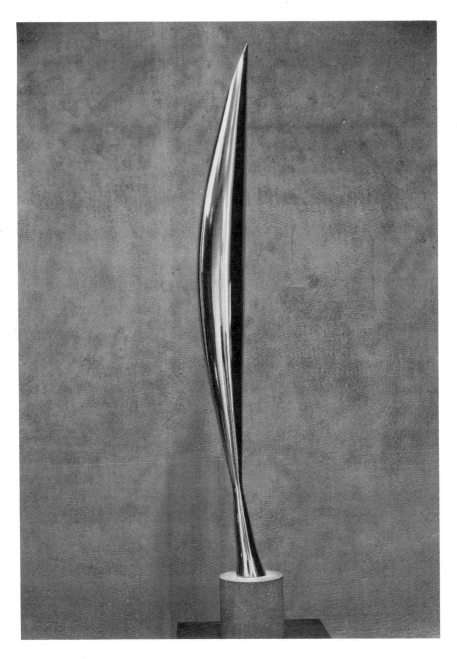

1. Brancusi, Constantin, *Bird in Space.* 1928 Bronze.
The Museum of Modern Art, NY. Anonymous Gift.

2. Lascaux Caves, France. Paleolithic painting. 15-10,000 BCE. Editions Arthaud-Giraudon/Art Resource, NY.

3. Lascaux Caves. "Well Scene".

4. "Venus" of Willendorf. Paleolithic sculpture, 15,000-10,000 BCE. Naturhistorisch Museum. Vienna. Foto Marburg / Art Resource

5. Neolithic pot, 11-12 cent. BCE. Paris, Musee Cernuschi.
Giraudon/Art Resource

6. Stonehenge. Megalithic. ca. 1650 BCE. Salisbury Plain, England

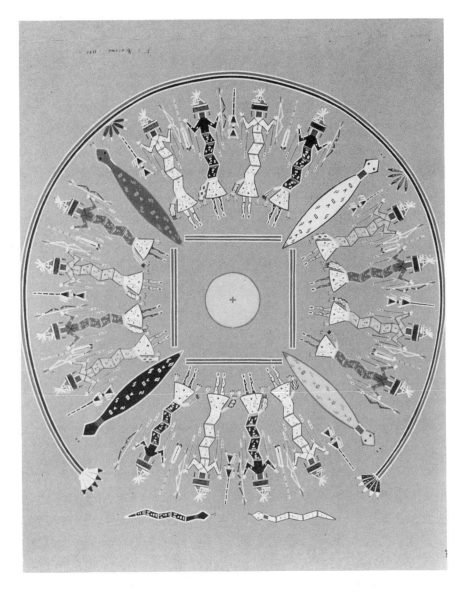

7. Navaho dry painting. *Crooked Snake People* from
the Male Shooting Chant.
Wheelwright Museum of the American Indian, Santa Fe, NM.

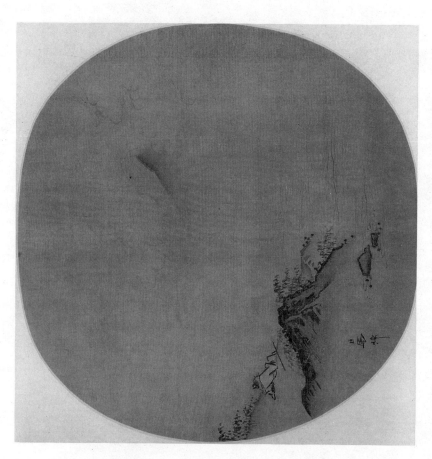

8. Ma Lin ca. 1180-ca. 1256. *Scholar Reclining and Watching Clouds.*
China, Southern Song Dynasty. The Cleveland Museum of Art. John L. Severence Fund.

9. Giovani Bellini, *St. Francis in the Desert.* (*Ecstasy of St. Francis*) Venice, c. 1485. The Frick Collection, NY.

10. Catacomb Painting, Orant Figure and worshippers.
Chiesa di Ss. Giovanni e Paolo, Rome.   Alinari/ Art Resource.

11. Werner Sallman, *Head of Christ.* 1940
Jessie C. Wilson Gallery, Anderson University, Indiana.

12. Pyramids of Cheops and Chephren, Gizeh, Egypt.
4th Dynasty (2689-2565 BCE). Art Resource, NY.

13. Pantheon, Rome. c. 118-128 CE. Interior view. Alinari/Art Resource. NY.

14. Ajanta, India. Interior of chaitya hall.
c. 2nd Cent. BCE-7th Cent. CE

15. Kandariya Mahadevi Temple, Khajuraho, India. c. 950-1028 CE.

16. Kandariya Mahadevi Temple. Detail of sculptures.

17. Ictinos and Callicrates, Parthenon, Acropolis, Athens. 448-432 BCE.

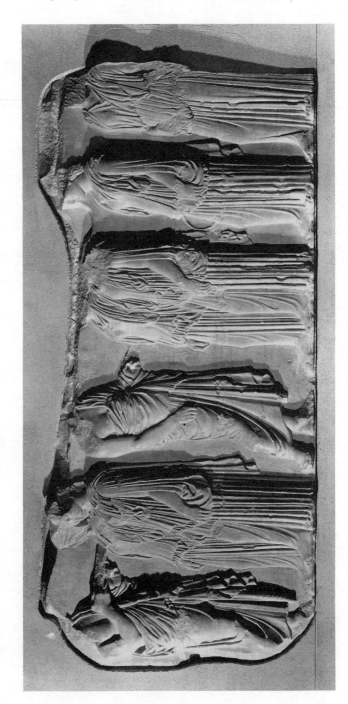

18. Phidias, Panathenaic procession, Parthenon frieze. Louvre, Paris. Giraudon/Art Resource.

19. St. Sernin, Toulouse, France. Interior. c. 1080-1120

20. Amiens Cathedral, Amiens, France. West front. 1220-36

21. Amiens Cathedral, Interior.

22. Amiens Cathedral, central portal, west front.

23. Hagia Sophia, Istanbul (Constantinople). Interior. 532-537.

24. Mosque of Sultan Ahmet. Istanbul. 1609-16.

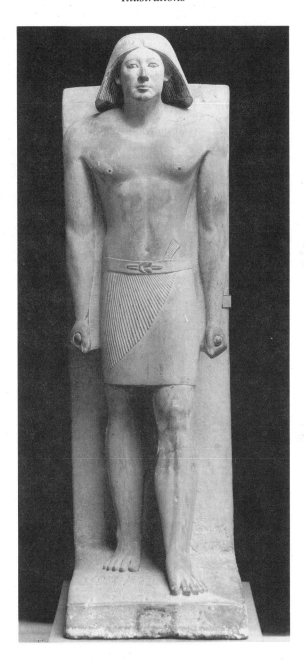

25. Ranofer, from Saqquara, painted limestone.
5th Dynasty (2550-2400 BCE).
Egyptian Museum, Cairo. Foto Marburg/Art Resource

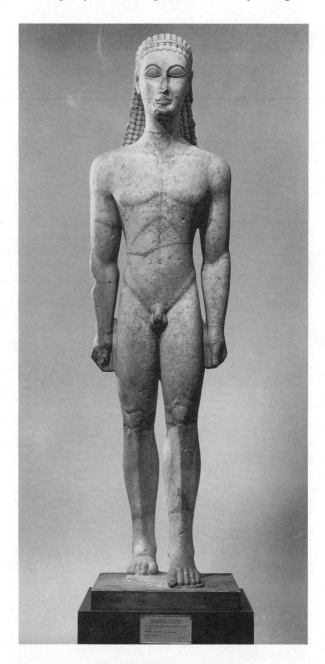

26. Kouros, Archaic Period. c. 600 BCE. Greece.
The Metropolitan Museum of Art. Fletcher Fund. 1932.

27. *Isaiah*, Abbey church, Souillac, France. c. 1100–1150.

28. Kings and Queens of Judah.
Chartres Cathedral, Royal Portal, west front. 1145-1170.

29. Donatello, *Zuccone*, 1423–25. Museo dell'Opera del Duomo.
Florence, Italy. Alinari/Art Resource, NY.

30. Agbonbiofe, and Assistants. Veranda Post from Palace at Efon-
Alaye. Nigeria, Yoruba people. 1912-1915. Ackland Art Museum,
The University of North Carolina at Chapel Hill. Ackland Fund.

31. *Natarajah: Siva as King of Dance.* Bronze. South India, Chola Period. 11th Cent. Cleveland Museum of Art. J.H. Wade Fund.

32. Great Buddha of Kamakura, Kamakura, Japan. Bronze. 1252.

33.. Titian, *Venus and the Lute Player*. Late 1550s. The Metropolitan Museum of Art. Minsky Fund., 1936.

34. Titian, *Danae*. 1554. Naples, Museo Nazionale. Alinari/ Art Resource.

35. Bernini, *St. Theresa in Ecstasy.* Cornaro Chapel, Sta. Maria della Vittoria, Rome. Alinari/Art Resource, NY.

36. Christos Pantokrator, interior of dome, monastery church.
Daphni, Greece. 11th Cent.

37. Giotto, *Expulsion of Joachim from the Temple.* Padua, Arena Chapel. Before 1305. Alinari/Art Resource. NY.

38. Giotto, *Meeting of Joachim and Anna at the Golden Gate.* Padua, Arena Chapel. Alinari/Art Resource, NY.

39. Pablo Picasso, *Acrobat's Family (Les Saltimbanques)*. 1905. National Gallery of Art. Washington, D.C. Chester Dale Collection

40. Wasily Kandinsky, *Improvisation 31 (Sea Battle)* 1913.
National Gallery of Art, Washington, D.C.,
Ailsa Mellon Bruce Fund

41. Mark Rothko, *Untitled 1953*. National Gallery of Art,
Washington, D.C. Gift of Mark Rothko Foundation.

42. Barnett Newman *First Station* from *Stations of the Cross*. 1958.
National Gallery of Art, Washington, D.C.
Robert and Jane Meyerhoff Collection.